OUR CARIBBEAN KIN

CRITICAL CARIBBEAN STUDIES

Focused particularly in the twentieth and twenty-first centuries, although attentive to the context of earlier eras, this series encourages interdisciplinary approaches and methods and is open to scholarship in a variety of areas, including anthropology, cultural studies, diaspora and transnational studies, environmental studies, gender and sexuality studies, history, and sociology. This series pays particular attention to the four main research clusters of Critical Caribbean Studies at Rutgers University, where the coeditors serve as members of the executive board: Caribbean Critical Studies, Theory, and the Disciplines; Archipelagic Studies and Creolization; Caribbean Aesthetics, Poetics, and Politics; and Caribbean Colonialities.

SERIES EDITORS
Yolanda Martínez-San Miguel, Michelle Stephens, and Nelson Maldonado-Torres

Giselle Anatol, *The Things That Fly in the Night: Female Vampires in Literature of the Circum-Caribbean and African Diaspora*

Alaí Reyes-Santos, *Our Caribbean Kin: Race and Nation in the Neoliberal Antilles*

OUR CARIBBEAN KIN

Race and Nation in the Neoliberal Antilles

ALAÍ REYES-SANTOS

Rutgers University Press

NEW BRUNSWICK, NEW JERSEY, AND LONDON

LIBRARY OF CONGRESS CATALOGING-IN-PUBLICATION DATA

Reyes-Santos, Alaí.
  Our Caribbean kin : race and nation in the neoliberal Antilles / Alaí Reyes-Santos.
    pages cm.—(Critical Caribbean studies)
  Includes bibliographical references and index.
  ISBN 978-0-8135-7200-0 (hardback)
  ISBN 978-0-8135-7199-7 (pbk.)
  ISBN 978-0-8135-7201-7 (e-book (epub))
  1. West Indies—Ethnic relations. 2. Antilleans—Ethnic identity. 3. Antilleans—Race identity. 4. West Indies—History—20th century. 5. West Indies—History—21st century. I. Title.
F1628.8.R49 2015
305.8009729—dc23

2014040077

A British Cataloging-in-Publication record for this book is available
from the British Library.

Visit our website: http://rutgerspress.rutgers.edu

Manufactured in the United States of America

THE
AMERICAN
LITERATURES
INITIATIVE

A book in the American Literatures Initiative (ALI), a collaborative publishing project of NYU Press, Fordham University Press, Rutgers University Press, Temple University Press, and the University of Virginia Press. The Initiative is supported by The Andrew W. Mellon Foundation. For more information, please visit www.americanliteratures.org.

A los que subieron de la costa a la montaña
A los que de la montaña bajaron a la costa
A los que cruzaron océano y mar
Y a Olokún, porque desde las profundidades del mar nació el saber

Contents

PREFACE

This book is about a quest for political communities, for solidarity. It is for those of us Antilleans who feel foreign at home and for those who must find a home somewhere where they are always seen as foreign. It is about the chosen families that we Antilleans have imagined for ourselves; it is about our tensions, secrets, complicities, silences, our longings for joy, belonging, care, and kinship.

It responds to an ancestral call to recognize those who have always been here: the Taíno, the Arawak; a call to recognize all those who came over by sea: the Congo, the Yoruba, the Fon, the Chinese, and even the European; and a call to those who continue to travel across land and water to the unknown, driven by the need to survive and thrive, many forced by dire circumstances.

It recognizes those ancestors that crowd the room and surprise us because they do not fit into our imagination of who we are, of who our people are. Those people who belong to us by blood, those who have adopted us, those we have adopted, those who are our family even when we cannot see ourselves in them.

This book comes into existence as a result of these ancestral calls to recognize the complex, beautiful, yet often painful imagination of kinship in the Antilles. It is not exhaustive, but it does hope to widen an already existing path for others also wondering how we Antilleans imagine ourselves as kin, how we care for one another, how we count on each other, or not, as we face the legacies of colonial and imperial histories.

And There Is a River

June 2013. It is a rainy afternoon on the outskirts of the city of Santo Domingo. Around thirty people gather next to a riverbed. A retired journalist, professors, peasants, farmers, dancers, a scientist, young and old, lesbian, gay, and heterosexual, dark- and light-skinned, men and women. We all stand under a tree, protecting the rice, beans, *pollo guisado*, and cakes from the rain. We huddle together, the heavy tropical rain on our shoulders.

A Dominican *palo* group has been invited to play for Anaísa, a *misterio*, the beautiful force that is the sunlight reflected on river water. A group of mostly Cuban migrants, Russian migrants, Ugandan visitors, some Dominicans from the island and the Diaspora, as well as a Puerto Rican (myself) have gathered to celebrate Ochún, an *orisha* of the Afro-Cuban tradition, *santería*. Ochún also lives in the movement of river waters. Dominican *palos* take the place of the Cuban *batá* drums usually played at similar festivities in *La Habana*. The *santeras* and *santeros* want to celebrate Ochún on this land, a land where most of them are foreigners, where they must learn to honor Ochún in other ways, as the land itself has taught its people, as Anaísa.

Altars have been set. One of the altars is dressed in magnificent golden and blue regalia honoring Ochún and her sister Yemayá, the mother of the seas and all living creatures: it is covered in bright blue and yellow fabrics, molasses, honey, sweets, and flowers. A second altar presents Anaísa with her candies, perfume, flowers, and her favorite fruits. A third one by the river holds a place for the *indios* who live in the sweet waters of the Dominican Republic.

This gathering is new for everyone. The *paleros* arrive and are taken aback by the Cuban altar. "We have never seen an altar like this. Hmm," they say. The *santeros* are nervous, hoping to have correctly honored both their ways and those of the musicians they have invited; some are also unsure about this altar that resembles but also departs from those built back at home.

The only question that remains, which is repeated by both Dominican and Cuban elders, is:

Are they the same?

Are they the same?

Anaísa and Ochún, are they the same?

And so says the *iya de ocha*, the main priestess in the *ilé*, the *santeros'* spiritual home.

And so says *la cargadora de misterios*, the Dominican healer and elder accompanying the *palos* musicians.

Vamos a ver. Let's see.

And the music begins. As soon as the drums play, the river hears the name and the song it has heard across generations calling for her, Anaísa Pié, Anaísa Pié. Anaísa/Ochún arrives through the body of the *iya*. She showers her guests with her *aché*, her blessing, honey pouring out of her hands, anointing everyone with its promise of health, happiness, joy, healing. Everyone dances and laughs, recognizing immediately the river woman among them, Ochún/Anaísa.

Te lo dije. I told you, says *la cargadora de misterios*. She is the same.

For an afternoon, suspicions and fears melt away under the influence of the river and the sacred cadence of the *palos*. As young people listen, the elders share healing stories, stories that illustrate their understanding of who Ochún/Anaísa is. We all wonder if we will ever get together again.

Along the river's edge, migrants, foreigners, and one of the island's *pueblos originarios* (original peoples) cross the waters that separate them. Together we offer sunflowers to the river. We attempt to build bridges across traditions and across class, racial, ethnic, gender, and sexual differences. The sense of kinship, of camaraderie, of belonging to a shared history of struggle, of being the descendants of those who survived the horrors of genocide and slavery is palpable. But questions linger in people's eyes, in their paused manner of reseeing and recognizing each other after the drums and dancing have stopped.

The heart of this book rests in our shared experiences and the questions provoked by moments of tension and mutual recognition. The river reflects back its light, allowing Antillean peoples to see ourselves and recognize ourselves in each other. The question is whether we dare to respond to the ancestral call, to face both the ugly and the beautiful truths of our coexistence, to respond to ancestral demands to build kinship aware and inclusive of our ethnic, racial, class, sexual, and gender diversity as peoples of the Caribbean Sea.

Acknowledgments

The research for and writing of this book have been possible due to a series of kinship networks that have sustained me in the Caribbean and the United States since the beginning of my research ten years ago. At the University of California–San Diego I was lucky to be welcomed by an intellectual community that valued the questions that drive my research.

There I received the intellectual support, training, and funding for the initial field research trips and writing. I am deeply grateful to the Center for the Study of Race and Ethnicity led by Ramón Gutiérrez, the Institute for International, Comparative and Area Studies, the Center for Iberian and Latin American Studies, and the Department of Literature at UCSD for enabling me to study the Caribbean while far away from it; for providing amazing intellectual communities that enriched my growth as a Caribbeanist through comparative conversations with incredibly engaging scholars working on all regions of the world.

At the University of Oregon I was honored to receive an Oregon Humanities Center (OHC) fellowship and a Center for the Study of Women in Society (CSWS) grant that bought me much needed time to write and produce the first draft of the manuscript. Along with the UO College of Arts and Sciences, OHC has also graciously supported the publication process itself, and CSWS provided travel funds when I needed to access primary sources in the Dominican Republic, as well as funds to acquire research materials and attend conferences. Both centers have created invigorating intellectual spaces where my work received much needed feedback. The Women of Color Leadership Project at CSWS has been a creative mentorship community. The Latin American Studies Program, the Center for Latino and Latin American Studies, and the Wayne Morse Center for Law and Politics at UO—and their respective directors, Carlos Aguirre, Lynn Stephen, and Margaret Hallock— have also been much needed accomplices and cosponsors in projects that have allowed Caribbean Studies to flourish in this corner of the world.

The Department of Ethnic Studies at UO has mentored me and fed my intellectual life for over eight years now. Michael Hames-García, Lynn Fujiwara, Ernesto Martínez, Brian Klopotek, Donella-Elizabeth Alston, Dan Martinez-HoSang, and Charise Cheney, and our affiliated faculty have made ES an enriching intellectual home for this Caribbeanist. Michael and Lynn have been supportive chairs and mentors. They gave me the right kind of mentorship when a debilitating health condition threatened to end my academic career. Sometimes one has to stop to be able to get to the finish line.

Away from the West Coast, I have been lucky to experience a series of encounters with similarly minded scholars who oftentimes became interlocutors, friends, companions. The Ford Foundation Interrogating the African Diaspora Summer Seminar organized by Jean Muteba Rahier at Florida International University brought together an incredible group of junior scholars willing to ask difficult questions about what it means to study people of African descent while honoring the specificity of location; it also required us to think seriously about the interventions of feminist and queer studies scholarship in the field. For me that month spent at the beautiful campus in Biscayne Bay was a revelation of how one's work can truly be pushed through collaborative, open, generous coexistence. Questions and comments raised by Xavier Livermon, Chantalle Verna, Devin Spence, Kai Mah, Andrea Queeley, and Maziki Thame, among the rest of the crew, have stayed with me throughout this journey, and finding them at conferences or through intermittent email has kept me in good company with other people invested in our desire to build a world where we can be truly free.

The Future of Minority Studies Consortium has also been an intellectual home for me since Michael Hames-García and Ernesto Martínez incorporated UO into its midst. Its Transnational Queer Studies Summer Institute facilitated by M. Jacqui Alexander and Minnie-Bruce Pratt and organized by Satya Mohanty at Cornell University was a life-changing experience that altered the course of the manuscript. In those lively conversations with fellow institute participants (Micaela Díaz-Sánchez, Erica Williams, Eng-Beng-Lim, Andrea Smith, Nadia Ellis), through creative exercises led by our facilitators, and over shared meals on the beautiful Cornell campus, I realized that intimacy, kinship, and solidarity were core concepts of the book. Our at times difficult conversations about sexuality, race relations, and politics reminded me of the painful tensions I was trying to document in the manuscript; our joyful moments of sharing reminded me of the joy felt when people find common ground and solidarity with one another. I must thank in particular Nadia Ellis for her friendship, for sharing the writing process and our attempt to thrive as Caribbeanists so far away from home. I know that our lively exchanges over politics, migration, and literature, as Antilleans from different islands, live in this book.

The FMS Postdoctoral Fellowship in Women's and Gender Studies at Syracuse University was another opportunity that greatly shaped the book as well as other concurrent projects. I must thank Chandra Mohanty, Myrna García Calderón, Silvio Torres-Saillant, Elisabeth Apelmo, Kal Alston, Nancy Cantor, and Margaret Himley, among many others, for their warm welcome to Syracuse. Silvio and Margaret were generous mentors. Silvio's knowledge of the Caribbean remains an inspiration as I try to better understand the political and cultural dynamics of such a diverse and complex region. Those autumn days in Syracuse when I could just read, reflect, and write without distractions are some of my most precious memories as a scholar. Himika Bhattacharya and Dalia Rodríguez were the most gracious hostesses and interlocutors; their collegiality and friendship have sustained me ever since.

Many colleagues and friends have read portions of the manuscript, shared secondary sources, or simply supported me through enthusiastic exchanges of ideas: Nancy Mirabal, April Mayes, Humberto García Muñiz, Pablo Mella, Ruth Nina Estrella, Pedro Ortega, Shalini Puri, Ginetta Candelario, Kiran Jarayam, David Vázquez, Celiany Rivera Velázquez, Priscilla Ovalle, Jinah Kim, Ileana Rodríguez Silva, Digna María Adames, Jorge Duany, Cora Monroe, Amalia Cabezas, Dixa Ramírez, Leopoldo Artiles, Deborah Paravisini-Hernández, Irene Mata, Suzanne Oboler, Analisa Taylor, Christine Handhart, Lamia Karim, Sangita Gopal, Melissa Stuckey, Shireen Roshanravan, Chris Finley, Myriam J. A. Chancy, Fátima Portorreal, Kiany Lantigua, Dayo Mitchell, Raquel Rivera, Lyric Cabral, among many others. I have been lucky to have such generous interlocutors at every step of the way. Others have been supportive friends, such as: Pedro Pérez, Omar Naim, Awilda Rodríguez, Rita E. Urquijo Ruiz, Justine Lovinger, Jahaira Cotto González, Edwin Xavier Vega Espada, Steve Morozumi, and the UO Multicultural Center students.

Nicole King, Sarah E. Johnson, Rosaura Sánchez, Beatrice Pita, Winnifred Woodhull, Misha Kokotovich, Robert Cancel, Beatrice Pita, Ana Celia Zentella, Denise Ferrera da Silva, Peggy Pascoe, Ana Kothe, Lisette Rolón Collazo, and Roberta Orlandini all mentored me as a young scholar and trusted that I could one day publish this book; I frequently hear their voices as I write. Shari Hundhorf did a beautiful and generous reading of a first draft that helped me delineate its main questions. Susan Quash-Mah copyedited drafts of chapters over the years. Maram Epstein, a Chinese literature scholar, has been an exceptional mentor at UO throughout the publication process.

Chuong-Dai Vo accurately assessed the strengths and weaknesses of the manuscript at its final stages and for twelve years has remained an intellectual interlocutor and good friend. Her keen editorial eye identified the connective thread that ran through each chapter.

Ana-Maurine Lara accompanied me through the writing process, cared for me through an illness that stopped it for a while, and shared fruitful ideas and debates in a loving manner. The various families we share—Puerto Rican, Dominican, Cuban, Mexican, and Texan—are truly a gift in my life. Thanks for embarking on so many adventures with me in an attempt to, like this book, build nurturing kinship and solidarity networks with our peoples. Ana also gave incredibly generous feedback on the content and form of this book. Her inquisitive questions were invaluable.

Rutgers editor Katie Keeran has been amazing, communicating with me at every step of the process, patiently answering questions. It is truly an honor to be published by the Critical Caribbean Studies Series. Knowing that Nelson Maldonado-Torres, Michelle Stephen, and Yolanda Martínez-San Miguel—whose scholarship has deeply affected the field of decolonial and Caribbean studies—had faith in this project, inspired me through days and nights of revisions. Rutgers's anonymous reviewers provided useful, clear, feedback; their questions and suggestions helped me find what I wanted to say in the book's four chapters.

The Dominican Studies Institute, its director, Ramona Hernández, and its library—and staff, Sarah Aponte, Jessi J. Pérez, Greysi Peralta, Nelson— have warmly welcomed me over the past four years. I thank Ramona for always pushing me to question my initial preconceptions. At the Universidad Autónoma de México, Olivia Gall, INTEGRA, and Jesús Serna and his brilliant and inspiring students have recently been invaluable interlocutors.

This book would not have been possible without the communities that have welcomed this Puerto Rican in the Dominican Republic. Las Altagracianas housed me during my first trip to the country and introduced me to Centro Bonó. At Centro Bonó, Mario Serrano, Roque Félix, Milosis Liriano, Maite (María Teresa) Peralta, Ana María Belique, Digna María Adames, Euclides Cordero Nuel, and the rest of the staff made me feel right at home. Erasmo Lara Peña and Elizabeth Lara opened their home to me many times, provided intellectually stimulating conversations, and taught me how to navigate social relations respectfully in the Dominican Republic. Those moments dancing to palos at CEDOPAZ with the community of El Ramón, San Cristóbal, have inspired me many times to finish this book. My godmother, Iya Abbebe Ochún, and my fellow spiritual brothers and sisters in the Dominican Republic have emotionally and spiritually sustained me. I thank them for their prayers and for hearing about this book for so long. The *ilé* is an example of the kinds of cross-cultural communities and solidarities I examine in this book. Thanks also to all of the community activists with whom I have collaborated since my days in San Diego: Students for Economic Justice, the antiwar movement, Basic Rights Oregon, Community Alliance of Lane County, Latin American Solidarity Committee, MRG Foundation, reconoci.do, the People's Summit of the Americas, among many others. When I write about affect and political solidarity, I think of what we have shared.

The seeds for this book were planted during my initial explorations of black, Third World feminisms and African and Caribbean literature at the Humanities Department at the University of Puerto Rico, Mayagüez. Often it takes just one good teacher to set you on the right path. I had much more than that. You have my gratitude always.

I must also recognize the friends, teachers, *compadres*, and family members in Cidra, Puerto Rico, who always believed that I would one day tell this story. *Cidreños/as, aquí está.*

My family has been patient with me ever since I left Puerto Rico to go to graduate school in San Diego. They have quietly accepted my irregular work hours, endless drafting, and absences from family events, always believing that I could finish this book. I thank my parents, Lionel Reyes-Cotto and Elena Santos-Agosto, for teaching me that one should find one's passion in life and dedicate oneself to it, for having endless faith in me, and for instilling in me a deep love for the land that surrounds our small town in the mountains of Puerto Rico. As the children of peasants and sharecroppers and as first-generation college students, my parents' commitment to education and public service has always been an inspiration. I thank my aunt Irma Santos-Agosto, Mamá Nydia, a passionate and dedicated teacher, a woman who helped raise her twelve siblings and introduced me to the joys of reading, writing, and teaching that have never left me. My siblings, Alba Giselle, Liomarys, Elena, and Lionel Reyes-Santos, have been loving companions on a journey that seemed incomprehensible more often than not.

My grandmother Elvira Agosto-Rivera passed away as I finished this manuscript. I promised I would show it to her once it was done. *Abuela, lo pongo en tus manos. Bendición.*

OUR CARIBBEAN KIN

Introduction: Our Caribbean Kin

On May 14, 2013, an unprecedented meeting took place at the Universidad Católica in Santo Domingo, Dominican Republic. Approximately three hundred people witnessed the official launch and signature of the *Compromiso Social y Político por un Nuevo Modelo de Gestión de las Migraciones* (Social and Political Pledge for a New Model for Migration Policies). That day 150 organizations crowded into the university auditorium, lining up to sign the *Compromiso*. The *Compromiso* demands that the Dominican government implement the Ley General de Migración No. 285-04 (General Migration Law No. 285-04), approved by the Dominican Legislature more than nine years ago, which calls attention to the inconsistent, cumbersome, and discriminatory screening processes to which migrants are subjected. It points to the specific case of Haitian migrants, whose labor is crucial for sugarcane production, construction, and the service economy. Many Haitian migrants are undocumented and wait for years for a response to their applications for visas, residency, or citizenship. The *Compromiso* asks the Dominican government to implement migration policies that recognize the needs of the labor sector, as well as the human, civil, and labor rights of migrants.

These demands are not new in the Dominican Republic. Over the past forty years, social justice organizations—comprising Dominicans, Dominicans of Haitian descent, Haitian migrants, Europeans, and South Americans—have called attention to the vulnerable living and working conditions of a population that is constantly subjected to the fear of deportation, even at the hands of their employers. However, these organizations and efforts tend to be overlooked by transnational media and scholarly representations of the Dominican Republic, which construct the country as an exceptionally anti-Haitian and antiblack society.

The *Compromiso* challenged such preconceptions. It received widespread support from a variety of sectors, including labor unions, business, religious organizations, and peasant advocacy groups. Catholics, feminists, workers, peasants, business owners, diplomats, LGBT activists, Protestants, NGOs, and leftist radicals, all gathered in the same room to express their commitment to a common vision. The *Compromiso* brought together Dominicans, Dominicans of Haitian descent, Puerto Ricans, Dominican migrants in Puerto Rico and the United States, and Haitians, as well as U.S. and European ex-pats, NGO officials, diplomats, and international aid workers. The room vibrated as people looked for a place to sit or simply stand to witness this historical moment. It was a moment when people who do not necessarily see eye to eye on other issues agreed to commit to a public demonstration of support for the regularization of migration policies. The collective excitement was palpable as people milled about the auditorium, reconnecting with old friends and meeting new ones. Every interaction was permeated with a sense of common purpose and belonging—a sense of kinship.

As each person signed the *Compromiso*, some shouted their amazement at the turnout. Others were mobilizing the hesitant. What made this amazing moment possible? What understanding of solidarity, of kinship, could explain this encounter of such disparate sectors of Dominican society? Who was absent? Why? These kinds of questions move this intellectual endeavor. *Our Caribbean Kin* disentangles the affective component of political solidarity in the Antilles. I examine how feelings of kinship politically mobilize Antilleans to make decisions that impact their communities on local, national, and transcolonial/transnational levels. In particular, I seek to understand how Haitians, Dominicans, and Puerto Ricans imagine each other as kin, as their "own people"—or not—as they face ongoing colonial, imperial, and neoliberal violence.[1]

To claim others as kin is to believe that the difficulties and obstacles they face are ours too. Kinship entails caring, having an ethical concern for the well-being of those who belong to a family or community, and being willing to put ourselves at risk by standing next to those who may be different from us.[2] When Dominicans publicly demand respect for the human rights of Haitian migrants, they are imagining those migrants as their kin, as family, friends, or neighbors whose needs are theirs as well. This powerful experience of Haitian-Dominican kinship begs us to explore how, when, and why Antilleans choose to recognize each other as kin or as outsiders.[3]

To understand the inclusions and exclusions embedded in Antillean kinship narratives, I examine brotherhood, marriage, and family as tropes that have been historically mobilized to construct kinship among Antilleans.[4] These tropes reveal how people create cohesion across differences, as well as the conflicts, secrets, abuses of power, and internal hierarchies that characterize kin relations. They are also useful sites of analysis because they reappear through time in canonical and emergent Antillean cultural texts. Nineteenth-century and early twentieth-century political and literary imaginations of pan-Antillean brotherhoods and national families inform contemporary representations of kinship ties between Haitians and Dominicans, and Dominicans and Puerto Ricans. The ways those narratives reified notions of racial mixture, such as *mulataje* and *mestizaje*, along with a series of heteropatriarchal conventions and ideas about ethnic and class differences, help explain what kinds of kinship seem possible or impossible among Antilleans living the consequences of colonialism and imperialism.

In the first chapter I examine how nineteenth-century *antillanistas* imagined and acted on their ideas about the Caribbean region based on a sense of shared kinship. This manifested itself in the conceptualization of anticolonial projects for the Antilles as a region, fostering intra-Antillean solidarity networks, and the creation of black- and mulatto-identified brotherhoods to sustain each other in the revolutionary struggle. In the recent past this transcolonial impulse translates into a short story by the Puerto Rican writer Magali García Ramis (1995b), in which black-identified, working-class, Dominican–Puerto Rican brotherly ties enable a Dominican character to pass for Puerto Rican in order to migrate to New York.

The second chapter focuses on how Dominican and Puerto Rican canonical novels written in the 1930s imagine marriages and national families. The protagonists in these novels share political and economic interests with a community inscribed by national boundaries, but they also coexist with figures considered to be outside of it (such as Haitian and West Indian migrants in the Dominican Republic and poor and black-identified workers in Puerto Rico). The novels considered in this chapter speak to contemporary racist and xenophobic ideas about Haitian migrants in the Dominican Republic and Dominican migrants in Puerto Rico and the limits of the national family. I also consider how critiques of U.S. imperialism in the past render the inequalities that characterize neoliberal economies visible in the present.

The last two chapters compare how Haitians and Dominicans, and Dominicans and Puerto Ricans, see each other sharing work and communal spaces in the Dominican Republic and Puerto Rico, respectively, in the late twentieth and early twenty-first century. Transcolonial brotherhoods, marriage, and national families reappear as metaphors that describe Haitian-Dominican and Dominican–Puerto Rican relations in neoliberal contexts. These metaphors appear in the idea of Haiti and the Dominican Republic as being in a "marriage without divorce" or in the treatment of poor and dark-skinned domestic workers as "part of the family."[5] Heteropatriarchal notions of marriage and family permeate all of these representations. It is partly through heteronormative marriage that cultural productions like the Puerto Rican television comedy *Entrando por la cocina* (1986–2002) imagine Dominican protagonists incorporated within Dominican–Puerto Rican kinship networks. In the TV show these kinship networks are both recognized and dismissed through their comedic representation. In 2012, in an odd moment in TV history when boundaries between life and the screen disappeared, the show's protagonist, Altagracia (Yasmín Mejía), celebrated her silver wedding anniversary with her Puerto Rican husband, Tato (Pedro Juan Texidor). Bellas Artes, one of Puerto Rico's most important cultural venues, was packed. Hundreds had come to watch Mejía's comedic depiction of Altagracia, the Dominican female domestic worker whose caricature reinforces racial, ethnic, and elitist stereotypes about Dominican migrants in Puerto Rico.

In all the historical moments, texts, and locations considered, *antillanos/as* attempt to be in conversation with one another. At times it is intimate and easy; at other times it is tense and awkward. But every encounter, every moment of intimate sharing provides insights into what is at stake when kinship narratives incorporate or fail to embrace particular voices or perspectives.

In colonial and postcolonial studies, scholars such as Anne McClintock (1995) and Ann Laura Stoler (2002), have examined the intimacies embedded in colonial regimes. They have examined how colonizers saw themselves sharing sexual encounters, households, and

child rearing with the colonized. They have demonstrated how impe-
rial/colonial regimes attempted to regulate the sexual practices and
kin relations of the colonized, especially those born out of European-
Native sexual relations (Stoler 2002). A rich scholarship on neoliberal
globalization and kinship in the Caribbean has described how romantic and sexual relationships, child rearing, gender divisions of labor
in the household, and national and transnational communities are
reconfigured by the mobility of capital and populations that characterizes this stage of capitalism. For instance, scholars discuss how the
economic conditions created by neoliberalism change understandings
of marriage and family (Freeman 2000; Graziano 2013). Scholarship
on neoliberal globalization and sex tourism has examined how the
violence and inequities embedded in old scripts for colonial/colonized
intimate relations replicate themselves in sexual encounters enabled
by tourism (Kempadoo 2004; Sheller 2003). Scholars such as Amalia
Cabezas (2009), Denise Brennan (2004), Steven Gregory (2007), Mark
Padilla (2007), and Erica Williams (2013) have studied how kin relations
emerge and are reimagined within the context of sex work and how the
meaning of love, romance, pleasure, marriage, and reproduction shifts
with the growth of tourism economies in the Caribbean. Feminist and
queer studies scholarship interrogating Caribbean nationalisms and
their incorporation or rejection of women and non-gender-normative
subjects has also taken us into intimate sets of affective relations in
the household, in the bedroom, on the dance floor, and in political
movements to explain the racial, gender, and sexual imagination of the
nation and diasporic communities (Allen 2011; Briggs 2002; Chancy
2012; Edmondson 1999; Francis 2010; Horn 2014; Janer 2005; Martínez
Vergne 2005; Mayes 2014; Suárez Findlay 1999). In these varied spaces,
kinship gets reimagined beyond blood ties, for instance among LGBT,
queer-identified, or same-sex loving Antilleans (Decena 2011; Glave
2008; Rivera-Velázquez 2008; Tinsley 2010).

Our Caribbean Kin builds on these bodies of scholarship. It denatu-
ralizes kinship by undoing its conventional association with blood ties,
marriage, and reproduction and examines how kinship has been a con-
venient metaphor deployed to build a series of political solidarities in
the Antilles and beyond. Affective responses such as sympathy, empathy, harmony, compatibility, and love are invoked by metaphorical
renderings of kinship used to naturalize transcolonial/transnational,
national, and colonial allegiances. Notions of brotherhood, friendship, national family, and extended family are invoked by a variety of

Antillean interlocutors as they imagine communities in struggle tied by feelings of solidarity. Jossiana Arroyo's recent book *Writing Secrecy in Caribbean Freemasonry* (2013) brilliantly invokes the metaphor of a "masonic brotherhood" to describe nineteenth-century antislavery political solidarities built through masonic networks and across colonial boundaries. Danny Méndez (2011), in his reading of the Dominican novel *Cañas y Bueyes* (1938) by Francisco Moscoso Puello, analyzes how the feelings and emotions of Haitian and Dominican characters—hate, frustration, and hopelessness—as well as their shared feelings of dislocation due to the consequences of U.S. occupation in the island manifest affective ties that complicate conventional understandings of *antihaitianismo* as a hegemonic discourse in the Dominican Republic. My readings demonstrate that both Arroyo's "masonic brotherhood" and Méndez's rethinking of Haitian-Dominican encounters can be better understood if we look at how Antilleans have historically negotiated multiple notions of kinship. Those feelings documented by Méndez are manifestations of historical maneuverings of a variety of transcolonial, national, and colonial kinship narratives articulated by Antilleans since the nineteenth century. It is through those maneuverings that we can also approach how, as Arroyo documents, masonic brotherhoods impacted antislavery *antillanistas* seeking the vindication of blacks and mulattos, the creation of an independent Antillean Confederation, and liberal projects of nation building that were often not as radical in their racial imagination of national families.

Kinship is a productive site of inquiry that illuminates the construction of political solidarities in the region, their potential and limitations. It is evident that deploying metaphors of kinship can be an attempt to silence or ignore racial, ethnic, class, gender, and sexual marginalization. As I demonstrate, those inequalities are produced not only within the intimate, kin-like, exploitative colonizer-colonized relations imagined within the context of colonialism, as illustrated by Stoler and Karen Strassler (2010). Representations of unequal yet intimate affective ties are also characteristic of political and cultural narratives of kinship within the Global South.

Through its transhistorical, comparative approach, *Our Caribbean Kin* intervenes in a series of interdisciplinary conversations about the meanings of race, gender, kinship, the nation, and neoliberal globalization in the Antilles. It does so through its attention to narratives and to words. As Arroyo (2013: 6) and Carlos Decena (2011: 3) suggest, words create and sustain affective ties among people, their sense of community and solidarity with one another. In Antillean literature the power of the word to create the (un)imaginable is evident. We are able to recognize the decolonial models for kinship—brotherhoods, marriages, and families—developed by Antillean writers. The power dynamics that hinder kinship are frequently hidden, silenced, or ignored by those who can afford to do so, but they operate in the "political unconscious" (Jameson 1981) of our societies just the same. Reading fiction and other texts (speeches, letters, autobiographies, historical sketches) as literary representations allows us to delve into that which is silenced or ignored. Collectively these texts "stir things up" (Woodhull 2003: 220). They prompt readers and scholars to interrogate the choices Antilleans have made, often in dire circumstances, as we imagine ourselves and our kin facing colonial, imperial, and neoliberal histories.

Los Hijos Emancipados

Chapter 1, "The Emancipated Sons: Nineteenth-Century Transcolonial Kinship Narratives in the Antilles," introduces the reader to the racial and gender premises of nineteenth-century *antillanismo*, what I call transcolonial kinship narratives. I use the term *transcolonial* rather than *transnational* to describe nineteenth-century "alternative community formations that contested the racialized violence endemic to European imperialism and creole nation-building projects" (Johnson 2012: 5). Transnational, according to Françoise Lionnet (2000), privileges North-South relations as shaped by the mobility of capital, neoliberal states, and international aid agencies.[6] Although transcolonial kinship has been historically identified with antiracist, antixenophobic, and anticolonial/imperial struggles, at times distinctions between neoliberal transnational and transcolonial kinship are not simple. For instance, NGOs can engage in transcolonial agendas that assert the rights of Haitian migrants in the Dominican Republic while being complicit with the condescending, paternalist logic of the Dominican and Haitian states and northern international aid agencies and lending practices. Transnational plans to develop free trade zones (FTZs) along the Haitian-Dominican border (with the blessing of the United States, Europe, and International Monetary Fund debt relief efforts) can invoke a transcolonial spirit of interethnic solidarity and collaboration instead of xenophobic relations. At times transcolonial/transnational kinship narratives reveal how neoliberalism attempts to co-opt a historical legacy of struggles by antislavery, transcolonial, political communities.

Transcolonial kinship narratives are intrinsically decolonial efforts. They engage "processes of disruption, or symbolic, epistemic and/ or material violence, that seek to restore the humanity of the human in all orders of existence, of social relations, symbols and thoughts." (Maldonado Torres 2011: 66).[7] Transcolonial kinship narratives seek to transform the exploitative and dehumanizing social relations that characterized the European invasion of the Americas, and Eurocentric understandings of history, knowledge, power, citizenship, and humanity. The term *transcolonial* emphasizes the regionalist nature of decolonial efforts. In the Caribbean, it describes antillanista political communities that did not follow the tenets of Latin American and U.S. nation-building projects that privileged whiteness. The term is also useful for thinking about horizontal, South-South relations between people experiencing legacies of colonial subordination in the past and the present (Lionnet 2000). It suggests that Antilleans have historically faced the colonial/imperial projects of multiple metropolitan powers (Spain, England, France, the Netherlands, and the United States) but have seen each other across those colonial lines as kin sharing the desire to end colonialism, racial subordination, and the dehumanization of the region's black, mestizo, mulatto, and indigenous populations. Nineteenth-century transcolonial kinship narratives are characterized by a radical antislavery project against racial subordination, which reframes anticolonial struggles like *antillanismo* as decolonial efforts. These narratives circulated across the Spanish-speaking Caribbean and Haiti and also reemerged within the twentieth-century decolonization struggles of the Anglophone and Francophone Caribbean. The Garveyists, the pan-Africanists, the Negritude movement and Créolistes in Martinique and Guadeloupe, and the Trinidadians C. L. R. James and Eric Williams were also influenced by these narratives, as demonstrated by the enthusiastic advocacy of a Federation of the West Indies in the twentieth century.[8]

Invoking *antillanismo* as a kinship model is not a coincidental act but a strategic and deeply political move. *Antillanista* thought has a long and varied history in the Antilles. Addressing common experiences since the nineteenth century, *antillanistas* (pan-Antilleanists) have represented the Caribbean as a geopolitical and cultural space intimately tied by a shared desire to fulfill ideals of freedom. These desires have fueled antislavery, anticolonial, and anticapitalist movements. For the past two centuries pan-Antilleanists such as José Martí, Lola Rodríguez de Tío, C. L. R. James, Luis Rafael Sánchez, the

Créolistes, Edouard Glissant, Silvio Torres-Saillant, Kamau Brathwaite, Wilson Harris, and Ana Lydia Vega have attempted to develop a transcolonial consciousness, a shared sense of identity for the region. In the recent past Antillean intellectuals, state officials, and community organizers described the Caribbean as "our regional mansion within a global home," "a family of islands" sharing filial bonds and cultural cross-fertilizations (see Brathwaite 2009; Ramphal 2009). Transcolonial kinship narratives are present throughout the Spanish-speaking, Anglophone, and Francophone Caribbean.

Originally I hoped that by explaining how transcolonial kinship was imagined by *antillanistas*, one could then easily interrogate how the radical antislavery politics of *antillanismo* has been co-opted by transnational neoliberal projects. I meant to show that by invoking *antillanismo*, such projects falsely appear to be committed to racial inclusion and equality in the region. However, it quickly became evident that the premises of nineteenth-century antillanista projects, which emphasize the political integration of Antillean islands into a confederation, needed to be examined before being invoked as decolonial possibilities. Transcolonial affective relations were not the only models of kinship used by *antillanistas*. What in fact did emerge was the possibility of what I call a decolonial affective matrix, constituted by political leaders' and intellectuals' rhetorical maneuvering of transcolonial, national, and colonial kinship models.[9]

Chapter 1 concentrates on the writings of two *antillanista* men, the Puerto Rican Ramón Emeterio Betances and the Dominican Gregorio Luperón, who imagined their transcolonial ideals implemented through an Antillean confederation of independent political territories in the mid- and late nineteenth century. Though the idea of a confederation is not necessarily what moves all *antillanistas*, transcolonial, antiracist, and black-identified ideas of brotherhood and family characterize their thinking. Betances and Luperón represent this ideological tradition, and both have been recognized as forefathers of *antillanismo* in the Spanish-speaking Antilles and, I would add, the Antilles as a whole (Castro Ventura 2002; Cordero Michel 1998; Ojeda Reyes and Estrade 2000; Reyes-Santos 2013b; Torres-Saillant 2006). The nineteenth century is the paradigmatic moment of *antillanismo* in the history of the Spanish-speaking Antilles. It is when Dominicans, Haitians, Puerto Ricans, and Cubans articulate *antillanismo* as a decolonial alternative and as an embodied call for transcolonial kinship in the context of revolutionary independence networks. By analyzing

Betances's and Luperón's writings, we can trace how *antillanismo,* specifically its transcolonial kinship narratives, engages what José F. Buscaglia-Salgado (2003) calls *mulataje.*

Both Betances and Luperón narrate ethnically and racially heterogeneous political communities mostly characterized by the intermixing of Africans and Europeans. Their political praxis is also characterized by a rhetorical *mulataje* that, according to Buscaglia-Salgado (2003), was characterized by the contestation of Eurocentric notions of the citizen and the nation. These mulatto leaders shared an antislavery agenda that transcended claims of national sovereignty and sought the consolidation of an Antillean confederation committed to racial equality. This agenda required them to mobilize black, mulatto, and white Creole interests in the region. *Mulataje* was the racial narrative of transcolonial kinship models. It asserted Afro-descendants' rights to freedom and self-determination as agents of political transformation in newly emerging nations.

Betances's and Luperón's commitments to transcolonial solidarity, to an *antillanista* brotherhood (Arroyo 2013), also entailed expressing their affiliation with particular national communities (national kinship) and cultural and political relationships with European colonial powers (colonial/imperial kinship). To use Luperón's (1939: 1:31) words, as "hijos emancipados" (emancipated sons), these writers navigated their actual familial, cultural, and political relationships with Europe (colonial/imperial kinship), along with their desire to end racial subordination in the Antilles (transcolonial kinship), honor their black ancestors and the interracial relationships that constitute their families (transcolonial kinship), and fight for the right to self-determination of emerging nations (national kinship) and the desired Antillean confederation (transcolonial kinship). A necessary political pragmatism often informed which narrative of kinship—transcolonial, colonial/imperial, or national—prevailed in their discourse.[10]

The notion of a decolonial affective matrix complicates representations of *antillanismo* as the ideal alternative to Creole nation-building projects, projects that were invested in whitening narratives (Buscaglia-Salgado 2003). As Sara E. Johnson (2012) clearly states, transcolonial communities are not always simply emancipatory. Their transcolonial kinship narratives interrogated the Eurocentric logic of colonialism. And yet Luperón and Betances also narrate their kinship ties to European colonial powers. These narratives help explain who they describe as natural allies and friends of the Caribbean in Europe. At times these political relationships seem to be at odds with their anticolonial critiques of white supremacy and European rule over the Americas. Moreover, to varying degrees, their narratives of national families and kinship gender relations and marriage within anticolonial struggles illustrate potential shortcomings of pan-Antillean anticolonial projects (Lazo 2005; Toledo 2002). Betances and Luperón themselves gendered the revolutionary antislavery and anticolonial subject in masculinist and heteronormative terms.

The decolonial affective matrix points to the co-constitution of transcolonial, national, and colonial/imperial kinship narratives in nineteenth-century Antillean political and cultural thought. In my discussion of Betances's and Luperón's work, using this matrix as an analytical framework allows me to describe transcolonial affective models, at their intersection with nationalist narratives of kinship, and colonial identifications and political affiliations.

Mujer, Comida y Cama Propias

As the nineteenth century came to an end, *antillanista* activism lost its footing in Dominican and Puerto Rican political imaginations (Arroyo 2013; Buscaglia-Salgado 2003). In the early twentieth century the Dominican Republic, Haiti, Puerto Rico, and Cuba became ground zero for U.S. attempts to establish its imperial power over the Caribbean. In 1898, during the Spanish American War, the United States invaded Puerto Rico and Cuba. Puerto Rico became a U.S. territory, and Cuba eventually renegotiated the terms of its relationship with the United States. In 1902 the U.S. Congress approved the Platt Amendment, limiting Cuba's international commerce, requiring the lease of land for U.S. military bases such as the one found in Guantánamo, and removing military forces while enabling unilateral military interventions. In 1917 the Jones Act granted U.S. citizenship to Puerto Ricans, but the island remained an unincorporated territory of the United States without a voting representative in the U.S. Congress, and Puerto Ricans on the island were excluded from participating in U.S. presidential elections.

In 1915 and 1916 the United States occupied the Dominican Republic and Haiti. The occupations lasted more than a decade in each country (Haiti, 1915–34; Dominican Republic, 1916–28). Sugar industries grew and were further modernized by the injection of U.S. capital in Cuba, the Dominican Republic, and Puerto Rico. The U.S. occupation of Haiti actively recruited significant numbers of Haitian peasants to be sent to work in Cuban and Dominican plantations (García Muñiz 2010; Inoa 1999; Moreno Fraginals 1985; Roorda 1998). By the 1930s, when the economies of the region were feeling the effects of the Great Depression, government officials and media in Cuba and the Dominican Republic started representing these workers as scapegoats.

Chapter 2, "Wife, Food, and a Bed of His Own: Marriage, Family, and Nationalist Kinship in the 1930s," illustrates how Dominican and Puerto Rican novels in the 1930s imagined national families under siege by U.S. imperialism. Marriage emerged as the primordial but insufficient affective model for national kin relations. While the metaphor of marriage allowed for the articulation of an imagined national unity, it also required ignoring the continued reality of transcolonial struggles for racial and economic justice, and it reproduced heteropatriarchal conventions of national belonging. As *novelas del cañaveral* (plantation novels; Costa 2004; Graciano 1990; Méndez 2011), the Puerto Rican Enrique Laguerre's *La Llamarada* (1939) and the Dominican Ramón Marrero Aristy's *Over* (1939; 1963) speak directly to the consequences of U.S. imperialism on national subjects and their kinship structures.

I have chosen to discuss these novels because they represent a period when nationalist projects were consolidated in the Dominican Republic and Puerto Rico in response to the colonial/imperial tutelage of the United States. The era of U.S. economic and military hegemony over the Antilles had been concretized by then and posed a new threat to decolonization processes. These novels are paradigmatic examples of national kinship narratives. Moreover their canonization reveals that, as narratives of marriage and national families, they were conveniently invoked by certain political sectors. They were especially valued for their rendering of families as the model for protecting national land and territory. *Over* became a useful tool for the Dominican dictator Rafael Leónidas Trujillo, who sought to nationalize the sugarcane industry to maximize his own profit (Sommer 1988). *La Llamarada* represents the interests of an elite, intellectual class, whose historical economic interests and political clout had been displaced by the colonial government and U.S. investments in Puerto Rico (Ferrao 1993; Janer 2005). But these canonical nationalist novels also negotiate multiple notions of community and belonging as they attempt to imagine a national family that can overcome the material consequences of U.S. imperialism in the Dominican Republic and Puerto Rico.

At the time many narratives of national kinship mirrored the racial assumptions of elite Creole nationalist projects that sought to whiten and contain the political demands of poor, *mestizo*/mulatto, indigenous, and black populations in Latin America. *Mestizaje* as whitening (whitening through racial and cultural mixture) and *hispanidad* (the affirmation of Spanish racial and cultural legacies over others) are two of the predominant discourses on nationhood in the Caribbean and Latin America (Candelario 2007; Dávila 1997; Fuente 2001; Godreau et al. 2008; Mayes 2014; Wade 2010; Whitten and Torres 1998). These novels touch upon these currents and, at times, replicate them. However, they also present a sharp contrast to Creole nationalism by engaging elements of *antillanista* thought.

The affective matrix that informed *antillanismo* remained in place in the early twentieth century, though its axis had shifted from a focus on transcolonial kinship to the construction of national kinship. Both *La Llamarada* and *Over* deploy narratives of national kinship alongside experiences and memories of transcolonial kinship and colonial/imperial kinship (with Spain and the United States). The novels' attempts at building national families, however, indicate the failures and tensions inherent in national projects. To some degree families in the novels fail not only because of their inability to reconcile racial and class differences or because of U.S. imperialist encroachments on their desire for autonomy. They also fail because of an awareness of the antislavery, transcolonial solidarities that the narrator-protagonists wish to ignore but ultimately cannot.

Studies of 1930s nationalisms in the Dominican Republic and Puerto Rico have always considered colonial kinship and the tendency to celebrate Hispanic legacies to describe the racial politics of nation-building literatures (Belén Cambeira 2001; Fernández Olmos 1978; Gelpí 1993; Horn 2014; Janer 2005; Méndez 2011; Rodríguez 2003; Roy-Féquière 2004; Sommer 1988; Torres-Saillant 2000; Veloz Maggiolo 1977). But not many analyses have noted how transcolonial ideas about national communities emerge out of La Llamarada's and Over's political unconscious to form internal contradictions within these nationalist narratives. As an analytical framework, the decolonial affective matrix provides fresh insight into the significance of national modes of kinship within the sea of transcolonial discourses and colonial/imperial occupation.

What we also learn from these texts is that paying attention to race mixture in national kinship narratives requires entering the intimate domain of romantic and sexual relations and how they have been codified by the institution of marriage (Horn 2014; Mayes 2014; Suárez

Findlay 1999). The narrators need to marry the right woman, properly maintain her, and produce national subjects in order to assume their presumed roles as patriarchs of the national family. Their investment in marriage as the affective unit that reproduces the nation limits trans-colonial kinship relations. Labor organizers, black-identified migrants and local workers, and Garveyists pass through the texts, speak their truths, and provoke a series of moral crises for the narrators, but never are they seen as the protagonists' people. Constructing marriage as the central affective unit of nation-building projects limits the possibility of imagining and recognizing other kin relations, other chosen families (Weston 1991). *La Llamarada* and *Over* provide an opportunity to reflect on the political value of nationalism in the past and in contemporary neoliberal contexts. Though anticolonial nationalisms were integral to decolonization struggles in the mid-nineteenth and early twentieth centuries, in the twenty-first century their value has been interrogated. Antiracist, Marxist, feminist, and queer critiques of nations as cultural and political family have correctly signaled some of the pitfalls of nationalist projects (Allen 2011; Roy-Féquière 2004; Janer 2005; Negrón- Muntaner 2007; Rivera Velázquez 2008). In her study of Puerto Rican nation-building literatures, Zilkia Janer (2005: 96) concludes that nationalism is "an obstacle" to quests for social equality and alternative models to "United States–led globalization."

At the same time, nationalist claims call attention to the inequities that inform transnational neoliberal projects, inequities shaped by histories of colonial subjection and dependency, U.S. economic interests, and U.S. military interventions on both sides of the island. They call attention to the exploitation of natural resources by foreign investors, such as the current campaigns in the Dominican Republic against the Canadian gold mining company Barrick Gold and the genetically modified seed producer and exporter Monsanto or the protests against the potential development of Dominican natural reserves like Bahia de las Aguilas and Los Haitises.[11] Nationalist claims are also used by Dominican youth of Haitian descent to claim their belonging to the national family.

Shalini Puri (2004) and David Vázquez (2011) have argued that the nation continues to be an important analytical category even while transnational frameworks gain more traction. The nation mediates one's experience of transnational economic and political processes, and nationalism "may still be productive for aggrieved communities" (Vázquez 2011: 19). Nationalism can still be a productive site for

oppositional politics, and it is fruitful to examine different nationalisms in order to better understand their force and imperfections.[12] As
Negrón-Muntaner (2007: 14) reminds us, "the nation is not enough,"
but it is still here. Questions remain: How can we engage the nation
in order to effectively address neoliberal realities, such as the rights of
the children of migrants and the privatization of public lands in the
Dominican Republic and of public services in Puerto Rico? How do we
address what the nation tends to leave untouched: its racial, class, and
ethnic hierarchical structures; its commitment to heteropatriarchal
notions of kinship and reproduction?

Contemporary Narratives of Kinship in the Islands of Haiti/Hispaniola and Puerto Rico

The first two chapters lay out the basis for an analysis of contemporary narratives of kinship between Haitians and Dominicans, and
Dominicans and Puerto Ricans, as people who share borders within the
Caribbean. They help us understand a multiplicity of discourses about
Haitian-Dominican and Dominican–Puerto Rican relations. Though
Haitian-Dominican relations tend to be described as tense by scholarly research on *antihaitianismo* (Adames 2013; Jarayam 2010; Méndez
2011; Sagás 2000; Wucker 1999), and Dominican–Puerto Rican relations
have been represented recently as ambivalent (Pacini-Hernández 2009;
Martínez–San Miguel 2003), analyzing them through the lens provided
by the decolonial affective matrix deepens and at times complicates
our understanding of such descriptions of intra-Caribbean relations.
Racism, xenophobia, and solidarity can all be descriptors of Antillean
attitudes toward those of a different national origin. The Antillean transcolonial framework has always been a malleable tool that responds to the
pragmatic needs of a historical moment. In the late twentieth and early
twenty-first century, metaphors of brotherhood, marriage, and family
continue to be deployed by Luperón's *hijos emancipados* as they face the
realities of neoliberal economies. Almost in the same breath Dominicans and Puerto Ricans appear to affirm racist and xenophobic ideas of
national belonging, as well as horizontal kinship networks with other
Antilleans, while at the same time articulating the need to collaborate
with or question colonial/imperial powers: Europe and the United States.

In the last two chapters of the book, I explain the slippage of meaning between transcolonial and transnational kinship in the recent
past. That slippage is crucial to understand how Haitian-Dominican

relations and Dominican–Puerto Ricans relations are narrated by state officials, media, and cultural production in the two islands. Beginning in the late twentieth century various principles of *antillanismo* were co-opted by neoliberal advocates seeking to implement transnational economic projects, such as FTZs (sweatshops) on the Haitian-Dominican border and free trade agreements between the Dominican Republic and the United States. Puerto Rico and its people have been embedded in a series of economic collaborations between the United States, the Dominican Republic, and Puerto Rican investors and commercial enterprises. Transcolonial kinship models are then reconfigured in the context of narratives about working-class Haitian migrants in the Dominican Republic and working-class Dominican migrants in Puerto Rico.

The texts under consideration in chapters 3 and 4 elucidate ideological tensions between national and transcolonial/transnational paradigms. In my discussion of contemporary narratives of Haitian-Dominican relations, I make a distinction between transcolonial and transnational kinship narratives. On one hand, media coverage of state practices illustrates that official narratives imagine a present and a future characterized by transnational neoliberal projects such as CAFTA-DR (the free trade agreement between the United States, the Dominican Republic, and Central American nations) and commercial enterprises between Haiti and the Dominican Republic. On the other hand, Haitian-Dominican alliances over labor, peasant, LGBT, environmental, migrant, and women's rights—along with collaborations with social movements in the Caribbean and Latin America—serve as examples of transcolonial solidarity invested in social justice.

In this context the transcolonial references Lionnet's definition, and it also stands for horizontal, interethnic efforts invested in social justice and in addressing more specifically racial, ethnic, and economic disparities among populations. The term *transnational* serves to describe state-sponsored triangulated efforts among Antilleans and their northern colonial/imperial parental figures. *Transnational kinship* describes those colonial/imperial parental relations at a time when we have witnessed some of the failures of neoliberal globalization. For one, it has not leveled the playing field of economic relations, despite claims to this end. For another, the continuing and increasing disparities in countries like the Dominican Republic and Haiti demonstrate how the racial and gendered presumptions of colonialism/imperialism are deeply engrained in neoliberal projects. As *Our Caribbean Kin* will show, colonial legacies have not been superseded as a result of the unrestricted free market.

Family, home, and community are commonplace descriptors of transnational kinship among neoliberal advocates. For instance, the online publication "CAFTA Facts" (2005) rhetorically mobilizes affect in its representation of CAFTA-DR as an effort to support "growth, opportunity, and democracy in our neighborhood." Produced by the Office of the U.S. Trade Representative, this document describes the advantages of CAFTA-DR. It imagines the American hemisphere as a neighborhood that counts on each of its members to succeed through reciprocal and interdependent sets of intimate relations.

Throughout "CAFTA Facts" (2005: 3) terms like "freedom," "democracy," and "leveling the playing field" characterize and celebrate this project of regional economic integration: "CAFTA is a way for America to support freedom, democracy and economic reform in our own neighborhood." Upon closer examination, the images invoked by the document reveal that it is a project premised on a paternalistic relationship between the United States and Central America, which is depicted as "a region of fragile democracies that need U.S. support" (3). Though the Office of the U.S. Trade Representative suggests that all countries involved in the agreement participate on equal terms, it is clear that the political-economic playing field retains the power relations that have characterized U.S.-Latin American relations since the nineteenth century. The United States is represented as the country with the ability to govern itself and help others govern themselves; the Caribbean region gets imagined as a neighborhood with a benevolent paternal figure at its helm: the United States. Representing Central America and the Caribbean as a region in need of rescue by the United States invokes the paternalist overtones of colonial civilizing narratives.[13]

As "CAFTA Facts" demonstrates, developing nations are subjected to colonial, paternalist representations that deem them in need of rescue. Such paternalism, however, also has a violent streak, one that applies a "logic of obliteration" (Ferreira da Silva 2007: 267) to racialized and gendered others who do not embody Eurocentric notions of civilization and progress. These subjects are characterized as expendable within global political-economic processes. Through the implementation of structural adjustment programs and the liberalization of their economies, developing nations can partake of regional integration efforts—enjoying their intimate economic proximity in the global village—despite the high human cost for impoverished communities.

Disciplining their socioeconomic behavior through life-threatening austerity measures and permitting their demise from genocide, warfare, or hunger become feasible plot twists in narratives of neoliberal kinship.

In spite of such realities, advocates of free trade policies imply that all participants in a regional market share intimate bonds that must be actualized through the deregulation of national economies. Neoliberal theory requires free trade among nation-states so as to permit a presumably natural flow of commodities, capital, and labor (Harvey 2003; Karim 2011). Neoliberalism rejects the intervention of the nation in the protection of its resources unless it is necessary to protect capital flows (Trouillot 2003), such as the recent example of corporate bailouts in the United States. Allegedly the interests of transnational capital must be allowed to flourish without restrictions. Corporate profits then trickle down to the less privileged classes and nations (Friedman 2006). Neoliberalism, proponents argue, will deliver the economic prosperity that individual nations—especially formerly colonized territories of Latin America, the Caribbean, Africa, and Asia—have not been able to deliver. Neoliberalism purports to eliminate relationships of dependence between the wealthier nations and those nations still struggling to construct independent prosperity.[14]

International financing institutions, such as the World Bank and the International Monetary Fund, prescribe open-border policies, restructuring programs, the outsourcing of labor, and the privatization of national enterprises for developing countries like the Dominican Republic (Bergeron 2004; Benjamin 2007). Those in dire need have to acquiesce to the prevailing economic model in return for funds to service earlier loans. Developing nation-states must relax their regulation of and taxation on imports and exports and must often undertake structural adjustment programs. National industries—even those administering basic resources, such as water, electricity, and communication systems—are privatized for the sake of efficiency and to cut the state's expenses. Social welfare for the poor is reduced or eliminated. Neoliberal economic agreements reduce or eliminate taxation of transnational economic projects—such as FTZs, tourism industries, and industrial parks—and provide a workforce prepared to participate in these economic activities (Cabezas 2009; Gregory 2007). These nations focus on furthering export-oriented manufacturing and agriculture, as well as service-based economies. In the Caribbean, neoliberal development prescriptions imagine a region modernized through the iteration of FTZs and tourist destinations (Kempadoo 2004).

Transnational corporations from the Global North outsource certain segments of their production processes to locations providing cheaper labor. The neoliberal Antilles is one of those locations. Labor unions frequently lose their bargaining power with corporations protected by state subsidies and debt-relief programs. Migratory flows, for example from Haiti to the Dominican Republic and from the Dominican Republic to Puerto Rico, are impacted by these policies (Graziano 2013; Silié et al. 2002). As the cost of living increases and social welfare decreases, migrants hope to improve their lives by migrating. In the meantime racist and xenophobic national discourses enable the dehumanization of migrants, who are increasingly mistreated and economically exploited within these neoliberal economies. Clichés such as *the global village, leveling the playing field, interdependence,* and *reciprocity* configure transnational kinship narratives that refuse to recognize the economic, racial, ethnic, and gender inequalities exacerbated by these policies (Brennan 2004; Cabezas 2009; Gregory 2007; Grosfoguel 2003; Kempadoo 2004; Padilla 2007; Sheller 2003). The distinction between transcolonial and transnational kinship narratives requires us to keep asking: Who is attempting to create a sense of kinship between Haitians and Dominicans? Between Dominicans and Puerto Ricans? Whose economic interests are at stake?

Como de la Familia

Chapter 3 "Like Family: (Un)recognized Siblings and the Haitian-Dominican Family," engages these conflicting narratives of Haitian-Dominican relations in a neoliberal context through the analysis of newspaper articles, online publications, social science research, political organizing campaigns, and fictional literature. The methodology for this chapter, and the following one, builds upon Yolanda Martínez–San Miguel's (2003) study of a culture of migration in the insular Caribbean. Martínez–San Miguel compares how intranational borders are imagined by Cubans, Dominicans, and Puerto Ricans in Puerto Rico and New York City, two sites where these populations encounter each other. She delves into how migrations transform representations of national identities. I compare how Haitians and Dominicans in the Dominican Republic and Dominicans and Puerto Ricans in Puerto Rico imagine national and transcolonial/transnational families.

Martínez–San Miguel (2003: 39) creates a rich archive of cultural texts, including literature, film, graffiti, music, photography, paintings, and the visual arts, to address both popular and elite cultural artifacts. Her analysis addresses how multiple social groups negotiate their particular understanding of intercultural Antillean encounters through cultural practices. In conversation with her I briefly refer to graffiti as a visual site where both popular sentiments and state-sanctioned politically correct positions are publicly displayed; the graffiti illustrates the impossibility of asserting that *antihaitianismo* in the Dominican Republic is simply one or the other. I also consider newspapers, particularly because historically they have disseminated ideas of the nation and national belonging and created cohesion among national subjects with a variety of class, ethnic, and racial interests (Anderson 1991; González-Pérez 2004). My participatory research experience as a volunteer in Centro Bonó's intercultural education program in the Dominican Republic, intellectual and political discussions about Haitian migrants' rights in the country, and participation in political mobilizations with reconoci.do, the group that represents Dominican youth of Haitian descent, have helped me to better understand the political, economic, and cultural conditions described by the literary texts under consideration.[15] Other collaborations and interactions with social justice organizations, such as the Confederación de Mujeres Campesinas (CONAMUCA), Amigos Siempre Amigos, the Movimiento de Mujeres Domínico-Haitianas (MUDHA), Participación Ciudadana, and La Colectiva Mujer y Salud, also gave me a broader sense of the kinds of narratives of kinship at play in the present-day in the Dominican Republic, especially those not documented in existing scholarship about Haitian-Dominican relations. All these analytical sites allow me to better describe how literature intervenes in public debates and quotidian conversations about narratives of kinship in the Dominican Republic and Puerto Rico.

In chapter 3 there are two metaphors that aptly describe the affective ties that frame my analysis. The first was articulated by the former Dominican president Hipolito Mejía and the former Haitian president Jean Bertrand Aristide, who referred to Haitian-Dominican relations as a "marriage without divorce." The second is a phrase that describes cross-class relations between servants and employers in the literary texts under consideration: *como de la familia* (like family). This phrase describes servants and racial or ethnic outsiders deemed inferior by elite interlocutors as people who are understood to be family. Here marriage describes state-sponsored Haitian-Dominican collaboration but also opens the possibility for acknowledging unofficial, grassroots, transnational/transcolonial solidarity movements. *Como de la familia* elides internal class, ethnic, and racial differences within a household and within national and transnational communities, but still asserts a certain intimacy between subjects who belong to a collectivity, albeit on unequal terms. Poor, working-class, and dark-skinned Dominicans and Haitians, Dominicans of Haitian descent, women, and Haitian migrants can all be (un)recognized siblings within the metaphorical marriage between Haiti and the Dominican Republic. Certain people, because of their class status, ethnic origin, racial background, migrant status, gender, or sexual practices, are disowned by national and transnational families. They are considered outsiders, an excess, a drain on the system, invaders. But they cannot be denied as children of the same land on an island shared by two countries, an island that shares political, economic, and environmental concerns as well as cultural, familial, and communal exchanges across its border.

I examine how a series of narratives about Haitian-Dominican relations engage these metaphors of transnational/transcolonial and national kinship in order to articulate different degrees of intimacy between Haitians, Dominicans, and Dominicans of Haitian descent. Newspapers, online publications, social science research, and political organizing introduce us to the following narratives of Haitian-Dominican relations in the Dominican Republic: pacific invasion, acculturation, neoliberal multiculturalism, Haitian-Dominican solidarity, and *interculturalidad*. These narratives illustrate the variety of notions of national belonging and kinship in public debates regarding Haitian-Dominican relations in the Dominican Republic. Intercultural nationalism appears as an alternative to elitist, anti-Haitian narratives and as a framework that does not ignore each country's claim to particular national histories and cultural heritages.

The novels *The Farming of Bones* (1998) by the Haitian American writer Edwidge Danticat and *Solo falta que llueva* (2004) by the Dominican-born Santiago Estrella Veloz imagine affective, even if troubled ties between Haitians and Dominicans and among Dominicans themselves. The national and transcolonial/transnational families that emerge in these novels illustrate how representations of racial, gender, sexual, and class difference co-construct kinship narratives. The particular subjectivities, story lines, and formalistic components of the novels speak to concerns regarding the significance of the national and the transcolonial/transnational as paradigms that can be activated by foreign investors, the working poor, and social justice activists, among many other social actors. Engaging the theme of Haitian migration and Haitian-Dominican communities in the Dominican Republic, both novels are meditations on the political potential of national and pan-Antillean kinship.

By documenting a broad range of narratives of Haitian-Dominican relations, I hope to offer a broader vision of those relations than the one offered by the common attention to narratives of *antihaitianismo*. I challenge mainstream descriptions of the Dominican Republic as an exceptional example of antiblack racism and *antihaitianismo* in Latin America and the Caribbean.[16] I join the voices of Dominican studies scholars Carlos Dore Cabral, Rubén Silié, Franklyn Franco Prichardo, Ginetta Candelario, Isis Duarte, André Corten, María Filomena Gónzalez-Alcalá, Sara E. Johnson, Silvio Torres-Saillant, Danny Méndez, and April Mayes, among many others, who collectively unveil histories of Haitian-Dominican relations that transcend the limits of elite nationalist narratives invested in the whitening legacies of colonialism/imperialism.

In chapter 3 I demonstrate that "in sharp contrast to the black denial chorus, not all roads lead blindly to whiteness" (Mayes 2014: 141) in Dominican national and racial thought, in particular with respect to Haitian migrants and Dominicans of Haitian descent. I honor the work of the hundreds of organizations in the Dominican Republic that signed a public agreement in May 2013 demanding that the Dominican government take action to regularize the status of Haitian migrants in the country, as well as of the more than sixty Dominican organizations that met in December 2013 with the International Commission for Human Rights to denounce the September 2013 decision of the Dominican Constitutional Tribunal to denationalize Dominicans of Haitian descent going as far back as 1929.[17]

Family Secrets

The metaphor of family secrets aptly describes how Dominican–Puerto Rican relations are formulated through cultural production in Puerto Rico. Representations of national and transcolonial/transnational families in Puerto Rico at times require a series of *secretos a voces*, secrets known but hidden in plain view. Whether Dominicans are seen as outsiders to the great Puerto Rican family or are imagined as integral components of Dominican–Puerto Rican extended families, secrets are what keep these narratives of national and transcolonial/

transnational kinship at play in Puerto Rican cultural practices. My attention to metaphors and tropes of family secrets seeks to explain the inverse feelings of empathy and rejection toward Dominicans that Martínez–San Miguel (2003) and Pacini Hernández (2009) have described. Cultural analysis suggests that a series of negations and secret complicities embedded in competing narratives of kinship between Dominicans and Puerto Ricans explains such ambivalence.

This ambivalence is grounded in narratives of Puerto Rican national kinship that exclude Dominicans by imagining them as poor, criminalized, racialized migrants. This same image originally targeted poor Puerto Ricans. Anti-Dominican discourses such as those discussed in media, ethnic jokes, and literature attempt to keep the realities of poor and dark-skinned Puerto Ricans a secret in order to sustain claims of a united national family. But these claims do not succeed. Across a range of narratives Dominican and Puerto Rican characters interrogate and dismantle Puerto Ricans' collusion with the neoliberal agendas embedded in the U.S. war on drugs and the war on terror, which criminalize Dominican migrants. Dominicans register their awareness of Puerto Ricans' inconsistency as brothers who may at times act like loyal Antillean siblings and at other times disown them.

To understand how Dominicans are excluded or incorporated in *la gran familia puertorriqueña*, it is necessary to engage the dual reality of Puerto Ricans as Antilleans as well as citizens of the United States. Migrating to Puerto Rico, Dominicans seek wages in U.S. dollars to send home remittances and hopefully acquire the documentation, U.S. residency, or citizenship that will allow them to travel freely between Puerto Rico and the Dominican Republic and Puerto Rico and the U.S. mainland. Many hope to either migrate to the U.S. mainland or to benefit from the higher standard of living in Puerto Rico, while remaining in a geographical, cultural, and linguistic setting that is more familiar to them as people from the Caribbean (Duany 2011; Duany et al. 1995). Puerto Rico then becomes a bridge between the Dominican Republic and the United States that enables many Dominicans to sustain long-standing economic, familial, and cultural ties in all of these locations, what some have called the "transnational village" (Duany 2011; Levitt 2001). In this transnational village Dominican migrants must negotiate Puerto Ricans' perceptions of them as blacker, underdeveloped, non-U.S.-born, Antillean neighbors (Duany 2011; Martínez–San Miguel 2003; Duany et al. 1995; Rey 1999–2000; Reyes-Santos 2008).

Narratives of Dominican–Puerto Rican transnational kinship are conveniently deployed within neoliberal free trade agreements and require that all participants collaborate in the U.S.-led war on drugs and war on terror. Moreover, after 9/11 the Puerto Rican government, the U.S. Coast Guard, and the Dominican Coast Guard have collaborated to police maritime transit through the Mona Channel under the rubric of these wars (Graziano 2013). Pursuing a series of policies and surveillance strategies that seek to deter drug traffickers and potential terrorists becomes a requirement of any commercial agreement between the United States and the Dominican Republic, as well as their intermediary, the Puerto Rican government.

In chapter 4, "Family Secrets: Brotherhood, Passing, and the Dominican–Puerto Rican Family," I analyze the iconic short story "Retrato del dominicano que pasó por puertorriqueño y emigró a mejor vida en Nueva York" (1995b) by the Puerto Rican Magaly García Ramis; the autobiography *Mona, Canal de la Muerte* (1995) by the Dominican Luis Freites; the television show *Entrando por la cocina* (1986–2002); newspaper articles about Dominican migration; and ethnic/racial jokes about Dominicans in Puerto Rico. Each of these texts provides insight into the spoken and unspoken contours of kinship between Dominicans and Puerto Ricans. Ethnic/racist jokes act as quotidian cultural practices that negotiate Puerto Ricans' ambivalence toward their neighbors (Martínez–San Miguel 2003; Quintero Herencia 1996). I add television to Martínez–San Miguel's archive of intercultural contact among Antilleans because television in Puerto Rico incorporates migrants into the national family and questions and reproduces stereotypes about them (Rivero 2005). I find that an extended working-class, Dominican–Puerto Rican family is imagined as a kinship possibility in Puerto Rican television.

Freites's autobiography provides a Dominican perspective on how kinship is built among Dominicans and Puerto Ricans on the island and the United States. The account suggests that transcolonial solidarity is possible only when these populations find each other as migrants in New York City. In this context brotherhood emerges as a metaphor for Dominican–Puerto Rican relations that enable both to support each other materially and emotionally as they attempt to better their circumstances in neoliberal economies.

García Ramis's short story allows the reader to experience the ambivalent nature of Puerto Rican relations on the island. It tells the story of a group of Puerto Rican males who help their Dominican friend to pass as one of their own so that he can migrate to New York. But the story reveals that the racial and ethnic marginalization of Dominicans is not simply limited to imagining Puerto Ricans as whiter, more educated, and modern Antilleans. It suggests that Puerto Rican Afro-diasporic, male, heteronormative, and working-class aesthetics associated with rap and hip hop culture can also be deployed to marginalize Dominicans.[18]

Reading this short story through an Afro-diasporic lens offers an approach to Dominican–Puerto Rican relations that engages national kinship and colonial/imperial kinship narratives built not on whitening but on working-class, black-identified practices. If Puerto Ricans are not supposed to be as black as Dominicans, then this story of passing cracks open the secrets of definitions of the national family that attempt to whiten it vis-à-vis Dominicans. The Dominican–Puerto Rican brotherhood represented in the story emerges from a similar economic, racial, and gender experience. However, it is a brotherhood consolidated through the imposition of an Afro-diasporic masculine, Puerto Rican–identified aesthetic sensibility that becomes hegemonic and is built at the expense of the Dominican character's own ethnic and gender specificity.

Similar to the nineteenth- and early twentieth-century examples discussed in chapters 1 and 2, in García Ramis's story transcolonial brotherhood and national kinship—once again, though differently—assume conformity with heteronormative gender norms. The television comedy Entrando por la cocina complicates these earlier narratives of male brotherhood by introducing a Dominican female character, Altagracia, to commercial Puerto Rican television. The show features a Dominican–Puerto Rican extended family and marriage that reveals its secrets and airs the dirty laundry of Dominican–Puerto Rican communities to a public that can identify with the show's interethnic working-class characters.[19] The show's heterosexual, non-gender-conforming, male and female working-class characters challenge middle-class Puerto Rican notions of respectability. Their stories reveal the survival strategies of both Dominicans and Puerto Ricans who struggle to make ends meet in a rapidly declining economic environment.

Analyzing these texts using the decolonial affective matrix as a lens provides new insight into the study of Dominican–Puerto Rican relations in the neoliberal Antilles. It makes visible how Dominicans' integration into a neoliberal Puerto Rican society is informed by various narratives of filial, romantic, and sexual relations: how Puerto Ricans see themselves as whitened by the legacy of *la madre patria*, Spain, and by their U.S. citizenship (colonial/imperial kinship); how they often imagine themselves as a racially mixed family whose blackness is not as black as Dominicans' (national kinship); and the secrets of working-class pan-Antillean complicity and solidarity (transcolonial kinship). Transcolonial brotherhoods appear in defiance of the United States, its racist and xenophobic histories and immigration policies. Colonial/imperial kinship is complicated by these brotherhoods, as well as by national kinship narratives based on Afro-diasporic, urban youth cultures. Every narrative negotiates heteropatriarchal gender conventions and kinship that continue to limit the potential hidden in all sorts of chosen families.

On the Value of Affect and Kinship for Other Antilleans

This book illustrates the kinds of insights we gain from analyzing how a malleable decolonial affective matrix has been navigated by Antilleans in various historical moments and spaces. I concentrate on the Dominican Republic and Puerto Rico and pay attention to Haiti as an important interlocutor, though I wish I could have more deeply engaged Haitian history and cultural texts. Some of the most obvious absences in it are, to some extent, Haiti, Cuba, the other Spanish-speaking island in the region, the Anglophone Caribbean, and the French departments Martinique and Guadeloupe. One could also consider the Dutch Caribbean, which tends to be rendered invisible in Caribbean Studies scholarship. Due to the challenges of comparative transhistorical work, I had to make choices about which material to include. For instance, the fact that Cuba is a socialist country, currently with a mixed economy that includes private ownership, makes it a site with a vastly different historical experience of neoliberalism than its Spanish-speaking Caribbean counterparts. However, it is my belief that such analysis would be a fruitful expansion of this project; I hope to see it in the near future. I also felt that I could not do justice to the historical, political, and cultural specificities of the French, Anglophone, and Dutch-speaking Caribbean while attempting to closely read texts produced in various time periods. But as a variety of references to intellectual, cultural, and political work from the Anglophone and Francophone Caribbean demonstrates, this book seeks to be in conversation with the Caribbean as a whole.

I do believe that the questions raised by the transcolonial/transnational, national, and colonial/imperial kinship narratives discussed here are important for the rest of the Antillean region. As countries in the Antilles face demands to further neoliberalize their economies through a variety of political entities, such as the Caribbean Community, the Assembly of Caribbean Peoples, the People's Summits of the Americas, and the Bolivarian Alternative for the Americas (ALBA), the transcolonial/transnational, national, and colonial/imperial narratives that characterize Antillean history and the neoliberalization of the region must be addressed. Such narratives help to explain who Antilleans see as their allies, brothers, sisters, and kin in the early twenty-first century.

For instance, at the IV People's Summit of the Americas in April 2009, tensions between transcolonial and nationalist decolonial and anticapitalist traditions in the Antilles and Latin America complicated solidarity networks.[20] Social movements, labor unions, and nongovernmental organizations from the whole continent, including Haiti and the Spanish-speaking Caribbean, met in St. Augustine, Trinidad and Tobago, and openly critiqued neoliberal policies. Participants rejoiced in the experience of hemispheric solidarity. During the final day of the summit, a representative of the Venezuelan-sponsored ALBA wondered how culture could be mobilized to bring together the Caribbean and Latin America. Advocating for the incorporation of the Caribbean into ALBA, Venezuela sought to create a free trade area, one that fulfills the dream of Simón Bolívar, Betances, and Luperón: a hemispheric entity that works together to address the legacies of colonialism. In the example presented at the summit, it would be a free trade area infused with socialist ideals.

The Venezuelan speaker pointed to cultural and historical differences permeating conversations at the summit. These differences became most apparent during moments of small (and large) crises. For example, when the government of Trinidad and Tobago refused to allow a planned march through the capital and harassed and denied entry to Latin American activists traveling to the country to partake in the summit, indigenous South American, Puerto Rican, and other Latin American activists proposed a response to the state that widely diverged from the Trinidadian organizers' suggestions. Ensuing conversations required participants to be aware of the distinct histories of struggle and cultural experiences that have informed Latin American and Anglophone Caribbean politics, and those of particular nations, in order to develop a shared response to the state, one simultaneously fraught with tensions and deep feelings of solidarity. The need for translation itself was emblematic of this process. It was not simply a linguistic need but required making sense of cultural and political traditions in order to facilitate communication across a diverse array of political actors. What the summit demonstrated is that even when colonial/imperial kinship or transnational kinship is not a desirable model for community formation, Antilleans, as well as their Latin American neighbors, must negotiate their investment in particular national experiences in order to imagine transcolonial families, to conceive of each other as their own people. Transcolonial and nationalist kinship ties remain inextricably linked in our decolonial imagination. The question is how we choose to reimagine those kinship models in ways that are informed by and conscious of racial, ethnic, class, gender, and sexual differences.

1 / The Emancipated Sons: Nineteenth-Century Transcolonial Kinship Narratives in the Antilles

When the Puerto Rican duo Calle 13 performed their song "Latino-américa" at the 2012 Latin Grammy Awards, they tapped into a visceral memory of decolonial and anticapitalist movements that have attempted to build a sense of kinship and belonging among marginalized peoples in Latin America. These movements share roots in the nationalist struggles of the nineteenth century, the anti-imperialist struggles of the early twentieth century, and the antiglobalization struggles continuing into the present moment. Thousands of people throughout the Caribbean and North, Central, and South America listened to their call for continental solidarity and shared it widely through social networks. The song and its music video became immediate hits. Their critique of the privatization of natural resources and the expropriation of land from Afro-descended and indigenous peasants spoke to historical decolonial projects and contemporary struggles against neoliberal globalization across the continent. Engaging colonial, capitalist, and racist histories, Calle 13 inserted themselves into a history of Antillean thinkers and cultural workers invested in transcolonial kinship.

Nineteenth-century *antillanistas* such as Ramón Emeterio Betances, Gregorio Luperón, Antonio Maceo, Eugenio María de Hostos, Antenor Firmin, Louis Joseph Janvier, Lola Rodríguez de Tío, and José Martí have historically been celebrated for their transcolonial politics and their demands for full citizenship rights for nonwhite-identified populations. Their ideal of a confederation of independent Antillean territories has shaped the political imagination of Caribbean peoples into the twentieth and twenty-first century (Benítez Nazario 2001; González 1983; Ojeda Reyes 2000; Vega 1983). They circulated transcolonial kinship narratives between Antilleans and Latin Americans, including *antillanismo*. In this chapter I analyze the works of nineteenth-century *antillanista* thinkers in order to assess contemporary calls for Antillean unity. The premises of nineteenth-century *antillanista* projects, which emphasized the integration of the Antillean islands, as well as Central and South America, into a single political-economic unit, require examination before being invoked as decolonial possibilities. It is necessary to examine how *antillanistas* imagined Antillean brotherhoods, communities, and families bound by certain narratives of racial mixture, filial relations to European nations, and a series of gender and sexual conventions.

The Puerto Rican Ramón E. Betances (1827–98) and the Dominican Gregorio Luperón (1839–97) precede the "black and masculine global imaginary" examined by Michelle Ann Stephens (2005) in her remarkable historical study of Marcus Garvey, Claude McKay, and C. L. R. James. Like these men, Betances and Luperón demanded the political and economic enfranchisement of those of African descent by mobilizing people across national and colonial boundaries. In the midst of independence struggles in the Spanish-speaking Caribbean, Betances and Luperón dreamed of an Antillean confederation that would protect the independence of Caribbean island-nations and the political rights of non-Europeans. They led *antillanista* anticolonial and antislavery political movements that not only sought independence and the abolition of slavery but also challenged white supremacy across the continent.

Through their political rhetoric these revolutionary anticolonial thinkers sought to build regional brotherhoods and political communities that stood against slavery, colonialism, and racial subordination. The metaphors and historical references they deployed in their political writings were meant to create the political alliances needed to sustain the dream of a confederation. Such alliances mobilized particular imaginations of interracial and interethnic intimate relationships and narratives that valued Antilleans' filial ties between Afro-descendant communities and oppositional European colonial powers. These filial ties were marked by decolonial, antislavery imperatives.

The intellectual labor of scholars such as Félix Ojeda Reyes, Paul Estrade, Nancy Mirabal, Silvio Torres-Saillant, Ada Suárez, Ada Ferrer, Santiago Castro Ventura, Ismael Hernández, José F. Buscaglia-Salgado, Pedro L. San Miguel, Rodrigo Lazo, Josefina Toledo, and April Mayes, among many others, inspired my comparison and discussion of kinship narratives present in Luperón's and Betances's work. In particular Sara E. Johnson's (2012) and Josianna Arroyo's (2013) insights about comradeship, brotherhood, and cross-cultural exchanges and translations in the circum-Caribbean region in the nineteenth century have been instrumental in the conceptualization of this chapter. In *The Fear of French Negroes*, Johnson provides a model to study attempts at forging unity among Afro-descendant peoples in the U.S. South and the Caribbean in the aftermath of the Haitian Revolution that productively engages class, gender, and territorial differences. Johnson underscores transcolonial collaborations, or "alternative community formations that contested the racialized violence endemic to European imperialism and creole nation-building projects" (5), that predate yet clearly speak to the transcolonial kinship narratives analyzed by this chapter. Though Arroyo mostly concentrates on the mulatto radicalism that shaped Masonic practices in the nineteenth-century Antilles, her attention to the rhetorical strategies that characterized Betances's attempts to build unity among Antilleans informs my own analytical proposal. She argues that Betances "forges a new ethic of Masonic radical brotherhood" (2013: 100) that translates into a broader commitment to what I call transcolonial kinship.[1] This new ethic crossed class lines and colonial boundaries to foster political solidarities grounded in the assertion of Afro-descendants' political agency, the independence of the Antilles, and the ideal of an Antillean confederation. Betances found himself fighting alongside brothers, such as Luperón, inspired by a commitment to create what they deemed a more just world for all, beyond the barriers created by racism and European colonialism.

Betances and Luperón participated in a variety of *antillanista* and transatlantic networks committed to Antillean independence and the abolition of slavery. In 1875, in exile, Betances enjoyed the hospitality of General Luperón in Puerto Plata, Dominican Republic.[2] Along with Cuban and Puerto Rican exiles, they published the anticolonial newspaper *Las Dos Antillas* (the Two Antilles), later known as *Las Tres Antillas* and *Los Antillanos*. They actively collaborated with the New York–based Junta Central Republicana de Cuba y Puerto Rico (Republican Council of Cuba and Puerto Rico) in their efforts to secure the abolition of slavery and independence for Cuba and Puerto Rico. Both participated in the organization of the 1868 insurrections, the Grito de Yara in Cuba and the Grito de Lares in Puerto Rico, that attempted to free both islands from Spanish rule. Their exiles in various Antillean territories—including Haiti, Jamaica, St. Thomas, and Curaçao—as well as their support of abolitionist work in Spain, France, England, and the United States, speak to their affective and political commitment to antislavery politics and to the constitution of a confederation of independent Antillean nations.

Betances's and Luperón's *antillanista* rhetoric leads us to examine the political implications of how they answered questions that remain with us today: Who are we *antillanos*? How should we formulate a decolonial *antillanista* agenda engaged in racial, gender, and economic justice? What is the role of the United States, Europe, and Latin America in *antillanista* projects? In other words, who is our kin? Three aspects of Luperón's and Betances's political rhetoric shed light on these ideological and strategic questions. These include the mobilization of specific ethnoracial discourses, the reformulation of alliances with European colonial powers, and the construction of male heroes in service to the *antillanista* ideals of revolutionary struggles.

Their narratives of transcolonial and national kinship mobilize ethnoracial representations of the Caribbean to describe the region and its nations as communities tied by their racial mixture. Betances's and Luperón's representations of the ethnoracial composition of the Dominican Republic and Puerto Rico are of particular interest. They developed a decolonial critique of whiteness by articulating a creolized approach to Caribbean demographics and politics. They embody the spirit of creolization described in Nicole King's (2001: 10) *C. L. R. James and Creolization* as a constant questioning of "colonial systems of categorization and their emphasis on order, absoluteness, singular national narratives, and fixed identity." Through distinct conceptualizations of creolization, Betances and Luperón interrogated the equation of whiteness with the right to self-determination that justified the system of slavery and colonialism. Their regionalist political discourses were not invested in notions of purity or mimicry of European political models.

Both Luperón and Betances publicly acknowledged their black heritage to assert the political rights of non-Europeans, while drawing from European and Spanish American political thought. They narrate ethnically and racially heterogeneous political communities mostly characterized by *mulataje*, the intermixing of Africans and Europeans. Their political praxis is also characterized by a rhetorical *mulataje* that, according to Buscaglia-Salgado (2003), contested Eurocentric notions of the citizen and the nation. These mulatto leaders shared an antislavery agenda that transcended claims of national sovereignty and sought the consolidation of an Antillean confederation committed to racial equality. This agenda required them to mobilize black, mulatto, and white

Creole interests in the region (Arroyo 2013; Buscaglia-Salgado 2003; Ojeda Reyes 2000; Rama 2001).

Though at times they were forced to mask their own intentions and to seek uncomfortable alliances, they affirmed black and mulatto political agency as central components of an Antillean transcolonial community. Their transcolonial narratives of kinship disrupted the Eurocentric logic of colonialism. And yet Luperón and Betances also narrate their kinship ties specific to European colonial powers. These narratives help explain who they describe as natural allies and friends of the Caribbean in Europe. At times these political relationships seem to be at odds with their critique of white supremacy and European rule over the Americas. Later in this chapter I will discuss potential explanations for such alliances and their implications for studies of *antillanismo*.

Canonical transnational and nationalist imaginings of the Caribbean's racial composition continue to be productive sites of inquiry and inspiration for decolonial movements, but they are limited by their universalizing patriarchal framework. Along with Arroyo (2013), Nancy R. Mirabal (2001), Rodrigo Lazo (2005), and Josefina Toledo (2002), I note the masculinist conventions that inform how Spanish-speaking Caribbean men, like Luperón and Betances, come to be represented as national and regional heroes. This rhetoric reproduces heteropatriarchal conventions of regionalist projects that imagine men as the primordial revolutionary subject, simultaneously limits the political agency of women, and disciplines gender performance. Betances and Luperón themselves gendered the revolutionary antislavery and anticolonial subject in masculinist terms. To varying degrees their narratives of national families and kinship at times rely on Eurocentric notions of gender relations. Their imaginings of gender relations and marriage within anticolonial struggles illustrate potential shortcomings, then and now, of *antillanista* projects, shortcomings that have been mostly associated with the construction of the nation-state.

National Kinship and *Mestizaje* in Nineteenth-Century Spanish-Speaking America

In *Modernity Disavowed* (2004), Sybille Fischer asks the reader to think of what might have been lost when culture and emancipatory politics were finally forced into the mold of the nation-state. She also asks us to think of what might have happened if the struggle against racial subordination had had the same prestige and received the same attention as did the struggle against colonialism and other forms of political subordination (3). Fischer suggests that national sovereignty struggles did not subvert racial inequality but rather suppressed the potential of radical antislavery proponents to redefine what emancipation could be across national and colonial/imperial lines. National sovereignty became the privileged anticolonial alternative, one that did not value to the same degree the struggle against racial subordination.

Fischer joins other scholars, such as Buscaglia-Salgado, in questioning the Enlightenment-based biases and limitations of the nation and struggles for national sovereignty. As a Western construct, the nation-state has historically tended to marginalize populations that do not embody the prescriptive, Eurocentric notion of citizen as white-identified, male, heterosexual, and propertied. In the 1930s Dominican and Puerto Rican intellectual elites explained the political and cultural constitution of the nation through narratives of *mestizaje* (Sagás 2000: 3). Early twentieth-century narratives of *mestizaje* date back to nineteenth-century discourses on nationhood in circulation throughout the Spanish colonies (Castro 2002; Wade 1993, 2010). At that time *mestizaje* was employed by elite political and intellectual sectors to describe the Dominican Republic and Puerto Rico as whitened through racial mixture. In this manner elites sought to justify struggles for independence or autonomy from Spain and the United States (Candelario 2007; Godreau et al. 2008; Mayes 2014; Rodríguez-Silva 2012; Suárez-Findlay 1999; Torres-Saillant 2000). By the end of the nineteenth century in the Spanish-speaking Caribbean, Creole nationalisms invested in whitening ideologies and the uplift of Afro-descendant peoples had displaced the revolutionary radical *antillanista* projects as a potentially effective paradigm to mobilize people (Arroyo 2013; Buscaglia-Salgado 2003).

For Betances and Luperón, *antillanismo* as a mode of transcolonial kinship narratives did not suggest the whitening of Antillean populations but rather reframed *mulataje* as a basis on which to assert the right to regional self-determination. Buscaglia-Salgado argues that the mulatto desire for an Antillean confederation was an alternative to Creole nationalism and its "race-nationalist program." Had it been successful, the Antillean confederation would have prevented what Buscaglia-Salgado (2003: 184) calls the "undesirable process" of nation-building. Nonetheless *antillanismo* does not present an all-inclusive and coherent response to the racial, gendered, and class exclusions of elite nationalist discourses. Exploring Luperón's and Betances's political thought, their kinship ties to Spain and France, respectively, and the discursive constitution of national families, we find a complex convergence of nationalist and *antillanista* paradigms, which lay the groundwork for what became a decolonial alternative.

The critical engagement of Betances's and Luperón's *antillanismo* with Spanish American national narratives cannot be fully understood without considering how elites in the Americas imagined both the Haitian Revolution and Haiti as an independent state. The 1804 triumph of the Haitian Revolution and the consequent birth of the self-proclaimed black nation undermined justifications of slavery based on racialized attributes. The political independence of Haiti challenged the animalistic and barbaric qualities ascribed to nonwhiteness by Latin American nationalist discourses. In a more concrete manner, the success of the Haitian Revolution presented the real possibility of successful insurrections by nonwhite populations against the socioeconomic and political supremacy of *criollo* white-identified elites in the emerging Spanish American republics.

Through economic embargo, migratory restrictions, and lack of political recognition, European and American nations across the continent attempted to silence discussion about the success of the Haitian Revolution. As Fischer (2004), Johnson (2001b, 2012) and Juan R. González-Mendoza (2001) document, French and Creole planters from Haiti relocated to Cuba, Puerto Rico, and Louisiana. They were joined by many affluent Spaniards and Creoles from neighboring Santo Domingo. Together their stories enabled the "disavowal" of Haiti as a modern nation-state. Fischer argues that other nation-building projects came to be represented in contradistinction to Haiti, at times because of a fear of black insurrections, at other times to avoid the same material and symbolic price Haiti had to pay for its independence. Acknowledging the historical disavowal of Haiti from Western modernity, Betances's and Luperón's references to Haiti highlight other narratives of Dominican and Puerto Rican relationships to its neighbor. Both see the history of Haiti as tied to their own, and they purport that Haitians are necessary allies and fellow Antilleans struggling against European and U.S. colonial desires for the region, their kin.

Dominican studies scholars Carlos Dore Cabral, Rubén Silié, Franklyn Franco Prichardo, María Filomena Gónzalez Alcalá, Silvio Torres-Saillant, April Mayes, Pablo Mella, Carlos Andújar, Carlos Esteban Deive, and Ginetta Candelario, as well as Puerto Rican and Caribbean Studies scholars such as Arroyo, José F. Buscaglia-Salgado, Félix Ojeda Reyes, Ada Ferrer, Johnson, Angel Rama, Humberto García Muñiz, Alejandro de la Fuente, and Paul Estrade, have unveiled similar histories of transcolonial relations that transcend the limits of elite nationalist narratives invested in whitening. Mayes's (2014: 141) *The Mulatto Republic*, her historiography about Dominican national identity, demonstrates that "in sharp contrast to the black denial chorus, not all roads lead blindly to whiteness. When certain choices are made, there are specific, historically situated reasons that explain why." Mayes's argument about *dominicanidad* in the nineteenth century can also be applied to the rest of the Antilles. The political pragmatism that Arroyo (2013) names is evident when Betances seeks help from the United States and Britain while in exile and when Dominicans mobilize different articulations of national identity in response to shifts in regional power dynamics (Candelario 2007; Torres-Saillant 2000). Together these choices suggest that Antilleans have had to engage in complex rhetorical moves to survive and thrive within highly contested imperial struggles over the region. They present a complex picture of the local, regional, political, and racial imagination.

Neither Luperón nor Betances stopped returning to tropes that affirmed their political alliances with metropolitan "motherlands." In particular France played an important role in their imagination of an independent united Caribbean and Latin America. Betances and Luperón, along with mid-nineteenth-century Spanish American intellectuals and political actors, disseminated the idea of a "Latin race" to explain why France would be a natural ally of the Antilles and Central and South America (Mayes 2014; McGuinness 2003). The unification of all non-Anglophone territories under the rubric of Latin America posed a continental challenge to the United States and its Anglo-Saxon expansionist project. The idea of a Latin race proposed by *antillanistas* provided France with the ideological support for its proposal to build a transoceanic canal in Panama and Nicaragua, as well as to further their investments in the Caribbean. Preferred to the United States or Spain, France was reimagined as a benign colonial motherland. This motherland shared an imagined racial root with the region that came to be known as Latin America, but unlike Spain, *la madre patria*, the French monarchy did not intend to formally colonize the continent. This political relationship also had its roots in the affective kinship ties articulated by Antilleans who were of French descent and/or found political allies and refuge in France.

La Madre Patria, Haiti, and the Latin Race: Ramón Emeterio Betances

Betances was of Dominican and French descent.[3] He deftly maneuvered his own filial ties to France, while condemning Spain and reclaiming Haitian history as his own. His model of kinship relied on strategic affective relationships with France, while rejecting those with Spain. In doing so he challenged Puerto Rican autonomist writers who represented Puerto Rico as the legitimate daughter of Spain deserving autonomy from the mother country, as well as narratives of whitening that would persist in elite national narratives in the twentieth century.

Creole autonomists often disseminated the idea of a Puerto Rican culture that would explain differences between them and Spaniards, but they would also highlight their Hispanic heritage. In such narratives Spain is the generous motherland with which Puerto Rico shares permanent filial ties. For example, when Salvador Brau (1986: xi) introduced the book *El Gíbaro* by Manuel Alonso in 1884, he wrote that Puerto Rico is the "legitimate child of Spain who discovered, populated and educated him. His literature cannot be any other than the Spanish." Spain appears as a generous matriarch that has shared its Hispanic civilization with America.

Imagining themselves as the inheritors of a superior Spanish culture, Puerto Rican elite Creole writers posited themselves as the ideal intermediary between the Spanish colonial government and Puerto Rican popular classes (Janer 2005: 15). They had the task of affirming those Puerto Rican cultural practices that fit Spanish standards of civilization and of ridding the island of those that did not. In her study of Puerto Rican nation-building literature, Janer has demonstrated that "Creole watchfulness was geared towards establishing the existence of an original culture—a basic claim in favor of self-government—but without traces of what might be considered peasant backwardness" (13). A narrative of cultural and, at times, biological whitening tinged Creole desires for a culture that would deem them worthy of self-government in the eyes of Spain. In this way "Puerto Rican Autonomists hoped to subject plebeian men to moral reformation, which would 'whiten' their behavior, if not their skin" (Suárez-Findlay 1999: 59).

In contrast Betances (2001a: 73) saw Spain as the main obstacle to the fulfillment of his antislavery ideals: to obtain "not only the abolition of slavery, but rather the ascription, for the slave, of all the rights enjoyed by citizens." In response to those who praised Spain for its gradual abolition of slavery in Puerto Rico, Betances's 1872 (2001a) proclamation "La abolición de la esclavitud en Puerto Rico" unearths a history of Spanish political violence against abolitionists and pro-independence movements. Betances asserts that the emancipation of slaves was a victory of the Puerto Rican people who had been demanding it for centuries. He argues that Puerto Ricans should not be thankful to Spain for the decree that ordered the abolition of slavery but rather must recognize how other countries had for years imposed the diplomatic pressure needed to accomplish it: "The whole world has not ceased to demand reparations for a humanity abused by Spain; the first (country) that imposed slavery; the last one to abolish it" (73).

Betances's representation of Spain is a response to the metropole's whitening policies in Puerto Rico during the nineteenth century. The 1815 Cédula de Gracias privileged white settlers by granting them more land and resources to encourage relocation in the colonies (Chinea 2005: 67). According to José Luis González's (1993) analysis of Puerto Rican culture in *El país de los cuatro pisos*, immigration laws dramatically changed the racial demographics of the island and its socioeconomic structures. He writes, "A wave of immigrants fleeing from Spanish colonies fighting for independence in South America began building and furnishing this second story. They were joined almost immediately afterward, under the aegis of the *Real Cédula de Gracias* of 1815, by numerous foreigners (English, French, Dutch, Irish, etc.) and with a second wave, composed mainly of Corsicans, Majorcans, and Catalans, following them around mid-century" (12). Measures like the 1803 code regulating interracial marriages and the 1848 Bando contra la Raza Africana (Black Code) were developed to restrict the physical and social mobility of enslaved and free peoples of color (Kinsbruner 1996: 36, 42). The former was a response to the Haitian Revolution, the latter to the abolition of slavery in French colonies.

In his proclamation Betances also foresaw that the Spanish colonial government would continue to exploit the labor of people of African descent even after emancipation. Following the abolition of slavery in Cuba, Spanish *criollo* plantation owners engaged indentured Chinese labor in conditions equal to or worse than slavery. This confirmed Betances's sentiment that full political enfranchisement of *la raza de color* was not feasible under Spanish rule. He stated, "It is not improbable that slavery would reappear under a new name, as it has for the free Chinese in Cuba, and that this labor regulation would emerge as the Ku-Klux-Klan of liberty; in other words, a new organization that would remove the *raza de color* from the island" (2001a: 77). If free indentured workers—who were not legally defined as slaves—experienced slavery-like conditions under the Spanish colonial government in Cuba, then it is not surprising that Betances expected the implementation of postemancipation policies that would guarantee the continued subordination of free people of color in Puerto Rico. Such policies did come into existence after the abolition of slavery through laws that limited the physical and economic mobility of former slaves and peasants. For instance, vagrancy laws required poor people and peasants to demonstrate their contractual obligation to a plantation or business owner to avoid fines or prison (Rodríguez-Silva 2012).

He ascribed to Spain a white supremacist project that shared the ideological grounding of the Ku Klux Klan in the United States: the elimination of nonwhite populations. Denouncing Spanish racial policies, Betances was not interested in affirming the Hispanic heritage of Puerto Rico or the island's filial ties to its colonial motherland. He sought instead to underscore the role played by Spain in the slave trade and the institutionalization of racial subjection in Puerto Rico, as well as its refusal to abolish slavery in Cuba until 1886. Betances (2001a: 77) ends the proclamation warning Spain of its fate as a colonial power and slave trader: "May the dissolving, disorienting institution of slavery end up consuming [Spain], and on all its deeds weigh, with the weight of thousands and thousands of crimes accumulated during more than three centuries, the fair reprobation of the civilized world." While rejecting any filial loyalty or gratitude to Spain, Betances (2008: 165) affirms his family's *sangre Africana*, their black ancestry. In a letter to his sister Demetria Betances Alacán on March 30, 1879, he asserts that no one in their family had ever denied their *mulatez*; he claims, "We are black [*prietuzcos*] and do not deny it" (166). In her letter to Betances, Demetria had complained about a former friend who had grown distant because Demetria was one of the darkest members of the Betances family. Betances explains to her that the family had to legally whiten themselves to override Spanish regulations that limited interracial marriages: "To fall within the parameters established by Spanish law, they had to acquire documents that proved their blood's whiteness [*blancura de sangre*] and prove, to everyone's eyes, that we, black people, were as white as . . . an Irishman, if necessary" (165).

Betances extended the *mulataje* that constitutes his immediate family to his description of Puerto Rican demographics. In his 1872 proclamation he asserts that Puerto Rico is demographically constituted by the *raza de color* (colored race) (2001a: 77). His valorization of black and mulatto populations and his refusal to discursively whiten them through any affirmation of the *madre patria*'s racial and cultural legacy in Puerto Rico are the basis for his transcolonial vision of the Antilles. He advocates the need to build cross-racial alliances to attain the abolition of slavery and independence for Cuba and Puerto Rico.

As a mulatto who openly asserted Puerto Ricans' blackness, Betances saw Haiti, not Spain, as a precedent and ally for those demanding the right of self-determination for nonwhite populations. As Arroyo (2013: 87) points out, the parallels he establishes between the Haitian Revolution and the Cuban independence struggle departed from how other advocates of the Antillean confederation, such as the Cuban José Martí and the Puerto Rican Eugenio María de Hostos, represented Haiti. Arroyo argues that these *antillanistas* also saw Haiti as a necessary ally but disavowed its constitutional definition of Haitians as black citizens. The internal differences among Haitian political leaders that then plagued the country became a reason to dismiss Haiti's antislavery politics as an adequate intervention into Enlightenment ideas about the nation and national sovereignty (Arroyo 2013). White revolutionary leaders in Cuba were afraid of the potential rise to power of black leaders like Maceo (see Buscaglia-Salgado 2003). Betances, on the other hand, claims his family's mixed, mulatto ancestry, and from that site of enunciation imagines "las Antillas para los Antillanos" (the Antilles for Antilleans). His transcolonial narratives of kinship are deeply invested in the affirmation of blacks' and mulattos' humanity and right to self-determination.

In Betances's political rhetoric and praxis, Haiti became a natural ally to Spanish-speaking Caribbean anticolonial struggles. Haiti held an enormous symbolic value for antislavery and anticolonial struggles of the nineteenth century. While the constant uprisings of black slaves and indigenous peoples that had been occurring since the inception of the first colony kept colonial forces on guard, Haiti embodied one of the worst nightmares of the colonial imagination. Having abolished slavery, gained its independence, and defined itself as a black nation, Haiti challenged the racial premises of nation-building rhetoric in Europe, the United States, and Spanish America. Along with European colonial metropoles and the United States, white-identified elites of emerging Spanish American republics developed policies that sought to contain what became real at the time: the possibility of successful insurrections by nonwhite populations (Geggus 2001; Johnson 2001b, 2012). In contrast Betances's 1882 letter published in Paris as "Los detractores de la raza negra y de la República de Haití" (2001c) illustrates his support for the tenets of the Haitian Revolution and his rhetorical deployment of Haiti to assert the humanity of Afro-descendants in the Caribbean.

In 1882 Haitians residing in France, including the renowned intellectuals Louis Joseph Janvier, Clément Denis, and Jules Auguste (Rama 2001: xxxi),[4] asked Betances and the abolitionist Víctor Schoelcher to write a prologue for a volume challenging the French journalist Leo Quesnel's article about Haiti in the Parisian *Revue Politique et Littéraire*.

In his piece Quesnel dismissed the Haitian nation-state following the triumph of the 1804 revolution. Undertaking a historical critique of Quesnel's article, Betances argues against Quesnel's claims regarding the cowardly nature of the black race. He quotes from the U.S. abolitionist Wendell Phillips's laudatory 1869 speech on the Haitian revolutionary leader Toussaint Louverture and on Louverture's military successes against the three main colonial armies of Europe: "[Louverture] forged a thunderbolt and threw it, against what? Against the proudest blood of Europe, the Spanish, and vanquished it. Against the most combative blood of Europe, the French, and trampled it under its feet; against the most enterprising blood of Europe, the English, and this one too retired to Jamaica" (2001c: 100). In Betances's letter, Louverture represents Haiti and all blacks. His capacity to gain and protect the sovereignty of Haiti in the face of Spanish, French, and British invasions demonstrates that, like Europeans, Haitians and other Afro-descendant populations have the courage as well as the intellectual skills to lead a political and military movement. In response to Quesnel's comments about the alleged "cowardice of the black race" (99), Betances's example places Haiti—and, I would add, all Afro-descendants—on equal terms with white-identified European powers. Haitians outperformed the most recognized armies of Europe and therefore affirmed their right to self-government. Consequently all blacks could demand their independence and freedom from colonial rule and slavery. Affirming the independence of Haiti, Betances recognizes the rights of all African descendants to determine their political future.

His feelings of solidarity and filial ties with Haiti had been evident twelve years earlier, in 1870, when he and his family relocated to Haiti to avoid persecution from the Spanish government. That year, speaking to his Masonic brothers at the Great Lodge of Port-au-Prince, he proclaimed "The Antilles for the Children of the Antilles" (quoted in Rama 2001: 6). Speaking on behalf of Puerto Ricans and Cubans fighting for the independence of their islands and the abolition of slavery and Dominicans struggling to avoid the annexation of their country to the United States, he recognized Haitians as also sharing a transcolonial desire to be treated as the legitimate heirs of the Antillean land they inhabited, heirs with the right to govern themselves and undo the legacy of slavery. In Paris Betances's desires and *antillanista* dreams sustained his collaborations with Haitian counterparts there and back on the islands.

Betances signed the 1882 letter written on behalf of Haiti in Paris as *El Antillano* (The Antillean), claiming an *antillanista* identity that tied him to the region and each one of its territories, including Haiti. He saw himself sharing a fate not only with other Puerto Ricans or Dominicans but with all Antilleans. As another 1870 speech demonstrates, he was writing not only as an ally of Haiti; he identified with its history, he claimed it as his own and claimed it for the rest of the Caribbean by showing how Haiti was a significant member of a transcolonial community that made possible the independence of Bolívar's Colombia.

In an 1870 (2001b) speech about the life of the former Haitian president Alexandre Pétion, Betances—addressing Cubans and Puerto Ricans— traces the struggle for national independence and the abolition of slavery in Cuba during the Ten Years War (1868–78) to early nineteenth-century collaborations between Pétion and the South American liberator Simón Bolívar. In 1815 Pétion sent Haitian troops to support Bolívar's attempt at gaining South American independence. In return Pétion demanded that slavery be abolished in the independent territories: "In exchange of two valuable expeditions that left *Les Cayes* and took independence to Colombia, Pétion only had one demand: the abolition of slavery" (Betances 2001b: 61). Betances greatly admired the alliance between Pétion and Bolívar and affirmed the role played by Haiti in the attainment of independence and the abolition of slavery in Spanish American mainland territories. By highlighting their political alliance, Betances provided a successful example of an interracial, transcolonial alliance in the Antilles for Cuban and Puerto Rican abolitionists and anticolonialists: "Those are our precursors, oh Cubans! Could one believe that we are condemned to die as slaves?" (62). He infused a Cuban nationalist movement with an *antillanista* genealogy of struggle that emphasized the significance of interracial relationships for the future of the Caribbean. Angel Rama (2001: xxiii) convincingly argues that in this 1870 speech, Betances "recommends the fraternity of all *criollos* (white, black, or mulatto) as a way to prevent their domination by their common enemies."

In spite of Betances's adversarial stance toward Spain at the time of emancipation, his *antillanismo* and advocacy for the Haitian Revolution did not entail rejecting European political influences and support of his cause. The historian and anthologist of Betances's writings Félix Ojeda Reyes (2000: 32) asserts that similar to Latin American Creole elites, he sought resources and models in England and France.[5] In this way and others he was politically pragmatic. His personal connections to France, a country that became his home in exile, were key. His French ancestry, education in Paris in the 1840s, participation in the 1848 revolt that abolished slavery in the Francophone territories and established the

Second Republic, and final relocation to France in the 1870s informed his thinking and defined his political allegiances. He spent the last two decades of his life in Paris. There he further collaborated with European political movements, including anarchists and a transatlantic Masonic brotherhood committed to the ideal of the confederation (Arroyo 2013; Ojeda Reyes and Estrade 2000). His rhetoric is an affirmation of his affective ties to France and to the Caribbean and South America. After his scathing critique of Quesnel's racism, he crafted words of sympathy and friendship to describe political relationships between France and the Antilles in what appears to be an attempt to maintain a French readership supportive of his anticolonial projects. Sympathy and friendship could also speak to his own personal relationships with radical political activists in France.

Although in "Los detractores" he acknowledges that France was one of the colonial powers confronted by Haiti, Betances (2001c: 100) promptly affirms that "certainly no other nation enjoys deeper sympathies—not only from Haiti, but also from South America—than the French. Those sympathies are worthy of being cultivated." Such an affirmation of the need to cultivate amicable relationships between Haiti, Latin America, and France, despite French colonial history, could have been motivated by Betances's and Luperón's vision for a unified Latin America at the time. Betances finds in France not only political education and a refuge when in exile but also the financial and political support for his work.

In 1880, with Luperón, Betances created the Unión Latino Americana, which counted on the support of French businessmen interested in investing capital in Latin American countries (Luperón 1939: 3: 133).[6] The union was an initial step in what they saw as the inevitable constitution of a confederation of Latin American and Caribbean nations. During the 1880s the construction of the Panama Canal by the French was one of the investment projects that would have cemented relationships between the French and a future confederation (Ojeda Reyes and Estrade 2000). Along with other Latin American intellectuals and politicians, Betances and Luperón preferred to see the project undertaken by France rather than the United States, whose expansionist policies had been impacting the continent throughout the century. However, the French could not complete the project, the Unión Latino Americana did not lead to the desired confederation, and the Panama Canal fell into the hands of the United States in 1903.

Betances's and Luperón's maneuvering of French economic and political capital in the service of the Bolivarian ideal was meant to curtail the increasing hegemony of the United States over the continent. This was despite the fact that France had colonial holdings at the time in Asia, Africa, and the Caribbean. In their attempt to gain and protect the sovereignty of Latin American and Caribbean territories, and in order to affirm the political rights of non-European populations, Betances and Luperón were compelled to turn to resources made available within a colonial metropole. In Betances's case, being of French descent, having received his education in France, and having lived there for a significant portion of his life could also explain his reliance on French resources.

Writing his letter on behalf of Haiti, Betances crafted a transcolonial narrative of *antillanista* kinship to defend Haiti's sovereignty as his own, alongside a narrative in which he articulates his affective ties to a colonial motherland, France. In this manner we see him negotiating his critique of whiteness, his valorization of Antillean African ancestry, and the strategic demands of a regional struggle with scarce economic and human resources. He was also recognizing the real support he found within and the loving ties he felt toward a transatlantic Masonic brotherhood, a community that in Haiti, France, and Puerto Rico had helped him spread his messages about independence, the confederation, and the fight against racial subordination throughout the Atlantic world (Arroyo 2013).[7]

Interracial *antillanista* collaborations were crucial for the success of nationalist and regionalist struggles for independence and the abolition of slavery. Betances self-identified as *El Antillano* and articulated himself as the product of a process of creolization that populated Puerto Rico with a racial majority of *gente de color* (blacks and mulattos) who could claim Haitian revolutionary history as their own. According to Betances, Haiti exemplified the capacity of Afro-descendants, and consequently the rest of the Caribbean, for self-government.

In the meantime France became another home when the Spanish government forced him into exile, and the French emerged as useful allies for the antislavery, *antillanista*, and pan-American project at hand. For this reason Luperón too cooperated with the French, but, unlike Betances, he strongly affirmed the Dominican Republic's filial relationship with Spain. Luperón produced a narrative of creolization that decentered whiteness while simultaneously affirming a Hispanic Dominican ethnoracial heritage.

Mulataje, Hispanidad, and the Nation: Gregorio Luperón

Having been called "the indisputable leader of the Antillean Confederation" (Betances in Cordero Michel 1998: 10), it is remarkable that Luperón's ideological contributions to nineteenth-century pan-Caribbean antislavery and independence movements have remained mostly unexamined. Luperón's three volumes of *Notas autobiográficas y apuntes históricos*, written between 1892 and 1896 and published in Mayagüez, Puerto Rico, offer an exceptionally productive site of inquiry for exploring transcolonial, colonial, and national narratives of kinship that continue to shape debates about the future of the Caribbean. His narrative of transcolonial kinship between Haiti and the Dominican Republic celebrates the racial mixture that constitutes the population of the island, while his nationalist description of the ideal national family asserts the Hispanic cultural and moral legacy left by *la madre patria*, Spain.

Unlike most of the recognized figures of nineteenth-century *antillanismo*, Luperón's political thought was shaped by a fraught historiography of Haitian-Dominican relations: the Haitian unification of the island (1822–44), the struggles for Dominican independence from Haiti, the 1861 reannexation of the Dominican Republic by Spain, and the 1863–65 War of Restoration that achieved the independence of the Dominican Republic from Spain. He was a Dominican of Haitian ancestry (Castro Ventura 2002; Luperón 1939: vol. 1), and his politics were greatly shaped by his working-class background, military career, and attempts to consolidate a Dominican state amid continued struggles to contain internal political conflicts and gain international recognition. *Notas* highlight his conceptualization of an *antillanismo* at times at odds with the racial premises of nationalist narratives that became officially sanctioned by the Dominican dictator Rafael Leónidas Trujillo in the 1930s.[8]

Mayes (2014) and Torres-Saillant (2000) have contextualized the concrete elite interests and historical processes that led to the *antihaitianismo* and antiblack racism espoused and made official by the Trujillo regime, known as the Trujillato (1930–61), and have asked Caribbean studies scholars to acknowledge Dominican radical antislavery projects. While *antihaitianismo* and antiblack racism are common tropes in narratives about Dominican racial politics, scholars like Mayes, Torres-Saillant, and Pedro L. San Miguel (2005) have demonstrated that Dominican racial thought has been varied since the inception of the Republic. Torres-Saillant has established that the struggle for Dominican independence was not intrinsically an anti-Haitian or antiblack process.[9] The newly constituted 1844 Dominican government was acutely aware of the need to restate the abolition of slavery in its constitution and to incorporate blacks and mulattos in its ranks. San Miguel's discussion of Pedro Francisco Bonó's *mulatismo*, his assertion and valorization of the mulatto makeup of the Dominican Republic, gives us an early example of attempts to vindicate Afro-descendant populations on the island. And Mayes (2014: 22) demonstrates that only an elite sector pessimistic about the fate of the Dominican Republic as a nation espoused the virulent antiblack racism and *antihaitianismo* that characterized the Trujillato.

Mayes (2014: 7) argues that, along with the intellectuals Bonó and Eugenio María de Hostos, Luperón "crafted inclusive and forward-looking national project(s) that were neither anti-Haitian nor anti-black." His inclusive national project was also a transcolonial one that rhetorically deployed *mulataje* to explain the natural kinship ties between Haiti and the Dominican Republic. Luperón starts his autobiography by interrogating the racial basis of Dominican national narratives that referred to Haiti's blackness as entirely antithetical to the demographic constitution of the Dominican Republic. In *Notas* transcolonial kinship is rooted in the intimate sexual relationships between blacks and whites that, according to him, are the fundamental roots of both Haitian and Dominican society. Luperón imagines Haiti and the Dominican Republic as places undergoing the same process of *mulataje*:

> The natives having mostly disappeared, the population of the island is constituted by two races very different from one another due to their origin and appearance, as well as customs and concerns. These are the European and the African, which after cross-breeding, have produced a mixed race, which draws from both, and by natural law will become the primitive race of the island, and which already plays an important role for the well-being of these two heroic Republics, that must reach a definite agreement that allows them to guarantee each other their independence and national integrity as well as to develop without restraints the prodigious elements of wealth they possess. (1939: 1: 27)

Many Latin Americans, such as Argentine president Domingo Sarmiento (Janer 2005: 13; Wade 1993), and some Puerto Rican autonomists (Suárez-Findlay 1999: 59) turned to whitening narratives to solve what was seen as the degrading process of racial mixture. Luperón articulated a distinct narrative; in contrast to Latin American thinkers who expected the gradual whitening of their populations through *mestizaje* (racial and cultural miscegenation), he imagined Haitians and Dominicans as mulatto populations that replaced the indigenous inhabitants of the island as its rightful heirs. In this narrative Europeans continued to be outsiders trying to impose their rule in a land to which they did not belong.

We could say that, as a mulatto military leader of humble origins, Luperón engages in what Sylvia Wynter (1970: 35) has called "the indigenization of the black man" in the Americas. Describing the rituals and dances associated with *jonkonnu* in Jamaica, Wynter argues that blacks' adaptations to their new natural and cultural landscapes "had transformed that New World Negro into the indigenous inhabitant of his new land. His cultural resistance to colonialism in this new land was an indigenous resistance" (35). Wynter recognizes the exchanges between indigenous and black populations in maroon communities and how blacks learned to live on this land, the Americas, on their own terms and not those of the colonizers. Her reading assumes the decimation of Arawak Indian populations in order to assert blacks' indigenization.

I take objection with that interpretation because it closes the door to potential and existing explorations of black-Indian relations in the islands and how they have, for example, informed the development of Dominican vudú, *misterios*, and other spiritual and cultural practices.[10] However, it is clear that Wynter engages in a move similar to Luperón's. He describes Haitians and Dominicans as mulattos who have been indigenized and must claim their natural right to defend the land and its sovereignty. He naturalized his proposal of transcolonial collaborations between Haiti and the Dominican Republic by indigenizing their mulatto populations.

Luperón asserted that Haiti shares a racial legacy as well as geopolitical space, history, and political concerns with the Dominican Republic. This narrative of transcolonial kinship frames *Notas*. He focuses on describing the geographical space occupied by the Dominican Republic and Haiti. To preserve the national sovereignty of the Dominican Republic required, in Luperón's political praxis and rhetoric, acknowledging that the economic and political circumstances of one country affected the other. Luperón (1939: 1: 27) states that the fates of Haiti and the Dominican Republic were inextricably linked; these two countries must "mutually guarantee one another's independence and national integrity."[11] He joyfully describes the natural beauty and resources of both nations and asserts that they have been blessed by Providence.

One of the main concerns shaping Luperón's historical narrative is that Haiti and the Dominican Republic must confront, in unison, the legacies of colonialism on the island in order to succeed as independent nations: "Unfortunately iniquitous dominations passed through her [the island] like horrendous storms, leaving the vices and hatred of slavery and tyranny as an inheritance for new generations, to such extremes that its inhabitants are still suffering the consequences of those horrible scourges" (1939: 1: 26). Comparing colonialism to the disaster, chaos, disease, and death left by storms in the Caribbean, he suggests that a colonial inheritance is embedded in the landscape of the island. Luperón asserts that colonialism is not a relic of the past but is present in Haitian and Dominican nation-building projects. In Luperón's account it is a shared turbulent, violent, colonial legacy that would not allow these new nations to build stable democratic systems of government.

Luperón's assertion of their common colonial past and racial future served as a basis for the anticolonial alliances that he proposed and pursued between Haiti and the Dominican Republic. These collaborations were crucial during the War of Restoration (1863–65) against renewed Spanish rule and the revolts against Dominican presidents Pedro Santana and Buenaventura Báez, who sought foreign protection over the Dominican Republic.[12] In 1861 Santana submitted the Dominican Republic to Spanish rule, and in 1869 Báez tried to annex the Dominican Republic to the United States and to lease or sell Samaná Bay to U.S. investors. Anticolonial leaders in Haiti and the Dominican Republic understood that these plans endangered the independence of not only the Dominican Republic but also of Haiti and required that Haitians and Dominicans share the task of challenging them. The expansionist doctrine of the United States and Latin America was evident. Anticolonial Dominican and Haitian leaders searched for ways to keep the old colonial metropole, Spain, and the recently created United States off the island. For this reason Haitian presidents Fabré Nicolás Geffrard and Nissage Saget and other Haitian officials provided political asylum and resources when Luperón led military forces against these colonialist projects in the 1860s and 1870s.

Luperón's imagination of a racially unified island translated into a series of concrete political alliances with Haiti, as well as with Puerto Ricans and Cubans seeking independence and the abolition of slavery in their islands. The transcolonial kinship model that he articulated in his narrative of Haitian-Dominican relations was reflected in his broader vision of a Latin American and Caribbean community of independent nations committed to a radical antislavery project. Luperón wished to consolidate the hemispheric will needed to make possible the ideal of an Antillean and Latin American confederation, a confederation that included in the *antillanista* imaginary of the nineteenth-century Spanish Caribbean places such as Puerto Rico, Haiti, Cuba, Dominican Republic, St. Thomas, Jamaica, and any other territory in the region that had been under Spanish colonial rule.

According to Luperón, the confederation counted all possible human resources without discriminating against anyone on the basis of race, ethnic origin, or religious practice. His speech for the 1888 presidential campaign asked fellow Dominicans to "establish relationships of friendship and commerce with the nations of Europe and America, strengthen those precious ties to the Latin American peoples, our natural brothers, without excluding any race, since there is no element that gives the State as much benefit as what men can produce" (1939: 3: 247).

In the same speech Luperón demanded freedom of the press, freedom of association, and freedom of religion, among many other rights that would guarantee citizens' free participation in the protection of the constitution and the sovereignty of the country. Luperón tells us that "the Republic opens its arms to the friendship of all nations and to the migration of all people, and it counts, if needed, on the aid of all inhabitants [of the republic] for the defense of its national independence" (3: 248).[13] His proposal for a Dominican nation, open to all migrants, a friendly nation respectful of its inhabitants' political rights, reflected his *antillanista* vision. His affirmation of a racially inclusive *antillanista* community contested colonial/imperial policies that sought the continued exploitation of indigenous and Afro-descendant labor after emancipation, the infringement on indigenous property and cultural traditions throughout the continent, and to whiten Latin American populations.

While *Notas* documents Luperón's transcolonial *antillanista* kinship networks, the professed purposes of the three volumes are to produce a history of the Dominican Republic following the War of Restoration and to assert Luperón's contributions in the making of this national history:

> This work is not a complete history of the Dominican Republic's titanic War of Restoration, but it will be a powerful auxiliary for those historians who write it. In it you will find, as in a living source, the narration of true events. . . . Moreover, this book also serves as a declaration in favor of the character who motivates and makes this exposition, freely calumniated by those who are so invested in extinguishing the glory of the Dominican people; and [this character, Luperón himself] has never had as an ideal anything else but the happiness of the motherland, which he hopes to see free and glorious. (1939: 1: 32)

References to *Notas* tend to emphasize either its autobiographical qualities or its value as a historical document. However, it is not solely a piece
of autobiographical literature because it is committed to a historical narration of the nation, and it is not merely a historical account because it is
always mediated through Luperón's construction of his own nationalist
subjectivity. He expects his writings to help historians of the Dominican
Republic in the future. To fulfill his national duty he accompanies the
narrative with letters, government documents, sketches of historical figures, and speeches pertinent to the subject matter.

Notas constructs a symbiotic relationship between Luperón and the
Dominican nation. The story of his life—his coming to consciousness
as a national subject and his defense of the sovereignty of the Dominican Republic for four decades—becomes the history of the nation. The
triumph of the nationalist revolutionary forces that ended the reannexation of the Dominican Republic to Spain in 1865 marked a new stage in
nation building, as well as initiating Luperón's life as a statesman, as one
of the men who made the sovereignty of the nation possible. It is implied
that the nation would not exist without such a dutiful national subject. In
1895, when Ulises Heureaux exiled him, Luperón constructed himself as
a "personaje" (character) in this historical narrative whose contributions
to the glory of his country needed to be recognized in the midst of political turmoil. The nation needed him as much as he needed it.

The historical and personal project that motivates Luperón to write
Notas reveals tensions and contradictions in his thinking and political praxis in the late nineteenth century. Despite belonging to a pan-
American antislavery and anticolonial movement, at times the nationalist
aspects of the text reiterate elite national narratives that emphasize
Dominican Hispanic heritages over others. Imagining the kin relations
needed to sustain the independence of the Dominican nation, he resorts
to a narrative of filial kinship between Dominicans and Spaniards. For
instance, his description of Spanish colonial rule affirms the filial relationship between Spain and its former colonies. He expresses gratitude
to Spain for granting independence to the Dominican Republic: "Spain
does not have enemies in the nations that were its colonies in America,
but rather emancipated sons, who are true brothers for the Spanish"
(1939: 1: 31). Spaniards, Dominicans, and Latin Americans are brothers
of the family created by the Spanish motherland through its civilizing
project in the Americas. Dominicans have emancipated themselves, as
children do when they become adults and are prepared to pursue their
own paths, but they do not reject their colonial mother. Spain appears,

then, not as the destructive force that took away the land from its indig-enous inhabitants but rather as a generous mother who left her linguis-tic, racial, religious, and cultural legacy in the Caribbean. Therefore the racial, gendered, and sexual constitution of national families is informed by values inherited from Spain, not necessarily by the revolutionary val-ues espoused by Luperón's transcolonial kinship narratives.

After introducing the trope of a transatlantic Hispanic family, in the same text Luperón's narrative of Haitian-Dominican relations radi-cally departs from his previous representation of a population tied by the laws of nature and their coexistence on the island. Haiti becomes an enemy of the Dominican Republic and its Hispanic heritage. The quest for legitimacy, despite all proof to the contrary, relies on a disavowal of Haiti's revolution as a foundational fiction with little to no relevance for the emerging Dominican Republic. Luperón's political pragmatism—as someone who was so actively involved in nationalist, antislavery, *antil-lanista* principles—is unexpected. His zealous defense of a Hispanic Dominican legacy is incongruent with the idea that both Haitians and Dominicans share the same racial composition and must work together against colonialist schemes. In *Notas* Dominican struggles to achieve independence from Haiti are represented as necessary acts to maintain the Hispanic heritage that sustains the moral health of the country. Luperón writes, "The Dominican people defended more than their inde-pendence; [the Dominican people] defended their language, the honor of their families, freedom of commerce, the morality of marriage, hatred of polygamy, a better destiny for its race. . . . It was the solemn struggle between customs and principles diametrically opposed, of barbarism against civilization" (1939: 1: 34). Here Luperón relies on linguistic, cultural, religious, moral, and racial distinctions to describe the two countries inhabiting Hispaniola. According to this narrative, belong-ing to a Hispanic national family entails defending civilized attributes, not the barbarism ascribed to Haitians. And heteronormative marriage becomes a necessary element for the process of building the nation, for the reproduction of healthy national subjects.

In *The Imagined Island: History, Identity and Utopia in Hispaniola*, San Miguel (2005: 39) states that in certain nineteenth-century elite Dominican national narratives, "the definition of 'Dominican' became 'not Haitian.' This dichotomy could be seen in nearly every sphere: Hai-tians practiced voodoo, Dominicans Catholicism; Haitians spoke Creole, Dominicans Spanish; Haitians were black, Dominicans were of mixed race or white." These elite narratives of *mestizaje* and *hispanidad* were historically shaped by the unification of the island under Haiti in 1822 and replicated through the development of discourses of *Hispanidad* well into the twentieth century, though, as San Miguel also documents, other narratives of Haitian-Dominican relations and racial mixture continued to be articulated. Luperón engages such narratives while deploying the racialized dichotomy between civilization and barbarism that buttress Latin American proposals to whiten indigenous, black, and mixed-race populations.[14] Thinkers who espoused the need to whiten Latin America assumed that non-Europeans were barbarous people whose presence delayed the economic and political development of the newly constituted republics of Latin America. Luperón draws from a Latin American intellectual tradition that justified nation-building policies encouraging miscegenation (whitening), white immigration, and genocide. He reracialized Haitians as nonwhites who limited the Dominican Republic's ability to sustain the cultural attributes left by Spanish colonialism.

Throughout *Notas* Luperón conceptualizes and naturalizes a transcolonial relationship between Haiti and the Dominican Republic, as well as with the rest of the Antilles and Latin America, by representing them all as siblings, members of the same family of nations. He generates tropes that characterize nineteenth-century narratives of transcolonial kinship in the Antilles: the need to end racial subordination and colonial rule on the continent, the desire for an Antillean confederation and pan-American unity, and narratives of racial mixture and *mulataje* that lay the groundwork for nonwhites to assert their right to self-determination. In a problematic narrative of indigenization of mulattos, he articulates a critique of white privilege in the Americas.

However, he participates in the erasure of indigenous peoples and their contributions to Haitian and Dominican political and cultural histories, and his nationalist imagination of the Dominican Republic reproduces Eurocentric values that undermine the transcolonial project he initially proposes. Though he affirms the racial and historical ties between the Dominican Republic and Haiti—and questions the assumption that only Europeans can enjoy the benefits of self-government—Luperón ultimately cannot imagine a stable independent nation that does not reproduce European/Hispanic cultural practices and religious mores. The national subject he envisions is an indigenized Afro-descendant yet culturally Hispanic Dominican.[15]

I would like to suggest that Luperón's decision to emphasize both a process of *mulataje* on the island and Dominicans' filial ties to Spain is symptomatic of the complex political landscape he had to navigate. He asserts the *mulataje* of the island and the indigenization of its mulatto populations to embed his transcolonial ideals in the land itself and to naturalize his proposal for anticolonial collaborations between Haiti and the Dominican Republic. His ethnoracial imagination of Haiti and the Dominican Republic was revolutionary. If Dominicans and Haitians share the same racial composition, then they must together defend their national territories from foreign intervention and assert their capacity as people of African descent to govern the new nations. He simultaneously struggled with Haitian collaborators against Spanish rule on the island and advocated for the secularism of the state and freedom of religion, the political rights of people of color, and the need for interracial and international political solidarity. In the end Luperón always asserted that he was Dominican and Antillean. He considered it impossible to claim to be Dominican and not recognize the shared plight of the Caribbean (Torres-Saillant 2006: 144).

Publishing his *Notas* while in exile in one of the last Spanish colonies, Puerto Rico, Luperón may have found the need to reimagine himself as a child of Spain and brother of all Spaniards. Asserting Dominicans' filial ties to Spain, he can continue to defend Dominican national sovereignty without posing a clear threat to the Spanish government in Puerto Rico. What becomes evident in his rhetorical moves is that decolonial thought is not always embedded in struggles for independence. Such struggles could continue to articulate Eurocentric ideas about the nation and citizenship, as both Luperón's framing of Haiti and patriarchal representations of women in *antillanistas'* writings demonstrate.

Transcolonial and National Kinship: A Gendered Perspective

To further complicate scholarly attempts that posit transcolonial and nationalist projects as clearly distinct from one another, I turn to how women and gender relations figured in Betances's and Luperón's writings. Both figures' heteronormative representations of gender relations suggest that their negotiation of national, transcolonial, and colonial kinship narratives were informed by European ideas about national sovereignty, statehood, and citizenship. Their descriptions of models for revolutionary leadership reveal that they privileged the normative male as citizen.[16]

Throughout the nineteenth century, women organized fundraising events to support uprisings in Cuba and Puerto Rico, promoted the cause of independence and the abolition of slavery through social functions and writing, created spaces for political organization, called attention to conservative trends in the anticolonial movement, and contributed to male-only organizations. They created their own organizations to support their national independence struggles, such as the clubs La Liga de las Hijas de Cuba, Hermanas de Rius Rivera, Caridad, and Mercedes Varona in New York City (Toledo 2000). However, women's material and ideological contributions to *antillanista* and nationalist struggles did not necessarily translate into an appreciation of their womanhood by their male counterparts. Toledo, Lazo, and Mirabal have noted the gender biases that informed the incorporation—or lack thereof—of women in *antillanista* struggles in the Spanish-speaking Caribbean.

In *Lola Rodríguez de Tió: Contribución para un estudio integral*, Toledo (2002) illustrates how women involved in the revolutionary struggle were praised only in terms of their ability to be or behave like men, who were assumed to be innately courageous. One of her examples is General José Laclert Morlet's description of Lola Rodríguez de Tió (1843–1924), who was a friend and ally of Betances and one of the most important *antillanista* and nationalist thinkers of her time. She was the author of the 1868 revolutionary version of Puerto Rico's anthem, "La Borinqueña." Rodríguez de Tió helped organize various attempts to produce an anticolonial and antislavery insurrection on the island. Her efforts continued during her exile in Venezuela, New York, and Cuba. After a failed attempt to organize an armed invasion of Puerto Rico in 1896, General Laclert Morlet stated, "The only prepared man I have found in New York is Lola Rodríguez de Tió" (quoted in Toledo 2002: 58). Rodríguez de Tió's bravery symbolically turned her into a man. Her poetry was also deemed worthy by literary critics insofar as it could be attributed to two iconic men in Spanish-language literature: Luis de Góngora and Fray Luis de León (Toledo 2002: 40).

Rodríguez de Tió is not the only woman masculinized by her fellow *antillanos* during her lifetime. According to Lazo, another well-known woman writer of the period, the Cuban Gertrudis Gómez de Avellaneda (1814–73), received similar treatment from her male counterparts. For example, the renowned Cuban *antillanista* José Martí describes Gómez de Avellaneda's "potent and manly spirit; her body tall and robust, just as her poetry was rough and energetic" (quoted in Lazo 2005: 123). Gómez de Avellaneda was masculinized for the purposes of celebrating the quality of her poetry. These male writers and critics could not imagine that a good writer could be a woman. If a woman wrote well, then she had to at least be read as almost manly, closer to men than to women in her gender presentation and aesthetic sensibilities.

Betances's rhetoric was not an exception to this trend. In spite of a deep friendship with Rodríguez de Tío, as well as his lifetime correspondence with various female relatives and friends, he refers to men such as Louverture, Petión, Bolívar, Maceo, Luperón, and Máximo Gómez to represent his vision of interracial, transterritorial, *antillanista* struggles. While respecting and corresponding with women who participated in independence struggles, his *antillanista* politics were not necessarily engaged in challenging patriarchal notions of citizenship. His representation of masculine military men as models of regionalist revolutionary struggle reflected the gender and social conventions of his time, without offering visionary possibilities equal to his *antillanista* ethos.

In Betances's engagement with gender and sexual conventions, he often articulates notions of masculinity and femininity prevalent in nation-building narratives in Spanish America. For example, his descriptions of his fiancée, María del Carmen Henry y Betances, repeat nationalist tropes that equate women with the motherland. He writes, "We called her the Puerto Rican woman and she was the perfect type, the adorable ideal, the mysterious personification of our beautiful country; all love, all grace and all virtue" (2008: 2: 86). Her embodiment of the land's virtues is associated with her virginity, as Betances publicly stated in his French publication of *La vierge de Borinquen* (1: 165) after her passing in 1859 in Paris. Her virtue was also proven in his descriptions of her as a friend, daughter, fiancée, and companion, a clever woman whose intelligence and commitment to the struggle for Puerto Rican independence blossomed under his guidance: "She was going to be my companion and she had been my daughter, because I had birthed her and then she began to live with her heart and intelligence" (2: 66). In Betances's 1859 writings, Henry y Betances is the ideal Puerto Rican woman and ideal wife for a patriot like himself. She represents the nation and its liberation struggles placed under the care of its husband/father/patriot Betances.

The metonymic relationship Betances establishes between Henry y Betances and the Puerto Rican motherland speaks to the intersection of nationalist and *antillanista* discourses in his political work. While challenging representations that whiten Spanish-speaking Caribbean territories, he rearticulates understandings of womanhood common in nation-building projects in Spanish America. This is not to say that according to Betances women are only passive actors in the struggle for national independence. He does imagine women taking arms with men if the struggle requires it. But this is necessary only when the need for revolutionary change requires people to temporarily surrender any social norms that may restrict it.

Similarly Luperón's *Notas* emphasizes the deeds of the great military officials and statesmen of his time, such as Ulises Francisco Espaillat, Pablo Pujol, Máximo Grullón, and Buenaventura Báez. His history of the Dominican Republic is the story of those men's actions to protect or endanger the sovereignty of the nation. The sketches of military figures found throughout the *Notas* elide the participation of women in the nationalist and *antillanista* struggles. The role played by heteronormative notions of gender and sexuality in his historical narrative is significant as well.

As previously mentioned, Luperón states that Dominicans must protect themselves from Haitians to preserve their language and to regulate sexual relations through marriage, safeguard the honor of heteronormative families, and promote monogamous romantic relationships between men and women. According to Luperón, to protect the cultural heritage left by Spain in the island, it is crucial to discipline gender and sexual relations. Hispanicity is reproduced through the adoption of Catholic sexual conventions that require women to embody gendered ideals of virtue. Luperón ascribes to women a role that is characteristic of nation-building narratives throughout the Americas: women are solely the "mirror of the man, testimony of divine truth," who must be recognized and respected as the bearers and caretakers of the nation's children, its new citizens (1939: 1: 119).[17]

These examples demonstrate that these *antillanista* thinkers imagined the basis for decolonial kinship among Antilleans without necessarily including women as active agents of political transformation. Women widely respected in pro-independence circles, like Rodríguez de Tío and Gómez de Avellaneda, transgressed gender roles constantly—because of their appearance, successful writing careers, public interventions in political and intellectual debates throughout the Atlantic world, or love affairs outside of wedlock (in the case of Gómez de Avellaneda). However, their disruption of the social order did not seem to radically challenge or change how their comrades came to represent national subjects in their writings.

On Kinship and Politics in the Caribbean

Luperón's and Betances's political work is situated at the precise moment when the idea of developing a single political-economic unit out of the Caribbean islands emerges. They both supported the independence of individual Caribbean territories (and Latin American nations) and the constitution of an Antillean confederation. As *antillanista* revolutionaries they have been credited with pursuing a radical anti-slavery project, one that sought not only the abolition of slavery but the full political enfranchisement of what they understood to be a majority nonwhite population in the Caribbean.

Their narratives of *antillanismo* elucidate who they imagined to be natural allies of their territories of origin or the Caribbean as a whole. They both developed ideological and strategic alliances with Haiti as the first republic in the Antilles to assert the political rights of black citizens. Both counted on Haiti as a refuge and ally for antislavery and pro-independence movements, and Haiti counted on their support at a time when its legitimacy as a nation was questioned by Europe and the United States.

Haiti figures prominently in Betances's political writings as a nation whose interests and experiences are in line with Cuba's and Puerto Rico's, a precursor to the interracial relationships and alliances that should characterize nationalists' struggles for independence. Luperón imagines the Dominican Republic and Haiti sharing the same racial history in the process of becoming the same race, one that can govern the island without colonial interventions. But his valorization of Hispanic Dominican attributes—the Spanish language, religion, and sexual mores—represented Spain as the motherland of the Dominican Republic and Haiti as a threat to the cultural and moral integrity of the Dominican Republic. In Betances's writings, France emerged as a friend of the Caribbean and Latin America. Betances's understanding of Puerto Rican racial demographics and his personal experience of exile and persecution due to Spanish policies against abolitionist and pro-independence movements are devoid of Luperón's celebration of a Hispanic Caribbean heritage. But his appreciation for French political traditions and support of French investments in the Caribbean leave us wondering how he would have incorporated France's colonial holdings in Asia, Africa, and the Caribbean in a French-Caribbean or French–Latin American alliance.

The pragmatism that characterized both Luperón's and Betances's political strategies cannot be underestimated. Luperón was trying to further transcolonial ideals in the 1890s, two years before the Spanish-American War, when the threat of U.S. intervention in the Caribbean became imminent. Claiming the Hispanic heritage of Dominicans may have allowed him to stay in Puerto Rico until his return home, but it also may have served to legitimize Dominicans' capacity to govern their own country in the face of increasing U.S. interventionism in the Caribbean and Latin America.

Betances also made a home in exile in France, where he was educated, politicized, and found allies in the Masonic community, anarchism, and other social and political spaces. Having foreseen U.S. desires to expand south, he collaborated with the French in an attempt to thwart U.S. attempts to build the transoceanic canal in Panama. He also called on other metropolitan powers to aid him in his international campaign against Spanish colonialism in Cuba and Puerto Rico.

These are complex decolonial, though Eurocentric, moves that cannot be easily condemned or dismissed. After all, they emerge out of the economic and material needs of the anticolonial struggle and the creolization processes that constitute the Caribbean contours. In order to address the political challenges before them, *antillanistas* had to acknowledge and address the region's black, indigenous, Asian, and European heritages. They deployed a malleable affective matrix—constituted by transcolonial, colonial, and national kinship models[18]—that allowed them to sustain a broad range of brotherhoods and political communities throughout the Atlantic world.

Such communities, in this case those articulated by the *antillanistas* Betances and Luperón, are not always emancipatory (Johnson 2012). The affective matrix they deploy complicates representations of *antillanismo* as an ideal alternative to Creole nation-building projects invested in whitening narratives. To use Luperón's words, as "emancipated sons" these writers must navigate their actual familial, cultural, and political relationships with Europe, along with their desire to end racial subordination in the Antilles; honor their black ancestors and the interracial relationships that constitute their families; and fight for the right to self-determination of emerging nations and the desired Antillean confederation. Their representation of the racial demographics of Puerto Rico, the Dominican Republic, and Haiti and their filial ties and solidarities with the Antilles, South America, and Europe illustrate some of the complex decolonial moves that characterized their rhetoric. A necessary political pragmatism often informed which narrative of kinship—transcolonial, colonial/imperial, or national—prevailed in their discourse.[19]

As the Caribbean faces demands to further neoliberalize Caribbean economies through a variety of political entities, such as the Caribbean Community (CARICOM), the Assembly of Caribbean Peoples, the People's Summits of the Americas, and the Bolivarian Alternative for the Americas, it engages the same questions Betances and Luperón addressed when they articulated an *antillanista* agenda: Who are we? Where are we going? And with whom?

To revive *antillanismo* as a mode of political-economic action in the context of globalization requires analyzing historical struggles surrounding the conceptualization of Antillean integration projects. Often neoliberal integration efforts pose as the contemporary manifestation of *antillanista* ideals. Neoliberal calls to integrate the Caribbean often rely on the political memory of antiracist and *antillanista* projects in order to naturalize free market progressions. As a consequence contemporary racial and socioeconomic inequities are dismissed or denied.

Neoliberal multiculturalist rhetoric *seems* to address the concerns of previous antiracist *antillanista* struggles to end colonialism. In the twenty-first century Caribbean histories of racial and cultural mixture get mobilized to justify neoliberal demands to facilitate the flow of transnational capital. For instance, international financing institutions have argued that due to cultural intermixing, the Caribbean antecedes contemporary trends of globalization. Anoop Singh, former director of the Western Hemisphere Department of the International Monetary Fund, rearticulated this idea at a 2004 conference with Caribbean state officials. He stated, "The Caribbean region can be proud of its integration with the world community. In many respects, the region has been among the pioneers of globalization, with an intermingling of peoples from different parts of the world that began many centuries ago" (Singh 2004). In Singh's statements the cross-cultural exchanges and processes of miscegenation that characterize Caribbean societies are celebrated as inherent features of globalization. In other words, Caribbean creolization processes are equated with the implementation of neoliberal economic policies. If Caribbean people have embraced the racial and cultural mixture of peoples from Europe, the Americas, Africa, and Asia, then they are well suited to open their markets to the regime of unregulated capital flows.

However, an *antillanista* project that follows the logic of neoliberal globalization is doomed to fail to meet the needs of Caribbean working people and those who still experience the burden of racial subjection (Reyes-Santos 2008). Globalization subsumes the need to actively resist existing racialized socioeconomic hierarchies under the multiculturalist celebration of difference that has come to characterize the global market. Such celebrations of the Caribbean's racial and ethnic hybridities negate demands of social equality in the region (Puri 2004: 6). They fail to account for the ways *antillanista* discourses are mobilized to diminish regional autonomy.

I have turned to historical antecedents of regionalism in the Caribbean to complicate contemporary uses of *antillanista* discourses, in particular neoliberal multiculturalism, which has attempted to co-opt an antislavery *antillanista* agenda. By focusing on the works of Betances and Luperón at the turn of the twentieth century, I have not meant to diminish the importance of preexisting regionalist efforts. I position their work as significant to the contemporary moment because they engaged a legacy of transcolonial collaborations that emerged out of the challenge to white supremacy and colonialism. They also drew, explicitly, on the political possibilities generated by slave and indigenous insurrections, including the Haitian Revolution.[20] I also have intended to provide an overview of *antillanismo* as presented in their work. My intention has been to explore *antillanismo*'s internal negotiations of colonial, national, and transcolonial notions of kinship as articulated by two of its most ardent and well-known proponents in the Dominican Republic and Puerto Rico. The ideas generated by these two men have come to represent the dream of an Antillean confederation in the Spanish-speaking Caribbean. Their rhetoric engaged the anticolonial desires embedded in *antillanista* and nationalist narratives, which were replicated in the twentieth century throughout the Afro-diasporic communities in the Spanish-speaking, Anglophone, and Francophone colonies and emerging nations in the Caribbean.

Luperón's and Betances's kinship narratives underscore the political value of *antillanista* and nationalist paradigms and the need to pay attention to their historical contingence—how they get articulated in response to specific historical demands. Reading these works allows us to contemplate how we continue to negotiate colonial, regionalist, and nationalist notions of belonging, and how creolized identities might get mobilized in the Caribbean for the interests of capital, the state, and the peoples of the region.

For the past two centuries *antillanistas* such as Martí, Rodríguez de Tío, C. L. R. James, Luis Rafael Sánchez, the Créolistes, Edouard Glissant, Edward Kamau Brathwaite, Edouard Glissant, Wilson Harris, and Ana Lydia Vega have attempted to develop a transcolonial consciousness, a shared sense of identity, of kinship, that to some extent overrides nation-specific concerns and understandings of belonging in order to integrate the political and economic life of the region. For some the stronghold of nationalism may seem to pose insurmountable obstacles for such a project. Political observers have pointed to CARICOM's dilemmas in negotiating the creation of a single economy for its members while individual nations protect their own interests.[21] Racial, gender, class, and sexual norms continue to limit the scope of who can belong and to what extent in decolonial collectivities. And the racism and xenophobia experienced by Haitian migrants in the Dominican Republic and Dominicans in Puerto Rico are also clear examples of how nationalisms have created animosity among Antilleans. The often tense yet simultaneous negotiations of *antillanista* and nationalist narratives of kinship continue to be a concern for those invested in decolonial thinking. As this chapter has illustrated, *antillanista*, colonial, and nationalist narratives of kinship have coexisted and co-constituted each other historically.

By 1898 Betances's nightmare had come true. The Spanish-American War of 1898 dealt an almost lethal blow to *antillanismo*. The transcolonial kinship networks imagined and built by *antillanistas* such as Betances and Luperón faced the military and economic might of the region's northern neighbor and its expansionist, imperialist ethos. Moreover the most well-known representatives of the revolutionary *antillanista* movements lived in exile and passed away before seeing the consequences of the war. Many decided to put their energies into educational and nation-building efforts when it was clear that the United States would not grant independence to Puerto Rico or Cuba. Puerto Rico became an unincorporated U.S. territory, and Cuba eventually renegotiated the terms of its relationship with the United States. In 1902 Congress approved the Platt Amendment, limiting the island's international commerce, requiring the lease of land for U.S. military bases such as the one found in Guantánamo, and removing military forces while enabling unilateral military interventions. The 1917 Jones Act turned Puerto Ricans into U.S. citizens without the right to vote in presidential elections—unless they lived on the mainland—and without a voting representative in Congress.

Luperón died in 1897, before the triumph of U.S. forces in the region. Betances, who died in 1898, did not witness the Treaty of Paris that gave the United States control over Cuba, Puerto Rico, Guam, the Philippines, and other former Spanish colonies. The *antillanistas* Lieutenant General José Antonio de la Caridad Maceo y Grajales and José Martí died in the Cuban wars of independence. Lola Rodríguez de Tío dedicated herself to the Cuban educational system until her death in 1924. She became a member of the Cuban Academy of Arts and Letters and continued to use her poetry to express her dreams of transcolonial kinship and her love for Cuba and Puerto Rico. After the Treaty of Paris was signed, Eugenio María de Hostos advocated for Puerto Rican independence before the U.S. Congress. Failing to obtain it, he returned to the Dominican Republic where, until his death in 1903, he continued to dedicate himself to advancing the educational system in an effort to better enable Dominicans to fulfill their civic duties as national subjects.

As the nineteenth century came to an end, transcolonial activism also lost its footing in the political imagination of the Dominican Republic and Puerto Rico. *Antillanista* kinship narratives were displaced by nationalist anticolonial representations of Dominicans and Puerto Ricans after the triumph of the United States in the 1898 Spanish-American War. The national family became the trope that evoked Dominicans' and Puerto Ricans' rightful claims to political sovereignty or, in the case of Puerto Rico, political autonomy from either Spain or the United States. The affective matrix that informed *antillanismo* remained in place; however, its axis had shifted. But the real experiences of transcolonial solidarity, as well as old and emergent colonial/imperial loyalties, shaped the internal contradictions embedded in white/whitened Creole heteropatriarchal narratives of national kinship. The transcolonial brotherhoods, families, and friendships embraced by Luperón and Betances continued to shape nation-building projects into the twentieth century.

2 / Wife, Food, and a Bed of His Own: Marriage, Family, and Nationalist Kinship in the 1930s

In the twentieth century the Dominican Republic, Haiti, Puerto Rico, and Cuba became ground zero for U.S. attempts to establish its imperial power over the Caribbean. In 1898 the United States invaded Puerto Rico and Cuba. Puerto Rico became a U.S. territory, and Cuba eventually renegotiated the terms of its relationship with the United States. In 1902 the U.S. government limited the island's international commerce, required the lease of land for U.S. military bases, and removed military forces while enabling unilateral military interventions.

Approximately fifteen years later the United States occupied the Dominican Republic and Haiti. Peasants, laborers, and other disaffected parties across the island resisted, but the occupations lasted more than a decade in each country: in Haiti from 1915 to 1934 and in the Dominican Republic from 1916 to 1928. The U.S. occupation government pursued an official economic and migration policy that took thousands of Haitians and West Indians to work on sugarcane plantations in Cuba and the Dominican Republic.

In the Dominican Republic the sugarcane plantations, which included the *central* (the mill), the *batey* (workers' living quarters), and the cane fields, were frequently run by elite *criollos* and U.S. investors and managers but were mostly maintained by black (Haitian and West Indian) migrant labor (Inoa 1999). In Puerto Rico elite *criollos* and U.S. corporations owned and managed a sugar industry protected by the occupation government (García Muñiz 2010). Workforces in sugarcane fields and the mill were divided across racial and ethnic lines, which shaped how Puerto Ricans experienced the economic structure of the plantation.

Published in the 1930s, the novels *La Llamarada* by the Puerto Rican Enrique Laguerre (1939) and *Over* by the Dominican Ramón Marrero Aristy (1939; 1963) imagine national families in the cane field. These novels speak to early twentieth-century social struggles on both islands. These include the *gavilleros, liboristas,* and armed peasant uprisings in the Dominican Republic (Davis 2004; Davis 2005; Roorda 1998) and the nationalist efforts for independence led by Pedro Albizu Campos in Puerto Rico (Ferrao 1993). Collectively these struggles asserted Dominican and Puerto Rican claims to national sovereignty. Though Laguerre and Marrero Aristy do not assume the political position of these activists, their work reflected ongoing processes of nation building while under siege by U.S. imperialism. Both novels have been canonized as attempts to defend the nation and its national subjects from the economic exploitation and upheaval of traditional social relations resulting from U.S. imperialism. Both locate the U.S. Empire within the sugar industry. National families emerged as a primary trope in this context. Laguerre and Marrero Aristy imagine particular marriages and families representing specific narratives of racial mixture in order to define belonging within the national Dominican and Puerto Rican families. *La Llamarada* and *Over* are representative of the political, cultural, and economic transformations that characterized the turn of the twentieth century in the Dominican Republic and Puerto Rico.

As José F. Buscaglia-Salgado (2003) and Jossiana Arroyo (2013) have suggested, narratives of national kinship at this time prevailed as an anticolonial rhetorical strategy, in sharp contrast to nineteenth-century transcolonial narratives of mulatto alternatives, invested in the affirmation of Afro-descendants' right to self-determination throughout the Antilles. Many of these narratives of national kinship mirrored the racial assumptions of elite Creole nationalist projects that sought to whiten and contain the political demands of poor, *mestizo*/mulatto, indigenous, and black populations in Latin America. These novels touch upon these currents and, at times, replicate them. However, applying the decolonial affective matrix as a lens provides fresh insight into the significance of national modes of kinship.

These novels reflect the internal contradictions inherent in the nation-building projects of which they are a part. The protagonists espouse national ideals of kinship as a response to colonial/imperial impositions of kinship. These national ideals of kinship, in turn, marginalize transcolonial kinship possibilities and reassert the subjectivity of the propertied, educated, white-identified, and heteronormative man as bearer of the political agency of the citizen. Ultimately, however, there is both failure and crisis. This idealized masculine citizen cannot really resolve the social conflicts produced by racial and class differences and by the U.S. military and economic interventions in the Caribbean.

At the time these novels were published, colonial/imperial kinship narratives characterized dominant political discourses that located the Caribbean within a field of filial, political, economic, and cultural relationships to Europe and the United States. This was reflected in pan-American colonialist legacies and notions of belonging. For example, in 1933 President Franklin D. Roosevelt sought to mediate a previous history of U.S. unilateral military interventions in the Caribbean and Latin America. His Good Neighbor Policy represented the United States as a noninterventionist friend of Latin America, while the United States continued to offer itself as the ideal model for democratic, capitalist governance for Latin American and Caribbean nations (Horn 2014; Ovalle 2011; Roorda 1998).[1] Latin America and the Caribbean could be good neighbors by adopting U.S. notions of civilization, including their racial exclusions, and by incorporating the regulation of kin relations through the institution of marriage within their structures of governance (Horn 2014; Mayes 2014). On the other hand, belonging could also be defined as being part of a family of Spanish nations where nationalist traditions relied on ideologies of *mestizaje* as a narrative of biological or cultural whitening (Candelario 2007; Dávila 1997; Godreau 2006; Whitten and Torres 1998). Literary production in 1930s Puerto Rico and the Dominican Trujillato negotiate these discursive histories (Belén Cambeira 2001; Fernández Olmos 1978; Gelpí 1993; Gutiérrez 2004; Horn 2014; Janer 2005; Méndez 2011; Rodríguez 2003; Roy-Féquière 2004; Sommer 1988; Torres-Saillant 2000; Veloz Maggiolo 1977), aptly reflected in *La Llamarada* and *Over*.

Both novels feature a male protagonist-narrator and appear to follow the conventional plot lines of national romances in Latin America, or what Doris Sommer (1993) has called "foundational fictions," national romances that serve as integral components of nation-building processes in Latin America. But they actually illustrate the limitations of foundational fictions. Like mainland Latin American foundational fictions, marriage appears in *La Llamarada* and *Over* as the primordial organizing affective unit of emerging nations, where loyalties and notions of belonging are built, at the expense of the poor, ethnic and racial minorities, women, and nonnormative subjects. The male protagonists get married and build families; in this way both novels represent the unity of the nation and its ability to govern itself through the paternal figure. In *La Llamarada* the male *pater* represents the Puerto Rican *hacendados*, whereas in *Over* he represents the Dominican petit-bourgeois class.[2] But in both cases marriage does not prove to be a sustainable kinship model, as it conventionally does in Sommer's foundational fictions. Trying to apply the concept of foundational fiction to these 1930s novels of nation building is troublesome because in the face of U.S. occupation and imperial designs and the consuming nature of the plantation, these novels behave more like "failed romances" (Janer 2005). Marriage does not resolve the internal struggles between national subjects over resources; it does not assuage the tensions arising from economic and ethnoracial differences; nor does it diminish popular resistance to foreign investors and, in the case of Puerto Rico, colonial authorities.

Moreover these Antillean novels represent the struggle to unify national subjects and also represent a history of *antillanista*, antislavery, political solidarities that transcended colonial and national boundaries in the region; in other words, they mobilize transcolonial kinship narratives. This is a reality that does not fit Sommer's model of foundational fictions in Latin America. *La Llamarada* and *Over* demonstrate that deploying the trope of marriage as a metaphor and mode of national kinship requires ignoring the transcolonial collaborations and solidarities that historically resisted the exploitation of Afro-descendant labor in colonial regimes. The narrators must downplay the claims of antiracist, labor, and socialist movements and of the Garveyists in order to uphold their class privilege and what they understand to be their fundamental male rights: a wife, children, and property.

National Kinship, Transcolonial Kinship, and Negritude

When these novels were published, notions of national kinship had gained higher representational value in political and cultural nationalist projects throughout the Spanish-speaking Caribbean. But cultural workers were also witness to labor strikes and socialists advocating for the rights of workers and Afro-descendant people beyond colonial/imperial and national boundaries. Plantations everywhere were set on fire as cane workers protested the exploitative labor system.[3] Garveyists and their leader, Marcus Garvey, who founded the Universal Negro Improvement Association and its chapters in New York, the Dominican Republic, Cuba, Jamaica, Puerto Rico, and many other Afro-diasporic communities, spoke openly about black pride and against the racial oppression of Afro-descendants (García Muñiz and Giovanetti 2003; Guridy 2010;

Mayes 2014; Stephens 2005). All these acts of resistance to racism and the plantation system carried the seed planted by *antillanistas* like Luperón and Betances in the nineteenth century. In the early twentieth century, labor movements, unions, Garveyists, anarchists, and socialists traveled the Antilles, as well as the United States and the circum-Caribbean region, creating transcolonial alliances that defended Afro-descendants' political, economic, and social rights everywhere (García Muñiz and Giovanetti 2003; King 2001; Stephens 2005).

Literature was another site where antiracist, transcolonial, *antillanista* impulses found a home in the early twentieth century. Both *Over* and *La Llamarada* were published during the decade when *negrismo*, Negritude, and *afro-cubanismo* became internationally recognized literary expressions. Haitian *indigenisme* had flourished in the 1920s, and some Haitian authors had turned to *noirisme* as its alternative in the late 1920s and 1930s (Dash 1981, 1998; Lerebours 1992; Morejón 1982). Even if these literary movements could at times be construed as limited by Europeanist exotic notions of blackness (Dash 1981; Roy-Féquière 2004), they stand out as a significant counterpoint to and intervention in racist discourses and policies. The Cuban Nicolás Guillén, the Dominican Manuel del Cabral, Haitians Jean Price-Mars and Jacques Roumain, the Puerto Rican Luis Palés Matos, and the Martinicans Aime Césaire and Guianan Léon-Gontran Damas, among many others, asserted the shared black heritage of the Antilles.

These literary movements were always transcolonial in spirit. Like *antillanista* projects of the nineteenth century, these literary expressions were informed by and construed in encounters with other Antilleans, Afro-descendant peoples in the United States and Europe, and Africans. They often affirmed the black heritage of the Antilles as a region, advocated for blacks' political, economic, and social rights, and valorized black cultural practices and artistic expression. Antilleans were often imagined as people sharing similar historical processes: slavery, the sugar plantation, colonialism, and U.S. imperialism (e.g., Guillén's poem "West Indies Ltd.").

Over and *La Llamarada* are more subtle than these literary expressions in their attention to transcolonial political and cultural impulses, but their critiques of racism and their affirmation of the humanity of *mestizo*/mulatto subjects stand in sharp contrast to Creole elite narratives. This is best exemplified in the metaphor of the fires that consume cane fields in both novels and appears in Laguerre's references to Cuban–Puerto Rican black and mulatto insurrections in the nineteenth century and Marrero Aristy's attention to the plight of Haitian and Anglophone Caribbean workers. These stories appear as traces of *antillanista* kinship narratives, though the texts themselves came to represent the nation in Dominican and Puerto Rican literary canons.

The Canon: Land and National Kinship in *Novelas del Cañaveral*

When published, *La Llamarada* and *Over* were immediately incorporated into national literary canons.[4] Canonical readings of these fictional texts sought to explain the significance of economic, political, and social changes by seeking historical truth within their realist aesthetics.[5] As canonical texts, they were used to represent the unique character and traditions that constitute Dominican and Puerto Rican national communities. Juan Gelpí (1993: 15) reminds us that "the constitution of every canon is simultaneously a literary activity and a political strategy." Both texts served the interests of nationalists seeking to critique U.S. interventions in the Caribbean. In contrast to the purported aims of the Good Neighbor Policy, the United States appears in both novels not as a benevolent father, friend, brother, or neighbor but rather as an exploitative, repressive investor in an economic system that destroys national natural and human resources.

Over became a useful tool for the Dominican dictator Trujillo, who sought to nationalize the sugarcane industry to maximize his own profit (Sommer 1988). *La Llamarada* appeared to represent the interests of elite, Puerto Rican intellectuals whose historical economic interests and political clout had been displaced by the colonial government and U.S. investments on the island. They were then posited as an intermediary class between the U.S. colonial government and poor and working-class Puerto Ricans, "an intellectual group that conceived itself as the privileged spokesperson of a nationality, conscious of their mission as organizers of a 'national culture' threatened by the North American presence" (Ferrao 1993: 46).

Critics have described *Over* and *La Llamarada* as *novelas del cañaveral* (plantation novels; Costa 2004; Graciano 1990). These novels also resemble the *novelas de la tierra* (novels of the earth) widely studied in mainland Latin America. They collect rural regional modes of speech and folklore, represent the family as an essential site for the reproduction of cultural and social practices, and create a chronological contrast that "chronicles the decline of a group as a result of a specific form of exploitation" (González Echevarría 2004: 204). These telluric novels try to find myths that will "make whole the disparate fragments" (204) of a community shaped by cross-cultural contact.

Over and La Llamarada share these attributes with 1920s and 1930s Latin American novelas de la tierra, such as Segundo Sombra (1926), La Vorágine (1924), and Doña Bárbara (1929). However, their historical realities are different from those of Central and South America. As novelas del cañaveral they exhibit a series of attributes that reveal their profoundly Antillean character and differentiate them from mainland Latin America novelas de la tierra. U.S. imperialism and the consequences of occupation government move the plot in both novels. They focus on the cane field and sugar milling corporations to critique their exploitative working conditions and their racial, ethnic, and socioeconomic hierarchies. They show how U.S. investment in that economic sector displaced small farmers and petit-bourgeois classes in the Dominican Republic and the traditional coffee growers and haciendas of Puerto Rico as productive economic sectors. Transcolonial kinship haunts these nationalist narratives, illustrated by the exchanges between Haitians and Dominicans in Over and the recovery of black insurrections and cultural practices in La Llamarada.

Some clarifications will help explain the particular manifestation of the novela del cañaveral represented by La Llamarada and the novela de la caña represented by Over. The two subgenres are distinguished by the novels' subjects: the protagonist and those he represents, the workers in the cane field, and the organization of labor on the plantation. According to Berta Graciano (1990: 29), Over—as a novela de la caña—is characterized by its critique of U.S. imperialism, by realist depictions of the plantation landscape, and by its concern with the exploitative space of the bodega (plantation store) within the lands owned by the central itself. This is different from La Llamarada's attention to the protagonist's life as the manager of a colony subcontracted by the central to produce sugarcane—an element that has been used to define it as a novela de cañaveral. These differences in literary subgenres arise from a complex interplay between the historical specificity of national motifs related to the particular organization of sugar production in each territory. These national motifs are signaled by the needs and desires of certain classes as representative of the nation under siege by the United States. In spite of these differences, I read both La Llamarada and Over as plantation novels that share the concern with the ways the nation is transformed by

U.S. imperialism as well as a desire to create a national kinship narrative that will enable an epistemic response to these processes.

I refer to the sugar industry, its cane fields and mills, using the word *plantation*. *La Llamarada* and *Over* are concerned with the modification of the national landscape by the sugar industry, reminding contemporary readers of Antonio Benítez Rojo's theorization of the plantation in the Caribbean:

> Its inexorable territory-claiming nature made it—makes it still— advance in length and depth through the natural lands, demolishing forests, sucking up rivers, displacing other crops, and exterminating native plants and animals. At the same time, ever since it was put into play, this powerful machine [the plantation] has attempted systematically to shape—to suit to its own convenience, the political, economic, social and cultural spheres of the country that nourishes it until that country is changed into a *sugar island*. (1996: 72)

Though sugar industries in the Dominican Republic and Puerto Rico do not share the same history with Cuba or the rest of the Antilles, I find Benítez Rojo's description of the plantation useful to approach *Over* and *La Llamarada* as Caribbean plantation novels. Examining how the plantation comes to be imagined with respect to a national history is crucial for addressing its lived legacies in the Antilles. In Benítez Rojo's description, the plantation is a societal structure imposing itself, in physical and ideological ways, on the national landscape and psyche. His use of the term *plantation* refers to the cane fields and sugar milling process but also to the social, racial, and cultural dynamics that have characterized sugar production in the Antilles.

While demonstrating that the sugarcane plantation destroys the national landscape and causes damage to the national psyche, *Over* and *La Llamarada* imagine an ideal nation constituted by a productive relationship between the land and the national subject and by intimate relations that follow certain racial-gender scripts. Their narratives suggest how families and people of different socioeconomic, ethnic, and racial backgrounds must relate to one another and the land in order to properly reproduce the nation and its natural and human resources.

During colonial times both the Dominican Republic and Puerto Rico produced sugar in *ingenios* that used slave labor and processed sugarcane cultivated in land owned by the *ingenio* owner. By the late nineteenth century, after emancipation, one found mostly *centrales* in

Cuba and Puerto Rico that contracted cane farmers (*colonos*) to grow the sugarcane. In the Dominican Republic an *ingenio-central* system took shape during that same time period. The *ingenio-central* milled sugar produced by the estate and by *colonos*. Unlike Puerto Rican sugarcane fields and *centrales*, which mostly employed local Puerto Ricans, work-forces on Dominican *ingenio-centrales* in the early twentieth century were characterized by a large migrant population from Haiti and the Anglophone Caribbean (West Indians), as well as some Puerto Rican managers, investors, and workers (García Muñiz 2010; García Muñiz and Giovanetti 2003).

By the 1930s the modernization of the sugarcane industry by foreign capital had transformed the material relationship between nationals and the national territory (Moreno Fraginals 1985; García Muñiz 2010; García Muñiz and Giovanetti 2003; Inoa 1999; Mayes 2014; Méndez 2011).[6] In 1898 and 1917 U.S. military and economic interventions were formalized in the Dominican Republic and Puerto Rico, as well as in Haiti and Cuba. Since the U.S. Sugar Act of 1871 a series of economic agreements had tied the fate of Dominican and Puerto Rican, as well as Cuban, sugar industries to U.S. economic policies. During World War I and the consequent scarcity of beet sugar in Europe, sugar experienced an economic boom that attracted and, at times, required increased investment by U.S. banks and corporations. Monoculture and the displacement of peasants from their land led to proletarianization. This trend characterized this period in both places, and the deep economic recession of the 1930s heightened the vulnerability of workers in cane fields and *centrales*. The novels document the labor strikes and plantation fires that took place on plantations throughout the Caribbean in response to worsening labor conditions.

In Cuba and the Dominican Republic, Haitian laborers were received with ambivalence. On one hand, U.S. and local investors benefited from hiring a migrant workforce that could be easily exploited. Many of the Haitian laborers were without the resources necessary to advocate for themselves through official channels. On the other hand, intellectuals invested in claiming the whiteness and *hispanidad* of the former Spanish colonies imagined Haitian migrants as a threat to the racial order in both Cuba and the Dominican Republic. Caught within the web of labor exploitation and racism, Haitian migrants became scapegoats for the conditions produced by the Great Depression in the 1930s. They were blamed for the high levels of unemployment and for the harsh working conditions.

In both novels the male protagonists' ability to properly care for their families and the national land is impeded by the transformation and expansion of sugar industries in their respective countries. In *Over* the petit-bourgeois protagonist must sell his labor to the *central* instead of managing his own land and business. The *central* has created such a monopoly over land and commerce that working for it is the only hope for personal advancement. The *central* stripped people of their lands in order to grow sugar and created an indebted working class that could purchase products only at its stores (*bodegas*). In *La Llamarada* the *hacendado* class—owners of small agricultural plantations in the mountains—is the aggrieved social group caught between empire and the laborers of their land, the children and grandchildren of former slaves. The U.S. occupation government fostered the growth and modernization of the sugar industry through corporate investments and protectionist policies, at the expense of other economic sectors. *Hacendados* began losing land to due to their increasing debt to banks and *centrales*.

In my close reading of the novels I will focus on how the subjectivity of the protagonist-narrators are construed, noting the biases that hinder their ability to represent the nation as cohesive, united, and thriving families alongside the plantation. I reflect, in particular, on the authors' representations of cane fields, the land and its inhabitants, and the characters' survival and resistance mechanisms. I end by analyzing the narrators' quests for ideal wives and the underlying desire to reproduce healthy heteropatriarchal national families.

La Llamarada

Choosing *La Llamarada* to discuss Puerto Rican narratives of national kinship in the 1930s is important because it was published at a time when political nationalists were being silenced by "bullets and prison" (Alvarez Curbelo 1993: 35). Cultural nationalism, on the other hand, and its articulation in 1930s literary texts, the educational system, and music (Ferrao 1993: 38–39) survived within certain cultural and academic institutions, such as the Ateneo and the Department of Hispanic Studies at University of Puerto Rico.[7] Jorge Duany (2007: 52) claims a "careful distinction between political nationalism—based on the doctrine that every people should have its own sovereign state, and cultural nationalism, based on the assertion of the moral and spiritual autonomy of each people—as expressed in the protection of its historical patrimony as well as its popular and elite culture."

These two forms of nationalism often operate simultaneously, as has historically been the case in the Dominican Republic. But in Puerto

Rico, an unincorporated U.S. territory since 1898, cultural nationalism has survived and thrived on the island and in the U.S. Puerto Rican diaspora communities (Duany 2002; Flores 2009). This is so even when it is clear that most Puerto Ricans may not support an independent nation-state, the claim associated with political nationalism.[8] *La Llamarada* is a perfect example of the kind of cultural nationalist texts that commented on Puerto Rican quotidian realities as a nonindependent territory. It affirmed Puerto Ricans' national character as a people in the 1930s, when islanders defined themselves against the United States.

In 1917 Puerto Ricans became U.S. citizens through the Jones Act. Until 1948 they were still governed by military and civil authorities appointed by the president of the United States. In 1952 the United States granted the island the status of an *Estado Libre Asociado* (free associated state), vesting the local government with a higher degree of autonomy in exchange for the continued repression of *independentistas*. The Puerto Rican governor Luis Muñoz Marín negotiated the new agreement between the island and the U.S. government. In an attempt to maintain the status quo, members of the Nationalist Party, led by Pedro Albizu Campos, as well as workers and others mobilizing to either gain political independence or criticize the colonial regime, were incarcerated, tortured, and repressed by the Marín government.

In the 1930s Puerto Rican cultural nationalisms became the safe oppositional response to U.S. occupation (Roy-Féquière 2004: 4).[9] A variety of sectors—upper-, middle-, and working-class intellectuals, suffragists, labor activists, and radical independence movements—participated in the conceptualization of Puerto Rican cultural nationalism (Gelpí 1993; Ramos Rosado 1999; Roy-Féquière 2004). This process included campaigns to end the government's English-only policy, campaigns to amend the education system, claims to new cultural-national forms of Puerto Ricanness, and outright attempts to end U.S. colonial rule. The Generación del Treinta was the cadre of intellectual elites that required Puerto Rican writers to devote themselves to the exploration of what being Puerto Rican meant vis-à-vis North Americans. Among the *treintistas* were Antonio Pedreira, Margot Arce, René Márquez, Concha Mélendez, and Abelardo Díaz Alfaro.

A teacher from the western rural town of Moca pursuing his bachelor's and master's degrees at the University of Puerto Rico, Enrique Laguerre entered this circle of intellectuals in the classroom; Pedreira and Mélendez were his professors. After its first and second publications, in 1935 and 1939, Laguerre's *La Llamarada* was extolled as a manifestation of what *treintista* intellectuals had been calling for: a truly Puerto Rican literature. At the time of publication Laguerre received an award from the distinguished cultural organization Ateneo Puertorriqueño. *La Llamarada* became one of the most widely published Puerto Rican novels, with more than twenty editions, and today it is required reading in all Puerto Rican public schools.

Though their thought was quite varied, the *treintistas* recognized the racial mixture that characterizes Puerto Ricans but tended to define Puerto Rican national identity as another manifestation of *hispanidad*. Spanish cultural values and customs, such as Catholicism and the Spanish language, were understood by the *treintistas* as the root of Puerto Rican culture. From their shared perspective, Spanish culture strengthened Puerto Rican's "weaker" indigenous and African components (Ferrao 1993; Janer 2005; Roy-Féquière 2004). They also shared and were proponents of nineteenth-century understandings of *mestizaje* as a process that should lead to biological and/or cultural whitening. As intellectuals they asserted Puerto Ricans' racial mixture and political rights to land as fundamental components of a nationalist response to U.S. imperialism. The "great Puerto Rican family" was therefore *mestiza* but mostly Hispanic, at times with some traces from indigenous peoples, at times denying or trying to whiten its blackness (Blanco 1981; Godreau et al. 2008).

Ferrao (1993) has argued that this way of imagining Puerto Rico was not coincidental because most intellectuals of the Generación were the offspring of Spanish and other white European émigrés on the island. This class had shared similar filial, professional, and political ties for generations. Some were the children of Spanish businessmen, colonial administrators, and former military officers in the Spanish army, before 1898. Many of them were also members of the *hacendado* class that produced coffee, tobacco, and other agricultural products. *Hacendados* had relied on slave labor and nonpropertied peasants: *jornaleros* (workers) and *agregados* (sharecroppers) tied to the *hacienda* by debt and government policies against vagrancy that sought to control the mobility of free people of color (Rodríguez-Silva 2013).[10] The changes that occurred after 1898 eroded the *hacendados*' political and economic power across Puerto Rico (Ferrao 1993: 60).

The economic and political decline of the *hacendado* class was prompted by U.S. trade policies: the importation of commodity foods, the economic incentives given to sugar production, and the reallocation of labor to cane fields and *centrales*. It is not surprising, then, that these writers privilege the subjectivity of the *hacendado*, the coffee planter of the mountain, as the ideal national subject and intermediary between the colonial government and other Puerto Ricans.[11] The populist undertakings of the 1940s and 1950s, led by Luis Muñoz Marín, relegated the *treintistas'* imagination of the "great Puerto Rican family" to the Ateneo, the Department of Hispanic Studies at the University of Puerto Rico, and, in 1955, the Institute for Puerto Rican Culture. However, their ideological project (Rodriguez Castro 1993: 104) left an indelible mark on generations of Puerto Ricans (Dávila 1997; Roy-Féquière 2004).

As a student of and interlocutor with *treintista* thinkers, Laguerre joined these debates about Puerto Rican national identity. But his position was somewhat different. José Juan Báez Fumero (1999) says that Laguerre criticized *hispanofilia*, centering a Spanish cultural heritage in representations of Puerto Ricans' ethnic roots. He was not interested in retaining Spain's Spanish language but in documenting the linguistic diversity of Latin America. Laguerre conceptualized his writing as part of a broader Latin American literary tradition. In 1977 he called attention to the limitations of the Generación's project regarding the three roots of *puertorriqueñidad*. In response to *treintista* claims, he adopted what he called an *indafrispanismo antillano* (García Cabrera 1992: 55) to define himself as a Puerto Rican national writer.[12] Adopting the term *indafrispanismo antillano* , he asserted Puerto Ricans' and other Antilleans' indigenous, Spanish, and African ancestry to the same degree, without privileging one over the others.

La Llamarada introduces itself as a narrative written by a young man, José Antonio Borrás, from the Puerto Rican Cordillera Central (central mountain range). As a recently graduated agronomist, Borrás becomes an agricultural labor supervisor on a plantation financed by a U.S.-owned *central* in the 1930s. At the beginning Borrás describes how he is integrated into the world of the sugarcane plantation. On his way to the plantation by train, he meditates on all the sacrifices he had to make to obtain a degree in agronomy: his regret at leaving behind a young and poor girlfriend and his father, a coffee planter who did not support his getting a college education and from whom he is thus estranged.

Borrás narrates his experiences at the *central*, where he witnesses the abuse and exploitation of peasants while having to be an accomplice to the administration's efforts at maximizing profit. After having indirectly provoked the death of a rebellious worker, Segundo Marte, Borrás's guilt turns into anger against the administrators. As a result of expressing his emotions, he later gets fired. At the same time, after years of a conflictive relationship, his dying father asks him to return home and take his place in the administration of the family's *cafetal* (coffee plantation). Borrás marries Pepiña, a member of a prominent family of French émigrés, and brings her to the *cafetal*. This return represents the return to a land that will enable him to confront the effects of the U.S. plantation system and restore a harmonious relationship between the land, peasants, and landowners.

Borrás's first sight of the lands of the *central* reflects how his dreams of an independent and productive adult life reside in working there: "Very soon I was able to make out the *central*, with its high black chimney and its white buildings. As the bus advanced, my eyes traversed the humid plains of the valley, its green sugarcane, whose roots dug deep into the brown and easily flooded terrain. Ahead of us, behind the *central*, the mountain range, over whose greenery stood the peasants' picturesque houses" (Laguerre 1939: 34). In the 1930s the *central* was the mill where sugarcane was processed and also the mill's administration; it produced sugar for exportation and financed sugar plantations whose owners were subject to the direct supervision of the *central* in order to ensure debt payment. In some cases the *central* also owned plantations. The landscape of the *cañaveral* presents a beautiful, colorful, and pleasant view. Natural shades of green and brown dominate the scene and stand out against the plain white and black of the *central*'s buildings. Borrás's image juxtaposes the organized modernization of the *central* and its *cañaverales* in the valley against the traditional peasant way of living in the mountains. At the beginning of the novel the proximity of these two geographical and productive spaces mirrors Borrás's own emotional state. He happily describes the landscape of the *cañaveral* and its place in the national territory. The cane fields represent his brilliant future, while the mountains represent the past that he's enthusiastically leaving behind and to which he nonetheless remains nostalgically bound. It is a past containing the traditions espoused by his coffee-producing family.

Despite these initial possibilities, after a couple months' work on the plantation, Borrás comes to see it as a system that destroys the nation's natural resources and, by extension, the people's modes of subsistence. The plantation, then, is another manifestation of the reconfiguration of Antillean spaces resulting from U.S. imperialism through militarization, economic investment, or colonization. Borrás looks at a forest of *ausubos*, a tree native to the region that has been "marked by the axe, to make way for the sugarcane," and cannot avoid feeling resentment "toward that cane field of limber and slashing leaves, leaves like a million swords" (87).[13] The cane itself comes to signify the foreign exploitation of natural resources; the natural landscape has been replaced with a cash crop. Sugarcane represents the economic violence exerted by those who profit from it, as well as the physical violence experienced by an altered natural landscape and by the laboring hands that have modified it to meet the needs of the *cañaveral*.

Both Borrás and Compré, the narrator of *Over*, begin describing the plantation in these terms when they realize their own subjection to the mandates of the *central* and the exploitation of those beneath them. The novels' titles serve as tropes throughout the texts, signifying the malaise brought on by the plantation. In *La Llamarada* (The Blaze), Borrás uses the words *fire* or *blaze* to describe the hate that characterizes social interactions in the *cañaveral*. Alluding to the ignited exchanges, *la llamarada* characterizes the dysfunctional social exchanges of those inhabiting the *cañaveral*, as well as the concrete threat posed by workers' potential radical response to the daily violence in the *central*. It also characterizes the hate Borrás sees expressed by another supervisor, Florencio Rosado, toward the workers: "I became clearly aware of Rosado's hatred of the poor; it was the blaze that consumed him" (265).

Borrás himself experiences a similar blaze. He finds himself struggling between a moral call to be an ally to the workers and his ambitions for social advancement. For Borrás the blaze takes the form of a disease, a delirious fever, making him hallucinate about a circle of fire in the *cañaveral*: "Fire in the cane fields! Fire! The circle of fire surrounded me, inched toward me" (237). The disease is an embodiment of his feelings of self-consumption. His awareness of his complicity with the administration does not allow him to enjoy the promises of economic and personal success ostensibly offered by the plantation to an educated man like himself.

His hallucinations are a premonition of the real blaze later started by a worker named Segundo Marte, a man respected by Borrás since his arrival at the *central* for his commitment to the rights of working peoples. Inspired by communist ideals, Marte attempts to obtain better benefits for the plantation workers through a strike, but the corruption within the labor union neutralizes his efforts. As a consequence Marte's hate for the plantation and its administrators, what Borrás describes as his internal blaze, moves him to set the cane fields on fire. The sequence of fires represents a threat to Borrás's job security, in turn triggering an almost obsessive response from him. Consequently Borrás's own hate, or blaze, provokes Marte's murder, in spite of a previously stated sympathy for his struggle. Marte is killed during an ambush set up and led by Borrás. His death leads Borrás to a breaking point. He regrets the murder deeply, blaming the cane fields and the blaze it produces, which burns nationals and their potential for kinship with one another: "We could have been good friends, maybe brothers, but we let ourselves be consumed by the blaze of hate" (308). The cane fields require that Borrás ignore the struggle for labor justice led by Marte, a struggle connected to transcolonial labor, socialist, and communist organizing in the Caribbean. He must relinquish his desire to be (or fantasy of becoming) a caring patriarch to those "below" him, as members of a national family, to submit himself to the violent repressive tactics of the plantation. In doing so he must ignore historical *antillanista* fights against that same economic system and its exploitation of black populations.[14]

In "Enrique Laguerre y la memoriosa construcción del blanquito en *La Llamarada*," Lola Aponte Ramos's (2003) psychoanalytic analysis of Borrás's character reveals the novel's construction of a deracialized memory. She parallels Borrás's acts with his attempt at *hacerse el blanquito* (becoming a whitey). In *La Llamarada* the workers in the cane fields identify Borrás as a white man. One of the workers, Don (José) Dolores (mostly known as Don Chelores), complains about the silencing of black people's participation in independence struggles. He tells Borrás, "The black man was the first to handle the machete, son. Even if later the white man takes advantage of his struggles. Look at Cuba. After the triumph, they pushed blacks aside and you white people kept everything for yourselves" (Laguerre 1939: 185).

Borrás ignores the history chronicled by Don Chelores, who is referring to the interracial struggles for Cuban independence celebrated by the *antillanista* and pro-independence advocate Betances in 1870.[15] For Don Chelores, his plight as a farmer about to lose his land to the *central* illustrates what has historically happened to blacks in spite of their leadership in and commitment to anticolonial efforts. That history is alive for him. Meanwhile Borrás's college education has not taught him this history nor allowed him to understand his place in it.

For a moment, though, Borrás starts to wonder about his black ancestry, albeit not expressly but rather referring to "those who first handled the machete" (186). He does not usually think of those ancestors, who, he says, constitute a tiny part of who he is: "At another time I would not have remembered such a small portion of blood, but in light of the man's forceful affirmation, now I remember" (186).

Like *Over*, *La Llamarada* is a social protest novel. It represents the plight of the national worker. Both authors attempt to represent the workers' and peasants' manner of speech, customs, food, and housing. For instance, Borrás documents the houses, gardens, and traditional manner of speaking of peasant women during a celebration of San Silvestre: "Wow, they have really outdone themselves. 'Ujú, it smells like *pasteles*'" (166). Borrás appreciates the daily life of those who toil in the *central* and of those farmers who have to use their lands to sell sugarcane, but he is never one of them. He collects the women's sayings while letting us know that he is an outsider, a collector, not someone who speaks in such ways. He remarks, "And one often hears other phrases along those lines" (166). To the workers Borrás is a representative of the plantation administrators. He decides how the work is undertaken, gives orders to the people working on the ground, and is responsible for persecuting any form of resistance to the *central*'s plans. His socioeconomic background and status on the plantation allow him to share a privileged social space with landowners and the old elites, whose social standing has been undermined by their dependence on the machinery, prices, and financial resources of the U.S.-owned *central*. The imagination of the national landscape in *La Llamarada* and *Over* is shaped by the narrators' relative privilege vis-à-vis cane cutters. They do not merely represent the nation but construct it based on their own assumptions and desires. For this reason the narratives bring to light and encourage questions about the racial, gender, and class biases that foreground their stories.

Borrás proposes a series of affective relations as constitutive components of the nation. Race and gender differences are reimagined and embedded within narratives of national kinship that seek to be inclusive, while articulating clear social hierarchies. In an anthropological fashion, Borrás describes the subjects exploited in the cane fields in great detail, in this way conveying Puerto Rico's racial and ethnic heterogeneity. The impoverished working people of the *cañaveral* embody various shades of skin color and cultural practices. Aside from recording the customs and linguistic practices of the plantation workers, Borrás also describes how the European-descended landowner class suffers from the dubious management and financial practices of the *central*. In this context all Puerto Ricans are unified by their confrontation with U.S. imperial rule and by paternal-filial relationships between social classes. The attributes of civilization and whiteness are thus ascribed to the landowner class to justify its position as enunciator of a national project for Puerto Rico and protector of the economic, political, and cultural interests of all Puerto Ricans.

The narrative voice at the same time didactically argues for national acceptance of race mixture. Borrás calls attention to the academic success of his mixed-race peers in college. Despite himself, Borrás sees his history in Don Chelores, a character identified throughout the novel as representative of Afro–Puerto Rican experiences. Borrás also considers Don Chelores to be a role model. Along with the communist Don Polo, Don Chelores serves as a moral compass for Borrás: "José Dolores is a symbol for me. It is with him that I have shared the most pleasant moments" (60). It is Don Chelores who exposes Borrás to the Puerto Rico unknown to him, a Puerto Rico where the black-identified musical genres, bomba and plena, reign. Though consistently privileging Borrás's whiteness, the text recognizes and celebrates racial mixture as an integral component of *puertorriqueñidad* through physical and cultural descriptions of Puerto Ricans from different backgrounds.

However, the novel pathologizes the life of the worker and his family. The workers must be saved by the benevolent and educated class of native landowners, like Borrás, who allegedly treated them like family members on the idealized coffee *haciendas*. Borrás blames the workers' poverty on what he describes as irresponsible sexual and reproductive practices. The workers do not follow the gender and sexual conventions that, for him, would be ideal in the reproduction of national subjects. According to Borrás, "The field workers are gaunt and pale men. Effects of climate, arthritis, and negligence. Many seem helots, with their laziness. The poor lack the means to counter the effects of the tropics, due to the inadequate orientations they suffer, and to the moral, spiritual, and physical slavery in which they live. It's a great pity" (191). The peasants, unlike him, cannot survive the climate of the tropics. Nature, not circumstance or oppression, defines their subordinate position. Borrás's condescending tone demonstrates his sense of superiority, informed by Puerto Rico's colonial legacy and the role of the *hacendados* within the colonial economy.

Borrás's discursive treatment of the workers explains why none of the manifestations of the blaze seems to offer him any hope. He interprets them all as manifestations of a destructive hate, not of class conflict or struggles for social justice. He thus dismisses histories of slave resistance in previous iterations of the plantation in the Caribbean. His reference to slavery operates in two ways: on one hand, it denounces the coercive and repressive practices of the U.S.-financed *central*; on the other hand, it ascribes to the workers a distinct lack of will to rebel and an innate inability to enjoy spiritual freedom. His narrative of the plantation, and of the nation itself, erases genealogies of resistance not led by white-identified *criollos*.[16]

This rhetorical move, made possible by Borrás's conceptualization of the blaze as undisciplined hate, constitutes what Aponte Ramos (2003: 907) calls the act of forgetting, expressed in the narrative through two discursive mechanisms: "on one hand, to underscore his own racial and physical superiority; and on the other hand, to make sure that the space of counterpoint—blackness—does not lose its identity nor its locus." Aponte Ramos notes that the novel includes the point of view of black-identified Puerto Ricans, specifically Don Chelores, who relays to Borrás the histories of black struggles for emancipation and independence in the Caribbean. Don Chelores underscores how people like himself, after emancipation and the end of Spanish colonial rule, continued to be subjected to political and economic disenfranchisement by local elites. Borrás listens and remembers how his own lineage ignores his family's black ancestry. However, his imagination of resistance fails to incorporate Don Chelores's historical memory. His resistance against the ever-expanding and disease-ridden landscape forged by the sugar plantation does not rely on a genealogy of black resistance. His resistance will be contingent on the values and economic interests of a white-identified landowner class, whose origins are marked in the text by references to Europe and a colonial past.

Marriage and leaving the cane fields become his only hope because he cannot fully assume a transcolonial consciousness. He respects Don Chelores's ideas and allows him to question his self-representation as a white man. But he misses the opportunity to mobilize Don Chelores's antislavery transcolonial kinship narratives to explain the realities he faces in the cane fields. Borrás's Eurocentric racial and gender values do not allow him to forge another kind of relationship with Don Chelores, one that moves beyond recording his ideas. It prevents him from accepting his own black heritage and deepening the ties that could center the political potential of interracial and interclass solidarity historically advocated by *antillanista* thinkers. The national family he imagines does not draw from transcolonial kinship models to envision its racial composition but rather from elite, Creole, nationalist narratives in Latin America.

Borrás's investment in the European ancestry of native landowners, such as his own French and Spanish heritage, reveals processes of racialization experienced by the inhabitants of the *cañaveral*. Though the workers are phenotypically heterogeneous, descriptions of their alleged physical and spiritual slavery and their pathologized behavior make evident that they are ontologically identified with an othered, racialized blackness. Moreover Borrás's celebratory identification of the landowner class with whiteness, civilization, and Europe is highlighted by the counterpoint provided by black-identified, uneducated, and extremely poor nationals. Every time Borrás describes a landowner, his or her family's European background is mentioned; they come from France, Corsica, Spain, and Mallorca. For this reason Borrás's decision to marry into the Moreau family is informed by their embodiment of a civilized way of living that is perceived as innate (Laguerre 1939: 76). His love for French but creolized Pepiña is justified by her perfection, beauty, Christian values, refinement, and potential to produce healthy children. His marriage plans require "a healthy woman, because I am concerned for the fate of my future children. . . . One has to consider the biological element, which is as important as the emotional factor" (361). The young *criollas*, whose racially mixed background or Americanization he underscores, do not measure up to Pepiña. Neither does his poor ex-girlfriend Sara or the orphaned Delmira. He describes them as unhealthy, pretentious, or flirtatious and unfit to be wives and mothers.

Having faced the plantation's blaze, a deep moral crisis that almost destroys him, Borrás leaves the cane fields and the *central*, but he foresees a bright future. In his narrative he constitutes the island's interior as the productive space of the nation, given that the coast has been surrendered to foreign interests: "My existence is bound to the landscape. . . . Each mountain . . . becomes an ally. I will make of my vines a resistant cord with which to strangle my enemies" (372). His relatively successful project, seen by Luz María Umpierre (1983) as escapist, highlights the ways his retreat to the mountains transforms his privileged position as a white-identified, male, colonial subject into a *hacendado*. He is able to leave the plantation and not fear for his future because he owns the means of production, the land. Moreover the *cafetal* promises a better life for peasants, those who work for him, through the nostalgic remembrance of a past when everyone lived on what the earth offered. In a context where Puerto Rican agriculture was being limited by the encroachment of U.S.-owned sugarcane plantations that using up fertile lands, leaving the people to rely on imported food products—"Canned milk, canned meat, canned beans!" (Laguerre 1939: 187)—the novel supports this return to the land. The narrator and protagonist agrees with the words of a peasant: "I think that we must return to the Puerto Rico of the past. To use what the land offers. . . . Only the land can save us" (169). The path to salvation here refers to the act of producing the food needed by Puerto Ricans, especially peasants. That is, salvation is the well-being of the people and the survival of the nation. This return to the land allows for the severing of ties binding one's dependence to the metropole, thus reminding Puerto Ricans of their true national character. In this way the novel's ending represents the path toward fulfillment of the national dream, where all national subjects enjoy the freedoms of sovereignty and are not limited by the foreign exploitation of their labor and resources. However, Borrás's escapist option does not include recognizing blacks as full political subjects, nor does it address the legacies of slavery discussed by Don Chelores's recollection of nineteenth-century transcolonial struggles for independence in Cuba and Puerto Rico. The history shared by Don Chelores recounts that workers and black-identified Antilleans have not fared better working for *criollos* in the past, nor do they benefit in the present.

While the nation is created through inextricable ties to the land, the creation of new national subjects is also inevitable. The last section of the novel announces the arrival of Borrás's wife, Pepiña, on the coffee plantation, an event blessed by nature and in conjunction with the land's productive forces: "Nature in the mountains sang hymns of joy to our love and the moon bewitched our souls. Soon, the first coffee blossoms would arrive, as would the perfumed gift of the lemon trees" (378). Pepiña's reproductive capabilities are imagined in relation to the land, whose fruits, as the nation's natural resources, parallel her potential reproduction of the nation's human component, the national subject. In *Over* too the narrator cannot imagine a healthy family on the plantation. The plantation stands for the imperialist designs of the United States in the Dominican Republic and damages the physical and emotional constitutions of its national subjects.

Over

The involvement of the United States in the Dominican economy and its sugar industry dates back to the 1870s. During Ulises Heureaux's presidencies (1882–84, 1887–99), the production of sugar was encouraged by the government, but the infrastructure it required made the country highly dependent on foreign loans. In 1899 the assassination of President Heureaux led to a political crisis that endangered U.S. interests in the country. In 1904 U.S. foreign policy analysts concluded that the decline in sugar prices during that time and Dominicans' inability to pay their debt to European financial institutions could potentially lead to European intervention (Roorda 1998). This posed a threat to U.S. hopes for hegemony over the region and access to the trade routes the United States was hoping to open with the Panama Canal. That year U.S. investors bought the country's debt from Dutch bond holders, consequently leading to the U.S. takeover of the Dominican Customs Receivership (Hall 2000: 12). During those first two decades of the twentieth century, U.S. corporations also invested in plantations previously owned mostly by Cubans, Spaniards, and Italians. These families were not able to survive drops in sugar prices, nor were they able to surmount the country's increasing foreign debt (10).

But U.S. intervention on the island of Hispaniola/Haiti did not end there. The United States occupied the Dominican Republic from 1916 to 1924 and Haiti from 1915 to 1934. In both places the occupation authorities changed existing land tenure policies. These policies, developed in 1824, benefited peasants and guaranteed their access to communal land (*tierras comuneras*) for subsistence agriculture, without state intervention or official documentation. When the U.S. occupation government released newly issued property titles to these lands, U.S. corporations were able to acquire the land for the purpose of sugar production (Roorda 1998: 17).

Having been trained as a military officer during the U.S. occupation, in 1930 Gen. Rafael Leónidas Trujillo assumed control of the Dominican government. In the 1940s and 1950s, using intimidation and taxation, he nationalized a sugar economy that relied on a large workforce of mostly Haitian migrant labor (Acosta 1976; Corten 1976; Duarte 1976). While Haitian labor produced profit, Trujillo espoused an official state anti-Haitian and antiblack nationalism.[17]

In 1937, two years before the publication of *Over*, Trujillo ordered what has come to be known as *el corte*, the massacre of thousands of dark-skinned Dominicans and people of Haitian descent, to consolidate his ideological whitening of the Dominican Republic and his continued efforts to establish a clear border with Haiti (Mateo 2004; Moya Pons 1998; Pérez 2002; Rodríguez de León 2004). The border had been under dispute for almost a century, since Dominican independence from Haiti in 1844. The Haitian and Dominican governments negotiated an agreement in 1929, the Tratado Domínico-Haitiano, which delineated the contours of the border. This agreement was ratified by Trujillo and Haitian president Stenio Vincent in 1936. But the border's porosity (Derby

2009; Price-Mars 1953; Lee Turits 2002) and the constant movement back and forth of Haitian and Dominican populations in the border region complicated Trujillo's plan to *dominicanizar* the region and whiten it by introducing European, Jewish, and Japanese migrants. The massacre was justified by a discourse generating a newly minted historical fear of invasion from and reunification with Haiti. It is estimated that thousands of people pinpointed as Haitians—including Haitian citizens, Dominicans of Haitian descent, and other Dominicans—were murdered (Reyes-Santos 2008; Sagás 2000, 46; Lee Turits 2002).[18]

During his dictatorship (1830–61) Trujillo produced an official version of *dominicanidad* that emphasized Dominicans' Catholicism, Spanish language, and Hispanic traditions, differentiating them from their Haitian neighbors as well as from U.S. Protestant, Anglo-Saxon, economic, and political traditions (Candelario 2007; Mateo 2004). *Trujillista* ideologues, such as Manuel Peña Battle and future president Joaquín Balaguer, constructed an idea of the Dominican nation that whitened it with respect to Haiti, especially with respect to poor Haitians (Balaguer 1983; Price-Mars 1953; Rodríguez 2003). Haitians could be black, but Dominicans could not. The term *indio* (Indian) and its variations (*indio claro, oscuro*, etc.) were used to indicate the racial mixture of Dominicans and the degree to which people were considered to be light-skinned, dark-skinned, or different shades of brown. Trujillo propagated his idea of *dominicanidad*, and who belonged to the national community, through official propaganda in the schools, museums, newspapers, speeches, and all government institutions, as well as through the repression, incarceration, death, and exile of anyone who openly questioned him.[19]

Marrero Aristy's novel found its place in the work of *trujillista* intellectuals and their efforts to define the racial representation of those who belonged in the nation they were constructing. Under the Trujillo regime, and despite having professed socialist ideals earlier in his life, Marrero Aristy served as a journalist, deputy, diplomat, and state secretary. Still he was assassinated by the regime in 1959. In the 1940s the publication of *Over* benefited Trujillo's plans of expanding his monopoly over the national economy. Trujillo claimed to be "Benefactor of the Fatherland" (Sommer 1988). *Over*'s open criticism of U.S. administrators on plantations and its nationalist claims to the land's resources could be read as a call to reconstitute the nation under the protection of a paternal figure like Trujillo. It could also be read as a justification of Trujillo's nationalist stance toward the U.S.-owned sugarcane plantations and people of Haitian descent. The novel's descriptions of Haitian and West Indian migrant workers as people who are apathetic and uninterested in the Dominican Republic also served the state's antimigrant discourses and policies.

What Alán Belén Cambeira (2001: 252) calls *Over*'s "conciencia antillana-dominicana" (Antillean-Dominican conscience) is an important component of the novel and complicates its adoption and canonization by the Trujillato as an anti-Haitian, anti-imperialist novel. After all, the Dominican writer Marcio Veloz Maggiolo has classified *Over* as a representative text of "la literatura del haitiano compadecido" (literature of the pitied Haitian; cited in Fernández Olmos 1978: 235). Belén Cambeira notes that, while the novel's protagonist represents Haitian workers in a condescending, racist manner, Marrero Aristy also critiques the racism of both U.S. administrators and local Dominican *blancos* as another racist outgrowth of the legacy of Spanish colonialism against native/local populations. Janice-Marie McDonald (1991) pays attention to Marrero Aristy's critique of how Haitian migrants face the racism of all three kinds of *blancos*: Anglo-Americans, white Dominicans, and Spaniards. *Over* therefore is not easily complicit in perpetuating an idealization of Spanish-Dominican relations, representations of Spain as motherland, or incorporating the Dominican Republic within a Hispanic family without acknowledging the real violence enacted by the metropole on indigenous and Afro-descended peoples.

Along with Danny Méndez's (2011) analysis of another *novela del cañaveral* of the 1930s, *Cañas y Bueyes* by Francisco Eugenio Moscoso Puello, I demonstrate that the *trujillista* whitening project did not completely dominate the racial imaginary of the national family or cultural representations of Haitian-Dominican relations. Literature provides other alternative narratives produced under violently repressive political conditions. In his reading of *Cañas y Bueyes*, Méndez analyzes how affective feelings and emotions between Haitian and Dominican characters—hate, frustration, and hopelessness—as well as their shared feelings of dislocation due to the consequences of U.S. occupation in the island complicate conventional understandings of the Trujillato's *anti-haitianismo* as a hegemonic discourse in the Dominican Republic. My reading of *Over* demonstrates that the affective ties built and undone in the cane fields negotiate transcolonial and national kinship narratives in the face of U.S. imperialism and a dictatorship. Those feelings documented by Méndez are manifestations of historical maneuverings of a variety of kinship narratives articulated by Antilleans attempting to question colonial/imperial regimes since the nineteenth century. The narrators in both *La Llamarada* and *Over* conceptualize notions of kinship that carry traces of nineteenth-century *antillanista* brotherhoods and solidarity networks. They also attempt to imagine national families surviving or resisting the consequences of U.S. military occupations and economic interventions in the Dominican Republic and Puerto Rico.

Like *La Llamarada*, *Over* is a first-person narration. The narrator is a young man, Daniel Compré, who works for a U.S.-owned corporation. Besides financing some local sugarcane plantations, the *central* administers its own land and sends Compré to one of its *bateyes*. An aspiring writer, Compré becomes a *bodeguero* (store clerk) at a Dominican *batey* in the 1930s. In the course of his story he responds directly to the U.S. manager of the *central*. Hoping to create a better future for himself, Compré marries the daughter of an independent storeowner, and they live together at the *central's bodega*. When she miscarries, he must pay for the expenses of her treatment at the hospital. His wife's illness makes it impossible for him to produce the *over*, or surplus, expected by the *central*, and he is eventually fired. As a result his marriage ends. In the end, hopeless, he decides to leave town in order to avoid returning to the plantation for the next *zafra* (harvest).

The novel starts with Compré wandering around town trying to figure out how to sustain himself after his father, a businessman and small landowner, disowns him for reasons that are not clear. He cannot resolve his homelessness and unemployment: "If one has any pride, one does not beg, and these days, no one offers; because if one looks for work, one cannot find it, and because in this town any stranger steals all our souls" (Marrero Aristy 1963: 1). In Compré's view, he has no options because there are no available jobs. A person of his somewhat privileged condition is not supposed to ask for economic aid, people are not willing to help anymore, and the U.S.-owned *central* has changed people's way of being. While Borrás in *La Llamarada* believes that the plantation will make all his dreams come true, Compré turns to the plantation as his last recourse.

Compré does not enjoy Borrás's more privileged position in the plantation economy as a supervisor of a colony; he is a store clerk. However, he occupies a higher position in the *batey* hierarchy than do the field workers. He represents the interests of the *central* because he is the guardian and seller of all of the commodities needed by the field workers: food, clothes, and utensils. He also enjoys a guaranteed daily meal, provided by the *central*, while subsistence for the field workers is never a guarantee. In addition Compré is in charge of producing *over* by deceiving his customers. His association with the *bodega* further highlights his relative proximity to the plantation's daily administration. The *bodega* in the *batey* is one of the exploitative tactics of the *central*. Since the workers get paid with vouchers instead of cash, they can purchase what they need only at the *bodega*; therefore their wages return directly to the *central*. The *bodega* constantly sells workers less than what they pay for in order to produce a surplus, or *over*. Compré in turn must produce *over* in order to retain his job.

While Borrás is eager to find what the *cañaveral* holds in store for him, Compré has a more skeptical approach to the *central*. As he walks toward the *central* in search of a job, he thinks, "It is true that in front of me is the *central* with beautiful avenues and dream houses, but they only offer their 'dead season' like a door slam to everyone who applies for work" (10). Once again the disciplined organization of the *central* presents an appealing image to the viewer. However, Compré, more than Borrás, is somewhat aware of the limitations of working on the plantation. He knows that during the "dead season" between harvests many workers are given an unpaid vacation. He has also heard of the racist and rude attitude toward locals exhibited by the *central*'s main administrator, the Anglo-American Mr. Robinson. Nonetheless the landscape of the *central* promises a better life, one where food is available and where a life partner may exist who can take care of him after a day of work: "They [the *central*'s employees] undertake their work in various departments of the company and when they finish their work days, they go to their houses, kiss their young wives, caress their children, take a bath, and then, play the radio, and read a newspaper. . . . That's a happy and humble life!" (14).

The U.S. *central* brings the project of modernization into the national landscape, replete with the machinery, capital, and operational mechanisms needed to maximize the profit of sugar production. Spatially the *central* is marked by its portrayal of a *central*-worker relationship that is reflected in the landscape and articulated as a paternal-filial bond. From the outside this landscape seems to offer good housing, a secure salary, and a heteropatriarchal dream of domestic bliss; given its organizing of time and space with respect to work and leisure, the landscape holds the possibility of Compré's entry into modernity, albeit through his own proletarianization.

Simultaneously Compré denounces the plantation as a space that does not allow the national land to nourish its subjects. The relationship between the land and those who work it has been disrupted; the workers are not receiving the products of their labor and of the land that is right-fully theirs as nationals. Compré describes the workers as displaced farmers who have been dispossessed by the reign of the U.S. plantation. The workers have no choice but to work in the cane fields. The capital-ist logic of the *central* even forbids its starving workers from growing food staples in any vacant lots: "poor folks, almost all of them farmers, amazed at the sight of so much uncultivated land" (56). Compré notes that the *central* kills regional economies and does not respond to any interests but its own. For Dominican nationals the space of the planta-tion becomes characterized by disease, misery, hunger, and destruction.

Like Borrás, Compré does not want to embody the hate that seems to consume the soul of the plantation's inhabitants. However, the *over* forces him to take a stand for his own survival: "I never believed that at such short distance from my home, and after having made such great plans for my future, I would find myself needing to serve these people here, and obey those others there, whom I must consider my absolute masters" (52). Compré sees his whole existence revolving around the need to produce *over*. First, he has to count everything the *central* sends, and he must take into account the difference between what he will be expected to pay and what has actually been sent to him. He suffers con-stant distress and fear of being audited by the administration. Sugarcane cutters insult him and treat him like a thief. The need to produce *over* turns him into a hostile man who sees his moral burden reflected in the workers who come to buy provisions at the store.

As the fire in *La Llamarada* manifests the social conflict and hate per-meating the plantation, in Marrero Aristy's novel the *over* represents the mechanisms set in place by the central to maximize its profits. *Over* pro-duces relations in excess of a healthy and productive life within the confines of the plantation's environs. The *central* undermines Compre's capacity to fulfill his duties as a respectable, normative, masculine, national sub-ject. The anxieties produced by the required *over* and Compré's inability to fulfill his economic and emotional responsibilities as a husband cre-ate a moral debacle that turns him into a man seeking refuge in alcohol and other women. His young wife suffers the brunt of his unhappiness and silence and miscarries their baby. Compré's salary and benefits at the *central* hardly cover her care in the workers' wing of the hospital, and he struggles to produce *over* to cover the expenses. Every day is a nightmare. Under constraints similar to those in *La Llamarada*, in *Over* fires destroy the cane harvest. They come as no surprise. Compré himself wishes for fire to consume everything contained within the boundaries of the *central*.

Compré, like Borrás, imagines a family in racial terms, but not white like the Anglo-Americans nor black like the Haitian workers in the cane fields. His family is *indio*. The constitution of this family is informed by his critique of the whiteness and racism of the U.S. administrators, Spanish colonialists, and local whites, as well as Trujillato nationalist narratives about poor Haitians' blackness. In Compré's narrative, the plantation becomes a foreign space and a threat to national subjects, as a U.S. enterprise that requires foreign labor from Haiti and from the Anglophone West Indies. Compré describes the workers in the *batey*:

> The native who lives on the plantation is a worn out subject, lacking moral equilibrium, incapable of responding in any way. . . . And if it's the foreign workers of which we speak, we can say the same and even more. Those people come from Haiti and the English islands every year, in hopes of working to return to THEIR homes in six months' time and they cannot—even if they did not have the slavery of centuries in the soul and still possessed the ability—concern themselves with reforms, because they are not from here and the fate of this country does not matter to them. (Marrero Aristy 1963: 67)

In his references to the cane workers Compré tends to underline their blackness and their (mostly) foreign background. As evidenced in his references to slavery, his paternalistic description of the workers has racial overtones. In his view foreign workers do not seem to have the will or even an interest in changing their circumstances. According to Compré, their racialized stagnation explains why the communist activism feared by the *central* and the government will never take place in the Dominican Republic.

Compré simultaneously recognizes the racism of the *central*'s administrators. He introduces the character of Mr. Robinson, the *central*'s Anglo-American manager, by describing his arbitrary, disrespectful, and authoritarian treatment of Dominicans seeking work at the *central*. Mr. Robinson is characterized by "his habit of not looking at or greeting anyone who does not belong to his race" (21). In this way it is clear that his Anglo whiteness marks his position of power in the *central*. Compré's derogatory depiction of Mr. Robinson reveals his understanding of the *central*'s U.S. owners and managers. When Compré approaches the *central* for the first time, he sees "a kind of white sack whose size creeps up over the avenue" (24). The administrators are ordinary "americanos" (Americans) who take jobs abroad in order to improve their less than desirable circumstances in the United States. Their whiteness is associated with an imperial takeover of the nation, racism, exploitation of local labor, and greed. Compré imagines his compatriots as a product of racial mixing, subjected to Mr. Robinson's racism for not being racially pure (white).

In Compré's understanding, Dominicans would ideally be neither black like Haitians or West Indians nor white like the Anglo-Americans or former colonizers, the Spanish.[20] *Hispanidad* is not necessarily an important component of his imagination of the ideal constitution of the nation. The Spanish are characterized as "blancos" (whites) who decimated the Native population and exploited the island. Compré also criticizes the *central*'s hospital for failing to properly treat poor nonwhites—Dominicans, Haitians, or West Indians—while providing all medical services to "the misters, the whites" (Belén Cambeira 2001: 248–49). These critiques of Spanish colonialism, U.S. imperialism, racism, and the mistreatment of Dominican, Haitian, and West Indian workers as Afro-descendant peoples place Compré within antislavery, transcolonial narrative currents.

Compré articulates a transcolonial narrative kinship between poor Dominicans and their Antillean coworkers and neighbors in the *batey*. He refuses to engage in narratives of colonial kinship that praise Spain as a colonial motherland and erase the violent history of colonization. He does not forget or ignore racist histories. As Belén Cambeira (2001) and McDonald (1991) note, he critiques the racial exploitation of indigenous and black people under Spanish colonial rule. He also seeks a wife who represents the racial mixture of the island, an *india*, unlike Borrás, who chooses a wife identified and praised for her European ancestry.

But as he places all hopes for himself in the creation of a family, he must distance himself from those same workers and migrants with whom he sympathizes. He must exploit them to produce the *over* that will allow him to be a proper patriarch, provider, and guide for his family. Marriage in *Over* requires moving away from transcolonial kinship models to concentrate on the task of reproducing proper and healthy national subjects.

Compré's in-laws represent a promising beginning for a national family. His father-in-law is "an old, easygoing mulatto with a healthy soul," and his future mother-in-law is "a very beautiful, white woman" (Marrero Aristy 1963: 113, 114). The couple owns a small business at the margins of the *central*. They are constantly under siege for posing a challenge to the *central*'s monopoly over the workers; they represent the national spirit and local enterprise being threatened by U.S. imperialism. Their daughter is the synthesis of racial mixture in the Dominican Republic. Compré immediately desires her: "She was not white, nor would I have wanted it, she was a bright, cinnamon-colored little Indian woman" (114). In this description of his future wife, Compré privileges what Candelario (2007: 235) has termed an Indo-Hispanic notion of Dominican racial and ethnic identity. His prospective wife represents the product of a process of racial mixing that cannot be identified as either black or white.

Compré chooses her over the women in the *batey* whom he pejoratively describes as "rickety and alien" Dominicans and "ugly and smelly Haitians" (Marrero Aristy 1963: 112). While expressing outrage for the plight of Dominican and Haitian women on the plantation, his elitist and xenophobic biases explain his choice for a bride. She, unlike the Dominican women in the *batey*, has not had to work in the fields and enjoys the relative privilege of being the daughter of a self-employed man. The repressed potential of the nation resides in families like hers.

Despite having found the right marriage partner, Compré is denied a happy ending. His complete dependence on the plantation hinders his attempts at creating a functional family. He marries the nameless *indiecita*, who lives with him in two rooms of the *central*'s store. But his happiness is disturbed by his economic reliance on the *central*: "Because it is fine for a man to be satisfied with having a house, food, and woman, to complete his existence, but a wife, food, and a bed of his own, subject to his will alone. And me, what do I have?" (137). Not owning the means of production, the land or the store, disrupts their life and draws attention to the ever-present prospect of poverty. He cannot claim to own that which he believes must be under his control: subsistence, housing, and a wife. In addition his constant feelings of guilt and anger for the injustices committed in the *batey* create a rift in his marriage. He describes his wife as a little girl who cannot understand his feelings and interpretations of the world surrounding them.

Compré expects his wife to be subservient to him because she has not acquired his level of education. He ignores her and spends time drinking rum and conversing with other store clerks. When she attempts to seek his attention, he demands, "Don't bother me! If you educated yourself, if you wanted to be of use to me, I would not need any friends to hang out with" (143). At the end of the novel he regrets the way he treats her, which is implicitly explained by his own psychological distress and his need to steal more from the workers to cover not only his expenses but hers too. The plantation corrupts the economic and emotional stability

needed for the constitution of a family able to reproduce heteropatriarchal gender norms for men and women, husbands and wives—the family unit expected for the reproduction of national subjects. It takes away
from Compré the woman, property, and children promised by marriage.

Along with the loss of their baby, the weakened constitution of Compré's wife signifies the nation's losses vis-à-vis imperialist interests. The
plantation spoils anything that enters its territorial boundaries. Nothing
is allowed to grow naturally; all is corrupted. Only the cane continues
to grow, harvest after harvest. When Compré loses his job, he and his
wife move in with her sister's family in town. The dependency of towns-
people too on the *central* renders him useless to his family. He cannot
return to the *central* and consequently leaves his wife and begins living in the streets. A woman, who also remains nameless, falls in love
with him; we know her only as "his lover, the prostitute" (222). She offers
him a place to stay, but in the end Compré does not deem her worthy of
a relationship and leaves her behind. He encounters a friend from his
childhood who nostalgically remembers his life working on merchant
boats that took him to places like New York and Cuba. Compré suggests
leaving to find a better future elsewhere. Foreshadowing future waves of
Dominican migration, he and his friend dream of going to Puerto Rico
and becoming U.S. citizens.

Compré does not leave the country but does decide to leave town. He
still has some constructive energy that he believes cannot flourish in the
town but might be productive somewhere else. One day he listens to a
voice in his head:

> The history of your town, of your region, is that of the sugar
> cane. . . . Do not attach yourself to that which is no longer yours.
> You yourself are not from here anymore. You gave your *over*, what
> are you waiting for? I believe that the only thing that keeps you
> here is the obsessive belief that you are no longer anything at all.
> You have seen so many men worn down, destroyed. You have seen
> so much *bagasse!* . . . You cannot understand—you do not want to
> accept—that you are not in the same condition. But don't you see
> your path? Be vigilant of the monster's current slumber, and leave
> before the new harvest begins. Go, brother! (223)

The only option left for Compré is leaving the region that has been transformed by sugarcane and escaping to an undetermined location. He
must, however, leave before the *zafra* begins, lest it lead him again to
impending destruction.[21]

Plantation Novels: A Comparative Perspective

While engaging different historical, economic, and racial experiences, as plantation novels *Over* and *La Llamarada* give us a glimpse at the boundaries that were created to open and limit national kinship in the face of U.S. imperialism. Through their representation of the national family under siege by the plantation, they share realist aesthetic conventions widely admired by their critics and that explain, to some extent, their incorporation into the Dominican and Puerto Rican literary canons, respectively. Marithelma Costa (2004: 128) argues that *La Llamarada* is "a historical document that recreates life in the coastal plains during the Great Depression." Critics also emphasize *Over*'s description of the working conditions of Dominicans, West Indians, and Haitians in sugar plantations of the past and the present. McDonald (1991: 37) writes, "In the Dominican Republic a form of slavery still exists. . . . In the novel Marrero paints a vivid picture of the dehumanization of the employees of the great sugar company in the Dominican Republic." The literary value of both novels resides in their ability to represent the reality of the nation in a recognizable manner.

The developmentalist character of the narratives also legitimized these novels as texts that provide historical knowledge of and justification for nationalist projects. The novels' narrative structures consist of the introduction to a setting and characters, a crisis produced by struggles over political and economic power, and a resolution. The protagonist, the first-person narrator, undergoes personal transformations that parallel those experienced by the national territory. He represents the nation in transition.

These two narrators are young men who face the responsibility of building their own future and, by extension, the future of the nation. Through the narration of their inner thoughts, feelings, and actions, their investment in becoming the rightful patriarch—the provider and caretaker of a woman, children, a family, and the land itself—is made evident. Like the nation, they are shaped by the plantation and must find a way to survive it, lest they perish in it.

These two narrators imagine the national landscape through the lens provided by their intermediary role between foreign capital and the working classes. Due to Borrás's responsibilities for supervising agricultural work in the fields and Compré's position as a plantation store clerk, they are middlemen in social structures that characterize labor and social relations on the plantation.

Their incorporation into the social space of the plantation signifies their transition into adulthood. They must now confront the world and survive on their own. The nation is also in transition, unable to achieve full adulthood or independence. The plantation, then, holds the men and the nation captive. As the narrators tell their personal stories, they reveal personal fates bound to the nation's destiny. These parallels underline the textual privileging of Borrás and Compré as sites of political agency within the nation-state. They can enunciate the nation. Their full subjectivity as national subjects is asserted through their role as narrator. Our acquaintance with the narrators' most intimate thoughts allows us to understand their transformations and see, through a first-person narrative, a lived, personal experience of the spiritual and economic condition of the national territory.

The narrators' authoritative voices, voices that circumscribe their narratives as national narratives, inherently privilege them as educated, whitened subjects. They are the true citizens of the nation who are called to constitute it symbolically and literally. Through the novels' canonization, then, these literary subjects become national subjects. Since the narrators speak for a national experience, they are read by the canon as true representatives of a unified national body. However, they are national subjects in crisis. The blaze, the *over*, and the desire of an all-consuming fire represent the moral decay of national subjects who find themselves trapped in the cane fields. Borrás's and Compré's responsibilities on plantations require them to keep a physical and emotional distance from other workers. They must primarily satisfy the demands of the administration to keep their jobs. Borrás must repress any worker demands for better working conditions, even if he himself acknowledges the truth behind their claims. Compre's social circle consists of other store clerks, the *batey*'s policeman, and the administrator of vouchers. He must ignore his moral predicament to be able to steal from the workers in order to produce the required *over*. The narrators' inability to live with these unexpected ethical dilemmas leads them to a series of moral and psychological crises, and eventually to their dismissal from their respective positions. In *Over* and *La Llamarada* the plantation does not make possible the productive use of land, nor does it sustain the family unit deemed necessary for the nation. For their survival, national subjects should be united in their common struggle against the plantation's never-ending expansion, but they are not. As the narrators' intermediary positions attest, plantations establish socioeconomic hierarchies that replicate the structure of power within the nation. On each plantation national subjects relate to each other across racial, gender, ethnic, and class differences. Compré's and Borrás's relationships to those who share their work spaces illustrate the racial, class, and gender premises of the anti-imperialist discourse the narrators come to represent.

Compré's and Borrás's marriages illustrate their ideal imagining of a national family and its racial demographics. In both texts women are a rhetorical and reproductive device through which the national project might be accomplished. Ultimately women are equated with the land and reproductive capacity. The fates of women and the land are feminized in normative terms. In order to ensure their (re)productive capacity, both must depend on the actions of men. Compré and Borrás are the men who must plant the seeds—literally and symbolically—in the land to produce resources for the nation and in their wives to produce national subjects. Thus their attempts at creating homes and families foreshadow the fate of the nation.

Both Borrás and Compré imagine national families under siege by U.S.-financed cane fields and *centrales*. The plantation emerges from the destruction of the geographical, demographic, moral, and spiritual landscape of the nation. The siege disrupts the necessary relationship between the national subject and the national land. The land stops being productive for the national subject, becoming a locus of his exploitation.

As narratives *Over* and *La Llamarada* behave like "failed romances" (Janer 2005: 27). Neither of these novels succeeds at creating a myth of national unity and prosperity. The families that should bring the nation together are not the ideal models for national kinship for three reasons. First, healthy marriages require property ownership in both novels. In *Over* Compré and his wife's affective bond is broken as a result of his proletarianization. The *cañaveral* makes it impossible for him to fully assert his right as an educated, petit-bourgeois national subject to determinate the fate of the land he inhabits. And even if it did, it would still entail the exclusion of unpropertied Dominican men from the personal bliss, economic autonomy, and political agency that should characterize marriage.

Second, deploying marriage as the ideal affective unit of the nation elides the elite and imperialist interests invested in the institution. Eileen Suárez Findlay (1999) and Laura Briggs (2002) have documented how both U.S. colonial government and nationalist intellectuals in early twentieth-century Puerto Rico insisted in the regulation of sexual and romantic relationships. For U.S. colonial authorities, instilling the bourgeois idea that family constitutes the heterosexual couple and their children was meant to help document, regulate, and discipline social relations (Suárez Findlay 1999: 111). Bourgeois feminists and elite nationalists and reformists, on the other hand, sought to protect the honor and respectability (i.e., whiteness) of the nation by formalizing romantic and sexual bonds through marriage (203–4). So-called dissolute women and illegitimate children allegedly posed a threat to these groups' demands to be incorporated into decision-making processes on the island and to their political sovereignty.

In the Dominican Republic both anti-occupation nationalists and *trujillistas* deployed marriage to limit the political agency of women and to control sexual and reproductive practices (Horn 2014; Martínez Vergne 2005). April Mayes (2014: 124) argues that elite male nationalists during the U.S. occupation "idealized domesticity and the family as the new foundation of the nation. Women were present as daughters, wives or mothers but invisible as independent agents or political actors." In turn Dominican women from the professional and intellectual classes had to be protected from U.S. influences that loosened their social and moral behaviors. Mayes draws attention to how in the 1930s and 1940s, while educated feminists managed to gain the right to vote for women, the Trujillato placed women squarely in the home so as to fulfill their patriotic duty as mothers: "By mobilizing activist women, Trujillo appropriated a nationalist rhetoric centered on harmonious but hierarchical ideals regarding marriage, domesticity, and family life. He amplified this vision, transforming the entire Dominican nation into a single household of which he was the head" (137). Deploying marriage as an analogy for anti-imperialist national kinship replicates elitist, sexist, and heteropatriarchal hierarchies both in Puerto Rico and the Dominican Republic.

Third, the practices of racial, ethnic, and class subordination that marriage requires contradict the desire for anti-imperialist national kinship. It is noteworthy that Pepiña and Borrás's wife are possible only because a *peón* (a worker) at the *central* carries letters between them (García Cabrera 1992) and because Borrás can take his wife away from the sugar-plagued coast to the idyllic land he has inherited. Assuming his role as *hacendado* is what enables their marriage. Marriage in this way also requires that the narrator-protagonists in both novels ignore any identification, empathy, love, and feelings of belonging that fall outside the realm of heterosexual romantic love. Borrás distances himself from the sugarcane cutters, impoverished coastal farmers, black-identified Puerto Ricans, and socialist organizers who have taught him to understand the exploitative realities of the plantation. Compré must disavow his own empathy for Haitian and West Indian workers, labor organizers, socialists, and West Indian Garveyists to produce *over*. Both Borrás and Compré find themselves in deep psychological turmoil, their patriarchal tendencies in crisis. They cannot coherently address their desires and identifications. They cannot rectify their desire to reproduce a national community through marriage and their often problematic identification with other inhabitants of the cane fields and the *central*. They do not recognize in other narratives of kinship the hope they seek for the nation in the face of U.S. imperialism. In the meantime, as the novels suggest, transcolonial kinship had not fully dissipated as an affective model for Antillean political communities. Labor and socialist organizations, Garveyites, and intra-Caribbean encounters in plantations throughout the region continued to build resistance to exploitative labor conditions and racism across colonial/imperial and national boundaries (Guridy 2010; Mayes 2014; Stephens 2005). These narratives were rendered visible not through the heteropatriarchal voice of the narrator but through the voices of those with whom they were in a working relationship.

Despite the nationalist focus on marriage, it was not the only available affective model for romantic and sexual relationships, family and nation building. In the 1890s young women of African descent migrated to the southern Puerto Rican city of Ponce, where they "lived and loved outside the limits of the patriarchal family" (Suárez-Findlay 1999: 202). By 1918 working-class women in the city were at the forefront of labor mobilizations. Early twentieth-century male and female working-class activists "saw the prostitute, a figure targeted by reformists in the late nineteenth century and by U.S. colonial hygiene campaigns in the 1910s, as a sister and comrade, the quintessential representative of an oppressed, multiracial working class" (204). The renowned working-class, feminist, anarchist, and labor organizer Luisa Capetillo spent the first two decades of the century advocating free love, free unions, women's sexual pleasure, women's right to abandon abusive romantic relationships, men's responsibility to help care for their children outside of wedlock, and cross-class solidarity among women. And nonnormative gender subjects constituted their own understandings of each other as kin, as demonstrated in Carlos Decena's (2011: 1) vignette about Pedro René Contín Aybar's publication of thirty copies of the first documented Dominican novel with a homoerotic theme, *Biel, el Marino*. The novel, published in 1943 in the midst of the Trujillato and its Catholic moral conventions, was dedicated to an unidentified small group of friends for whom copies were made.

Non-gender-normative kinship coexisted alongside dominant affirmations of heterosexual marriage, even as marriage was heralded as the quintessential affective model that would unify a nation with disparate class, gender, and racial interests.

Transcolonial and National Kinship: Lessons for the Present

Both *La Llamarada* and *Over* deploy narratives of national kinship, alongside experiences and memories of transcolonial kinship and colonial/imperial kinship (with Spain and the United States). Academic understandings of both *antillanismo* and nationalism as organizing tropes of Caribbean anticolonial movements must be considered within the rubric of the decolonial affective matrix. Colonial kinship and the tendency to celebrate Hispanic legacies have always been considered in studies of early twentieth-century nationalisms in the Dominican Republic and Puerto Rico. But not many analyses have noted how transcolonial kinship narratives emerge out of a collective political unconscious to form internal contradictions within nationalist narratives. The novels' attempts at building national families fail not only because of their inability to reconcile racial and class differences, or because of U.S. imperialist encroachments on their desire for autonomy, but also because of an awareness of the antislavery, transcolonial solidarities that the narrator-protagonists choose to ignore. Moreover transcolonial kinship narratives were not simply alternatives to whitened, elite, Creole nationalisms but were co-constituted by the *antillanistas'* need to create independent nations before creating their desired Antillean confederation. These narratives drew from the same European ideas about gender, race, sexuality, and class that limited elite nationalist definitions of citizenship and political agency.[22] Paradigmatic advocates of both *antillanismo* and nationalism wrote narratives of racial mixture to assert Antilleans' right to self-determination. The former relied mostly on *mulataje* as a model; the latter tended to deploy narratives of *mestizaje* as whitening. *Over* and *La Llamarada* demonstrate that these distinctions are not as clear-cut as they may first appear.

What we also find in these texts, as well as reading Betances and Luperón, is that paying attention to race mixture requires entering the intimate domain of romantic and sexual relations and how they have been codified by the institution of marriage. When the Spanish colonial government required Ramón Emeterio Betances's family to whiten themselves in paperwork before marriage, they were protecting the official representation of white people's rights to marriage and property. In this way property inheritance was regulated to privilege white-identified Spaniards, Puerto Ricans, and European émigrés. When Borrás and Compré propose a specific racial composition for their families, they are also negotiating the reality of racial mixture, miscegenation, of cross-racial sexual encounters, and trying to conceptualize a version that would ideally legitimate their political and economic claims as national subjects. Therefore deploying marriage as the central affective unit of nation-building projects limits the possibility of imagining and recognizing other kin relations, other chosen families (Rivera-Velázquez 2008; Weston 1991: xvii).

La Llamarada and *Over* provide an opportunity to reflect on the political value of nationalism in the past and today. Though anticolonial nationalisms were integral to decolonization struggles in the mid-nineteenth and early twentieth centuries, in the twenty-first century their value has been interrogated. Antiracist, Marxist, feminist, and queer critiques of nations as a cultural and political family have correctly signaled some pitfalls of nationalist projects (Allen 2011; Roy-Féquière 2004; Janer 2005; Negrón-Muntaner 2007; Rivera-Velázquez 2008). In her study of Puerto Rican nation-building literatures, Zilkia Janer (2005: 96) concludes that nationalism is "an obstacle" to quests for social equality and alternative models to "United States–led globalization." However, Shalini Puri (2004) and David Vázquez (2011) have argued that the nation continues to be an important analytical category even while transnational frameworks gain more traction. The nation mediates one's experience of transnational economic and political processes, and nationalism "may still be productive for aggrieved communities" (Vázquez 2011: 19). Nationalism can still be a productive site for oppositional politics, and it is fruitful to examine different nationalisms in order to better understand their force and imperfections.[23] As Frances Negrón-Muntaner (2007: 14) reminds us, "the nation is not enough," but it is still here. How, then, do we address what the nation tends to leave untouched: its heteronormative, patriarchal, racial, class, and ethnic hierarchical structures? Its commitment to heteropatriarchal notions of kinship and reproduction?

Gautam Premnath (2003) has argued that in a neoliberal Caribbean, the "fictions of sovereignty" deployed by Antillean territories, or claims based on national sovereignty, continue to be effective. Premnath points out that though the sovereignty of Antillean territories appears to be weak in the face of economic powers such as the United States and the European Union, the mobilization of nationalist interests within regional sites demonstrates affective autonomy. He cites CARICOM's 1999 negotiation with the European Union, which resulted in the economic protection of banana imports from the Caribbean, Africa, and the Pacific and closed Europe's doors to U.S.-led multinationals such as Dole and Chiquita. When the United States attempted to protect the multinationals, CARICOM ended its security and trade treaty with the United States. Premnath concludes by suggesting that "between a rock and a hard place, the nation continues to offer grounds from which to reassert an alternative future" (261). In this case national interests and fictions were mobilized on a regional level to secure trade agreements and protections.

While Betances and Luperón are paradigmatic examples of transcolonial solidarity in the nineteenth century, *La Llamarada* and *Over* ask us to meditate on the value of nationalist notions of kinship, of belonging to a land and a people. By paying attention to the articulation of marriages and families in the novels, I show that ideas of national kinship are troubled by transcolonial experiences and memories of kinship at the same time that the tenets of kinship are embedded in the affective, loving, violent, painful, joyful constitution of national communities. They are not simply political devices that can be easily disposed of, but rather live in Antillean hearts and bodies and have been inscribed in cultural imaginations of the land itself.

In 1997 and 1998 islandwide strikes in Puerto Rico attempted to stop the sale of the government-owned telephone company to a transnational consortium. These strikes invoked the generalized sentiment that Puerto Ricans have a duty to protect their national patrimony, public services, and workers. In 1999 the death of a security officer, David Sanes Rodríguez, in Vieques motivated a protest movement, Paz para Vieques, that led to the eventual exit of the U.S. Navy from the small island. Paz para Vieques drew from a broad range of social and political sectors, both on the island and in its diaspora. Across the board the movement's messages invoked Puerto Ricans' right to access to beautiful land (land that at the time was occupied by the navy) and to protection from death— either from military accidents or from the carcinogenic effects of U.S. military trials in Vieques. Since 2010 Puerto Ricans have also struggled against the dismantling of the island's public university system. The University of Puerto Rico is considered a national patrimony that should not fall into the hands of private interests. To this end students and laborers have used national frameworks to organize ongoing protests. The value of nationalist claims is also proven by Puerto Rican youth of Dominican descent who affirm that they are Puerto Rican, that they belong to the island, even as they and their parents are constantly discriminated against for their Dominican ancestry (Nina-Estrella forthcoming). They refuse to be considered outsiders of the national family and assert their right to be treated with dignity.

In the Dominican Republic nationalism is mobilized by those most marginalized by the state. In October 2009, when changes in the Dominican Constitution threatened to allow foreign ownership of coastal areas and further limit nationals' access to those natural resources, protesters chanted, "The beaches belong to the people, not to businessmen" (Associated Press 2009). Dominican protesters invoked their sense of belonging to a community tied together by specific cultural practices in order to protect their national patrimony: the beaches that they feared would be sold to hotel developers. Protesters dressed in beach gear, occupied the public spaces in front of congressional buildings, and shared a traditional Dominican beach picnic, spaghetti with chicken, inviting members of the Dominican Congress to join them. The act of sharing a traditional picnic demonstrated their understanding of each other as kin, members of a national family.

In 2013 a youth group comprising Dominicans of Haitian descent used nationalist claims to articulate their belonging to the Dominican Republic. During monthly protests in front of the Presidential Palace, they wore T-shirts with the slogan "Yo soy de aquí" (I am from here). For many of these young people, claiming to be national subjects is a radical act, especially given that they have been disenfranchised by documentation policies that render their Dominican birth certificates invalid. In September 2013 they found themselves denationalized by a decision of the Constitutional Tribunal. While the decision deprived thousands of Dominican citizens of Haitian descent of their nationality, *reconocido* youth kept asserting their Dominican national identity. Recently their voices appeared to be heard by lawmakers seeking to address the consequences of the Constitutional Tribunal's decision for this population that has always seen itself as Dominican. Nationalist claims enable marginalized populations to productively negotiate the circumstances created in neoliberal states. These neoliberal states tend to privilege the protection of capital, foreign economic interests, and private ownership over the civil and human rights of the citizenry. But this is not a new phenomenon. For this reason, considering 1930s narratives of national kinship within emerging nations can illuminate our understanding of nationalism, intra-Caribbean relations, and neoliberal globalization in the present.

These contemporary struggles are informed by nationalist discourses that have developed in conversation with twentieth-century nationalist literary canons. Whereas *La Llamarada* and *Over* highlight how sugarcane fields and *centrales* changed the physical and social landscape of the Dominican Republic and Puerto Rico in the 1930s, contemporary neoliberal economics have transformed the region's landscapes through other modes of labor. In essence there is a ruptured continuity between the sugarcane plantation, multinational sweatshops, and resorts. These spaces are characterized by monocultures, migrations, and exploited labor. The rupture emerges in the reorganization of space and time that maintains continuity via the types of bodies and modes of production.

Steven Gregory (2007: 7) has documented how Boca Chica, which used to be a *batey* in the Dominican Republic, has been converted into a resort town. Feminist scholars Amalia Cabezas (2009), Erica Williams (2013), Denise Brennan (2004), Mimi Sheller (2003, 2012), and Kamala Kempadoo (1999, 2004), have traced how colonial racial imaginations shape contemporary neoliberal racial imaginations. They show that the ways black bodies were imagined within the plantation system continue to shape how tourists imagine and treat Antilleans. The "global empire of capitalism [has conflated] emergent opportunities with old forms of oppression" (Cabezas 2009: 5). Neoliberal globalization has not solved the racist and heteropatriarchal legacies of colonialism; it has reproduced them in the service of capital. Seeing the consequences of neoliberalism through the lens provided by *La Llamarada* and *Over* provides an opportunity to examine the allure of nationalism as a continuously relevant political paradigm.

Finally, how *Over* and *La Llamarada* negotiate the three axes of the decolonial affective matrix urges us to dig deeper into contemporary representations of Haitian-Dominican and Dominican–Puerto Rican relations. Nationalism prevailed as an anticolonial paradigm in the Dominican Republic and Puerto Rico, and it currently manifests itself, respectively, in anti-Haitian and anti-Dominican sentiments. Even so, working-class, black/Afro, intercultural narratives emerge to describe other possibilities of kinship relations between these Antilleans. Transcolonial kinship survives, though complicated by neoliberal attempts to co-opt its decolonial value.

La Llamarada and *Over* and the struggles they represent have the potential to speak to the present moment, providing a possible tactic for contemporary struggles against neoliberal policies. They remind the reader of the sugarcane plantations that cover thousands of acres of land, one *batey* after another, throughout La Romana, Barahona, Azua, and Haina in the Dominican Republic. On those plantations workers continue to toil in the face of a deep disregard for their rights and an absence of secure access to food, housing, education, and health care. But they also warn us against romanticized ideas about the power of national kinship. As ongoing events lay bare, Haitian-descended people constantly face the fear of deportation even when they are Dominican-born. In Puerto Rico, Borrás's idealized coffee plantations often offer meager wages (US$100 to US$150 per week) to Dominican migrants, many of whom risk deportation if they attempt to leave the plantation site (Graziano 2013: 93).

Nationalist and anti-imperialist stances can, also, reproduce notions of racial-ethnic difference and gender-normative discourses on family and reproduction. This chapter has suggested that employing nationalist tropes may entail assuming paternalistic attitudes toward those whose political agency is undermined due to their racial, class, gender, and sexual difference. Such tropes can then limit the possibility of building a sense of national and regional kinship for collectivities in decolonial struggles and movements critical of and resistant to neoliberalism. Betances, Luperón, Laguerre, and Marrero Aristy provide us with a deeper understanding of two paradigms constitutive of the decolonial affective matrix: transcolonial narratives of *antillanista* kinship and national kinship. In the following chapter I will reference these literary examples, tropes, and narratives in order to further explore contemporary representations of Haitian-Dominican relations in the Dominican Republic and Dominican–Puerto Rican relations in Puerto Rico.

3 / Like Family: (Un)recognized Siblings and the Haitian-Dominican Family

Since the 1970s and 1980s the defining mechanisms of neoliberalism—privatization of natural resources, exorbitant external debt, free trade agreements, outsourcing of labor, and open border policies for capital—have been felt on the island that comprises Haiti to the west and the Dominican Republic to the east. In this context, interactions between their populations are represented in various highly contested state, grassroots, media-based, and literary narratives. Graffiti found near the western door of the first university of the Americas, Universidad Autónoma de Santo Domingo, at the center of the bustling Ciudad Universitaria in the capital city, Santo Domingo, illustrates the contentious nature of narratives about Haitian-Dominican encounters.[1] Placed right behind food vendors, many of whom are of Haitian descent, near construction sites that mostly employ Haitian migrant workers, and across from one of the main entrances of the university, the graffiti clearly engages the quotidian exchanges between Dominicans, Dominicans of Haitian descent, and Haitians in an area where Spanish and Haitian Krèyol can be heard simultaneously: *NO HAITIANO* (NO HAITIAN) has been crossed out and someone had added *NO RACISMO* (NO RACISM).

Drawing from Armando Silva's distinction between graffiti art and murals, Yolanda Martínez–San Miguel (2003: 164) has analyzed graffiti in Puerto Rico that similarly targets Dominican migrants in the island: *Muerte a los Dominicanos* (Death to Dominicans). This graffiti too was rewritten to critique racism in Puerto Rico. Another artist erased the original statement and wrote *Muerte al Racismo* (Death to Racism).

Martínez–San Miguel argues that the violence of *Muerte a los Domini-canos* constitutes graffiti: an expression of popular sentiment in Puerto Rico. The response is a mural: a politically correct answer that has become hegemonic and articulated by the state itself. However, break-ing historical conventions, the mural is signed by a minority political group and the graffiti seems to speak for the sentiment of most of the population.

Martinez–San Miguel's analysis illustrates the complicated discursive dynamics that characterize public debates about intra-Caribbean relations in Puerto Rico and the Dominican Republic and provides a useful coun-terpoint to the example found in the Dominican Republic. Both murals/graffiti speak to public struggles over signification that cannot be easily ascribed to particular political interests. Would a majority of Dominicans adopt an anti-Haitian position? Or an antiracist one? Which statement is a mural? Which one is graffiti? The narratives of Haitian-Dominican rela-tions documented in this chapter attest to the fact that there is not one answer to these questions. When I left Santo Domingo in June 2013 the graffiti still remained on the wall, reminding passersby of the quotidian discursive struggles over representations of Haitian-Dominican relations in the island, struggles that can be characterized by anti-immigrant and racist sentiments toward Haitians on the one hand and solidarity based on an understanding of shared experiences of colonial and capitalist histories and cross-cultural exchanges on the other.

The texts under consideration in this chapter elucidate ideological tensions between national and transcolonial/transnational paradigms mobilized for a variety of purposes. Considering contemporary Haitian-Dominican relations through the analytical framework of the decolo-nial affective matrix, the power dynamics embedded in transnational neoliberal and foreign aid projects on the island are made even more apparent. A distinction must be made between transcolonial and trans-national kinship narratives. On one hand, media coverage of state prac-tices illustrates that official narratives imagine a present and a future characterized by transnational neoliberal projects such as CAFTA-DR (the free trade agreement between the United States, the Dominican Republic, and Central American nations) and commercial enterprises between Haiti and the Dominican Republic. On the other hand, Haitian-Dominican alliances over labor, peasant, women's, LGBT, environmen-tal, and migrant rights, along with collaborations with social movements in the Caribbean and Latin America, serve as examples of transcolonial solidarity invested in social justice.[2]

These distinctions are not simple. For instance, NGOs can engage in transcolonial agendas that assert the rights of Haitian migrants in the Dominican Republic, while being complicit with the condescending, paternalist logic of the Dominican and Haitian states and northern international aid agencies and lending practices.[3] Transnational plans to develop free trade zones along the Haitian-Dominican border can invoke a transcolonial spirit of interethnic solidarity and collaboration instead of xenophobic relations. At times transcolonial/transnational kinship narratives signal the slippage of meanings between them and reveal how neoliberalism attempts to co-opt a historical legacy of struggles by anti-slavery, transcolonial, political communities.[4] However, the distinction between transcolonial and transnational kinship narratives requires us to keep asking: Who is attempting to create a sense of kinship between Haitians and Dominicans? Between Dominicans and Puerto Ricans? Whose economic interests are at stake?

Narratives of national kinship continue to be productive as well. They call attention to the exploitation of natural resources by foreign investors, such as the current campaigns against the gold mining company Barrick Gold and Monsanto, producer and exporter of genetically modified seeds, and the potential development of Dominican natural reserves like Bahía de las Aguilas and Los Haitises. Nationalist claims call attention to the inequities that inform transnational neoliberal projects due to histories of colonial subjection and dependency, and U.S. economic interests and military interventions on both sides of the island.[5] They are also used by Dominican youth of Haitian descent to claim their belonging to the national family. At the same time, elitist narratives of Dominican nationhood represent Haitian migrants and their Dominican-born and -raised children as invaders who can damage the racial, cultural, and moral fabric of Dominican society.

I engage these conflicting narratives of Haitian-Dominican relations in a neoliberal context through two metaphors that aptly describe the affective ties that frame my analysis. The first was articulated by Dominican president Hipólito Mejía and Haitian president Jean Bertrand Aristide, who spoke of Haitian-Dominican relations as a "marriage without divorce." The second is a phrase that describes cross-class relations between servants and employers in the literary texts under consideration, *como de la familia*. This phrase describes servants and racial or ethnic outsiders deemed inferior by elite interlocutors as people who are "like family." In the previous chapter, marriage constituted the nation. Here marriage describes state-sponsored Haitian-Dominican collaboration but also opens the possibility of acknowledging unofficial, grassroots, transnational/transcolonial solidarity movements. *Como de la familia* elides internal class, ethnic, and racial differences within a household and within national and transnational communities but still asserts a certain intimacy between subjects who belong to a collectivity, albeit on unequal terms.

I examine how a series of narratives about Haitian-Dominican relations engage these metaphors of transnational and national kinship in order to articulate different degrees of intimacy between Haitians, Dominicans, and Dominicans of Haitian descent. In an analysis of social science research, newspaper articles, and online publications, I identify five narratives of contemporary Haitian-Dominican relations in public discourse: pacific invasion, acculturation, neoliberal multiculturalism, Haitian-Dominican solidarity, and *interculturalidad*. These narratives illustrate the variety of notions of national belonging and kinship in public debates regarding Haitian-Dominican relations in the Dominican Republic. Intercultural nationalism appears as an alternative to elitist, anti-Haitian narratives and as a framework that does not ignore each country's claim to particular national histories and cultural heritages.

My analysis does not preclude the existence of other narratives, nor do I seek to simplify the complexity of others' work by placing it under a narrative category. However, this is an important and necessary intervention in the existing scholarship on Haitian-Dominican relations because it produces an account of kinship narratives that transcends and complicates the usual discussion of *antihaitianismo* as the quintessential narrative of cross-border encounters in the island. I seek to motivate other scholars to unravel the variety of affective relations that are invoked to narrate Haitian-Dominican relations. Moreover discussing these narratives places the literary texts under consideration in public discussions of Haitian-Dominican relations roughly contemporary to their publication and distribution.

The novels *The Farming of Bones* (1998) by the Haitian American writer Edwidge Danticat and *Solo falta que llueva* (2004) by the Dominican-born Santiago Estrella Veloz are in direct dialogue with these narratives of Haitian-Dominican relations. They incorporate nationalist and transcolonial/transnational narratives of kinship, at times simultaneously. The particular subjectivities, story lines, and formalistic components of the novels speak to concerns regarding the significance of the national and the transcolonial/transnational as paradigms that can be activated by foreign investors, the working poor, and social justice activists, among many other social actors.

Both *The Farming of Bones* and *Solo falta que llueva* imagine affective, even if troubled ties between Haitians and Dominicans and among Dominicans themselves. In these novels Haiti and the Dominican Republic appear to be *como de la familia* to one another. As a trope integral to these novels' representations of Haitian-Dominican relations, *como de la familia* complicates the metaphor of a *matrimonio sin divorcio* sponsored by the Haitian and Dominican states. Poor, working-class, and dark-skinned Dominicans and Haitians, Dominicans of Haitian descent, Haitian migrants, and women can all be (un)recognized siblings in the metaphorical marriage between Haiti and the Dominican Republic.

Ann Laura Stoler and Karen Strassler (2010: 183) have meditated on what it meant for Dutch colonials and their Javanese domestic employees to use the phrase *like family* to describe how they related to one another before the Japanese occupation that overthrew Dutch control of Indonesia (1942) and Indonesian independence (1945): "Whereas the Dutch invocation of family ties conjured an enclosed realm of cozy intimacy, former servants who spoke of being treated like family evoked their stance of respectful fear and deference." This description of colonizer-colonized kinship speaks to *como de la familia* as a trope that describes Haitian-Dominican relations in both novels. It makes visible the inequalities embedded in such kinship narratives. But those inequalities are produced not only in the context of colonialism or only in relation to colonizers, as Stoler and Strassler document; rather, as this chapter illustrates, *like family* serves to describe unequal yet intimate affective ties among nationals of different class, ethnic, and racial backgrounds, as well as among peoples of the Global South.

In the era of globalization, certain people, because of their class status, ethnic origin, racial background, migrant status, gender, and sexual practices, have been disowned by national and transnational families. They are considered outsiders, an excess, a drain on the system, invaders. But those (un)recognized siblings cannot be ignored. The narratives I discuss suggest that they cannot be denied as children of the same land, an island shared by two countries, an island that shares political, economic, and environmental concerns, as well as cultural, familial, and communal exchanges across its border. Their demands for inclusion produce other unofficial affective ties between Haitians, Dominicans of Haitian descent, and Dominicans that often transcend and critique neoliberal transnational agendas. Engaging the theme of Haitian migration and Haitian-Dominican communities in the Dominican Republic, both novels become meditations on the political potential of national and *antillanista* kinship and the usefulness of kinship metaphors as a lens through which we can assess inequalities and political solidarities whether we are studying colonialism/imperialism, nationalism, or neoliberalism.

The Farming of Bones was written and published in English. Danticat is a Haitian writer in the United States whose work is deeply relevant to island-based narratives of Haitian-Dominican relations because, as Juan Flores (2009), Martínez–San Miguel (2003), Myriam J. A. Chancy (2012), Donette Francis (2010), and Silvio Torres-Saillant, Ramona Hernández, and Blas Jiménez (2004) have documented, ideas travel throughout the insular Caribbean. What happens on the islands, and to U.S.-based Caribbean communities, is not contained by national boundaries but travels across the waters. As people in diaspora remain in contact and travel back and forth between different geographic locations, they retain their relationship with their Caribbean homelands. The Haitian-Dominican family imagined on the island finds itself rearticulated in diaspora by writers such as Danticat, Ana-Maurine Lara (2006), and Angie Cruz (2005) and their literary treatment of kinship ties among Haitians, Dominicans of Haitian descent, and Dominicans. This sense of family is also enacted in political practice, such as with the mobilization of young Haitian and Dominican students in New York City in 2013 in a series of educational events to address the recent denationalization of Dominicans of Haitian descent by the Dominican Constitutional Tribunal.

By documenting a broad range of narratives of Haitian-Dominican relations—nonliterary and literary, island-based and diasporic—I hope to offer a broader vision of Haitian-Dominican relations than the one offered by the usual attention to narratives of *antihaitianismo*. I challenge mainstream descriptions of the Dominican Republic as an exceptional example of antiblack racism and *antihaitianismo* in Latin America and the Caribbean.[6] I engage the Dominican Studies scholars Carlos Dore Cabral, Rubén Silié, Franklyn Franco Prichardo, María Filomena Gónzalez-Alcalá, Danny Méndez, Carlos Andújar, Pablo Mella, Digna María Adames Núñez, Ginetta Candelario, Sara E. Johnson, Silvio Torres-Saillant, Katerina Civolani, and April Mayes, who collectively unveil histories of Haitian-Dominican relations that transcend the limits of elite nationalist narratives invested in the whitening legacies of colonialism/imperialism.

Citizenship, Migration, and Neoliberalism
in the Dominican Republic

The irony of the 2013 decision by the Constitutional Tribunal Court is that it penalizes the children of Haitian migrants who have been integral to the economic history of the Dominican Republic since the turn of the twentieth century. As discussed in chapter 2, since the early twentieth century sugarcane plantations in the Dominican Republic have recruited Haitian laborers (Corten et al. 1976). Today most laborers at Dominican *bateyes* are Haitians or Dominicans of Haitian descent. Their labor is relevant because their lack of rights and benefits augments investor profits in an industry that is no longer competitive (Martínez 1995: 2).[7] In the 1920s and 1930s people of Haitian descent were recruited and sent to government-owned and private plantations (9). Today the recruitment of Haitian workers continues in the form of illegal trafficking of Haitians who cross the border or of people who are lured by recruiters' false promises (Corten 2013; Polanco 1994: 37). A 2012 survey of workers in the sugar industry found that 40 percent of Haitians in that sector are undocumented both in the Dominican Republic and Haiti (CEFASA 2012: 168). Changes in the economy of both countries in the past thirty years have prompted the creation of other work spaces for Haitians and Dominicans and the emergence of other migratory trends (CEFASA 2012; Corten 2013; Lozano and Báez Evertsz 2013).

According to *La nueva immigración* (2002) by Ruben Silié, Carlos Segura, and Carlos Dore Cabral, a large portion of these workers is from the urban proletariat and the lower middle classes escaping political turbulence and economic problems in overcrowded urban centers in Haiti. Dominicans also migrate from the countryside to the cities and abroad. *La nueva immigración* affirms that "the new [neoliberal] model essentially concentrated growth in urban zones, which in the eighties promoted the strong process of internal migration, and a strong tendency towards migration abroad, leaving spaces for Haitian immigration in nontraditional agriculture, in urban sectors like public works, the construction of houses, tourism, and in the informal sector, in a variety of activities" (66).

In the early 1980s the Haitian-Dominican Cultural Center in Santo Domingo had already documented that approximately half of the Dominican free trade zone's workers are Haitian-Dominicans ("Constituyen el Centro Domínico-Haitiano" 1983: 23). Due to Dominican emigration, workers of Haitian descent have occupied positions available in non-sugarcane-related economic sectors. The undocumented status of many migrants—and the assumption that Dominicans of Haitian descent do not have rights to Dominican citizenship or even identification documents—further heightens the vulnerability of these workers, who often find themselves without legal protection from exploitative labor practices. The devastation of Haiti after the 2010 earthquake left thousands homeless and left Haitian migrants with fewer human and economic resources than before (Alexandre 2013; Hurbon 2013; Silié 2013).

Economic neoliberalization in Haiti and the Dominican Republic occurred at times when both countries faced the weight of their external debts. It resulted in the development of new economic sectors into which Haitian migrants were integrated. Amalia Cabezas (1999: 94) asserts, "After three decades of employing the import substitution model of industrialization, in the nineteen-sixties international donor agencies urged the country to abandon this model and pursue the tourism route toward economic growth." By 1999 tourism produced 13 percent of the gross domestic product of the Dominican Republic. In the 1980s the Dominican Republic implemented the IMF's recommended austerity measures and established free trade zones within its national territory. Simultaneously Haiti fully entered the global market. After the fall of Jean Claude Duvalier's regime in 1986, the Haitian economy underwent a neoliberalization process following the recommendations of the World Bank, USAID, and the IMF. Haiti was required to abandon import-substitution policies and to open its border to subsidized imports without restrictions (Dupuy 2014). During this period rural-urban migratory trends and migration abroad increased in both countries (Corten 2013). The neoliberalization of the island also required cross-border economic collaborations. The partnership of Haiti and the Dominican Republic in neoliberal economic enterprises, such as free trade zones along the border, have shaped recent approaches to the border and to Haitian-Dominican relations.

Narratives of Haitian-Dominican Relations

Between 1980 and 2013 a variety of headlines, editorials, letters, and comments by Dominican legal scholars reproduced the idea that Haiti was invading the Dominican Republic in the form of a migrant population and was therefore contaminating the racial composition of the country. The racialization of Haitian migrants as black invaders is not new (Núñez 2001; Pérez 2002). Such characterizations date back to the

unification of the island under Haitian rule between 1822
Throughout the twentieth century nationalist narratives th
officially sanctioned by statesmen such as Trujillo and Balag
ated the idea that Haitians covet Dominican economic resources and
seek to blacken the island and transform the Hispanic heritage of the
Dominican Republic (Mateo 2004; Rodríguez 2003; Rodríguez de León
2004). The fear produced by such representations justified the massacre
of Haitians ordered by Trujillo in 1937.

In the twenty-first century the narrative of a Haitian invasion is found
in media outlets and online postings that justify massive deportations of
people identified as Haitian. In 2004 the Inter-American Commission
for Human Rights found the Dominican Republic guilty of violating the
human rights of Haitians and Haitian-Dominicans subjected to such
deportations, who are denied Dominican citizenship by birth. In 2013
the commission reviewed cases of Dominicans of Haitian descent whose
birth certificates and legal documents were rendered invalid by the Junta
Central Electoral through the application of Resolution 12 passed in
2007.[8]

Resolution 12 suspends any identification documents that appear to
be irregular. Nationality is not mentioned as one of those irregularities;
however, in practice, officials of the Junta Central Electoral cite parents'
nationality, a non-Dominican last name, dark skin, and anything that
signals Haitian ancestry as reasons to suspend or destroy identification
documents of Dominicans of Haitian descent (Civolani 2013). Those
affected are unable to register for classes, get married, open a bank
account, have access to health care and health insurance, vote, or work
in the formal sector. As Katerina Civolani (2013) asserts, they find their
lives suspended and their sense of identity questioned. More recently, in
September 2013, the Constitutional Tribunal determined that hundreds
of Dominicans of Haitian descent—the children of foreign-born parents
since 1929—could not be considered Dominican citizens. For many
people of Haitian descent in the Dominican Republic who were born
there and have had children there, this has created what some call a legal
limbo. They are suddenly considered foreigners by the law. Moreover, if
people of Haitian descent attempt to regularize their status, the decision
is in the hands of the general director of migration. Unlike other appli-
cants, Haitians and Dominicans of Haitian descent are subjected to a
different bureaucratic process, as documented by Centro Bonó.

The narrative of a pacific invasion underlines the application of
these policies. As Kiran Jarayam (2010) and Ernesto Sagás (2000) have

documented, the idea that Haitians are invading the Dominican Republic is not solely an anti-immigrant discourse but also tends to have very clear class implications. In his ethnographic study of the lives of Haitian migrants from a variety of social classes in the Dominican Republic, Jarayam (2010: 38) has demonstrated that class and skin color inform which Haitians bear the burden of being considered a nuisance to the state.

Sagás (2000: 124) argues that *antihaitianismo* is more than the product of racism. I agree with him in acknowledging that *antihaitianismo* is an elitist discourse employed to undermine efforts to improve the living conditions of working classes. He states, "Antihaitianismo has had one main objective: the protection of powerful personal and elite interests through the subjugation of the lower (and darker) sectors of the Dominican population. . . . Prejudice and racism—as expressed through *antihaitianismo* ideology—distract attention from class and economic issues" (119). Like other anti-immigrant discourses in the Americas, including those articulated in the United States, *antihaitianismo* disrupts possibilities of class-based kinship in poor and working-class communities. It attempts to impede interethnic solidarity and disrupt existing affective, filial, and political ties within Haitian-Dominican communities facing similar challenges with regard to access to land, food, adequate housing, education, employment, a living wage, and health care.

According to the narrative of the pacific invasion, Haiti will achieve the unification of the island through an invasion of the Dominican Republic undertaken by its poor migrants (Pérez 2002). The ideological work of *trujillista* intellectuals such as Balaguer and M. A. Peña Battle turned *antihaitianismo* and a Hispanicized notion of *dominicanidad* into the official narrative of intra-island relations in the mid- and late twentieth century (Mateo 2004; Price-Mars 1953; Rodríguez 2003)

Néstor Rodríguez's (2003) monograph "La isla y su envés: Representaciones de lo nacional en el ensayo dominicano contemporáneo" illustrates how *trujillista*, anti-Haitian, and Hispanic-centered representations of Dominican national identities permeate contemporary understandings of Haitian-Dominican relations. During his multiple, politically repressive terms as president of the Dominican Republic,[9] Balaguer expressed in both his speeches and his intellectual publications his fear of a Haitian contamination of Dominican Catholic values and morality, the pollution of the Dominican national family by immoral practices "contrary to the Christian institution of family" (1983: 94), and an overarching fear of the *africanización* of the country by Haiti. According to Balaguer

(1983), the Dominican Republic had to distinguish itself from Haiti and retain its status as a Spanish nation by asserting and protecting its religious, cultural, and moral inheritance from the former colonial motherland, Spain. While Trujillato racist and xenophobic ideologies have lost ground, they continue to be rearticulated. At times the racial component is not as explicit as it used to be, and *dominicanyorks* have become, along with Haitians, another enemy of the moral health of the national family (Rodríguez 2003: 41).

The 1822 unification of the island by Haiti is the historical referent most commonly cited to justify the fear of an invasion that could damage the demographic composition of the country. Torres-Saillant (2000) suggests that *antihaitianismo* emerged as a form of differentiation between Dominicans and Haitians. It is based on racial-biological and cultural attributes ascribed to *dominicanidad* and Haitianness after unification and Trujillo's state-sponsored whitening project in the 1930s.

These narratives, however, were not the only ones (Franco Pichardo 1977; Mella 2013; Torres-Saillant 2000). Some Dominicans favored unification as a strategy to protect the abolition of slavery and prevent the incursion of colonial powers on both sides of the island. Others saw in it the seeds for a confederation of independent Antillean nations. Those who fought for the independence of the Dominican Republic from Haiti did not necessarily explain their quest through a discourse of racial difference. Dominicans' resentment over taxation and questions of political representation underlie their desire for independence. In the midst of these debates regarding Dominican independence and the meaning of unification on both sides of the island, the narrative of the pacific invasion emerged as a means to target people of Haitian descent in the Dominican Republic. In a very different political context marked by assertions of state-sponsored Haitian-Dominican collaborations, the narrative of the pacific invasion has been rearticulated in present-day media.

For example, in the article "Hay que defender el país" (2004) in *Listín Diario*, the author asserts the need to defend the country from Haitians while differentiating the inhabitants of the western and eastern parts of the island. The whitening qualities of miscegenation are considered an improvement in the Dominican Republic's racial composition: "The Dominican Republic is a mulatto country whose skin coloration goes from *canela* [cinnamon]—of different degrees—to *marrón-negro* [brown-black]. Here we are all mixed, even those who look white, like me. That offers great advantages, because it is through fusions that racial improvement and development are born" (10). In the description of a multipolar racial identification system based on skin color, the author starts with *canela* and ends with *marrón-negro*, but not black. The mixed Dominican body can contain blackness but cannot be black in the same way the Haitian body and its cultural and political practices are. The author continues, "Loyalty to remote agricultural habits, understandable in African territorial extensions, but nonsensical in Haiti, have destroyed their soil. The cruelty of their rulers has continued just like the African tribal chiefs" (10). In contradistinction to Haiti, the Dominican Republic is represented as a place where people of all shades coexist in a civilized manner due to racial mixture. Haiti becomes a symbol of pure blackness, of African ancestry, that has not been civilized through racial mixture and an adequate European cultural heritage. Haiti's economic marginalization is relegated to an imagined blacker, more African nature: "Our neighbors represent a compact force, proud of its blackness and African culture, of its voudou and magic, even of its misery" (10).

In the end Haitians are also blamed for their exploitation at work sites in the Dominican Republic. Their proclaimed racial capacity to work without rest, accept low salaries, sleep on the floor, and eat meagerly explains their increasing numbers in various occupations. It also explains the consequent unemployment of Dominicans who are forced to abandon the island. Haitians are imagined as people trapped in another time by a primitive African heritage. The author calls for the defense of the national territory by making recourse to racist, colonial notions of blackness, a relatively whiter *dominicanidad*, and the alleged invasion of work spaces. But the author simultaneously acknowledges and claims blackness in the Dominican Republic as a blackness mediated by racial mixture. The narrative of the pacific invasion does not necessarily deny Dominicans' blackness but rather valorizes it differently from Haitians' black heritage.

The 2010 earthquake in Haiti mobilized thousands of Dominicans in relief efforts. *Antihaitianismo* also reemerged as certain sectors of Dominican society generated the fear of a new massive wave of immigration. In the opinion letter "Cuidado con la invasión haitiana," published by the newspaper *Hoy* on June 24, 2010, the author, José R. Martínez Burgos, warns readers, "Beware that they might become capable of dumping us from our own houses, and in future years place as President of the Republic one of our pacific invaders! I have the horrible intuition that at the rate we are going and the continuous increase of Haitian immigration, our sorcerers will displace and expel us from the country." The reference to witchcraft points to the constant media and popular vilification of the Afro-Caribbean practice of vodou. Even though this practice exists in a similar way in the Dominican Republic, voudou works as a metonym for the African legacy in Haiti. The letter reiterates the fear of a Haitian invasion by migration as well as a fear of the African heritage of the Haitian side of the island. Several of the responses to the letter support these ideas, articulating perceptions of an intrinsic difference between the two sides of the border. One critic of the letter points out its racist assumptions. Another commentator assumes that this critic is Haitian and responds by stating, "Well, that has precisely been the hazard of your nation [Haiti]. In contrast to the East side that is mixed in a *mestizaje* that makes us what I am: PROUDLY DOMINICAN." Once again the idea of racial mixture emerges as a divergent element between Haitians and Dominicans. Within this discourse a presumed difference resulting from miscegenation explains Dominican resistance to Haitian migration and confirms representations of migration as invasion.

The idea of a pacific invasion is also fomented by the sensationalist coverage of Haitian childbirth in Dominican hospitals, including headlines such as "Calculan que el gasto es de 24 mil pesos por parto, cada doce minutos nace haitiano en República Dominicana" (A cost of 24 thousand pesos has been calculated per labor, every twelve minutes a Haitian is born in the Dominican Republic; González 2013). Frequently it is implicitly or explicitly suggested in the media that Haitian women do not deserve medical treatment at the public health centers even if they are pregnant or in labor. These immigrants are seen as a burden on the state's economic resources; some also see them as a tool for an invasion in process. Media outlets in the Dominican Republic often vilify the demographic growth of a population seen as a political, economic, racial, and cultural threat. Haitian women of childbearing age become subjects who must be policed. It is important to state that *antihaitianismo* is not only a racial and class experience but also has gendered and sexual connotations that impact Haitian men and women differently. Haitian women's reproductive right to bear children is voided by their representation as instruments of an ongoing invasion. Whereas thinkers of all political strands—including the *antillanista* thinkers Gregorio Luperón and Eugenio María de Hostos, the nationalist writer Ramón Marrero Aristy, Trujillo, and Balaguer— have historically heralded the need to protect Dominican women's role as mothers and caretakers of national subjects,[10] women of Haitian descent find their motherhood and their children criminalized.

These children are undocumented according to the 2013 Constitutional Tribunal decision. The Constitution deems Haitian migrants "persons in transit" through the country and therefore ineligible for documentation. Being born in the Dominican Republic does not automatically grant Dominican citizenship, as the legal principle of *jure solis* used to allow, unless at least one parent is a Dominican national. Dominicans of Haitian descent can be easily deported to Haiti even if they have never been there and have no family ties there. Unlike the children of undocumented migrant women in the United States, derogatorily called "anchor babies," these children cannot anchor their migrant families to the Dominican Republic. They are not able to use Dominican citizenship to request visas, residency, or citizenship for their parents or extended family. Often they remain (un)recognized children of the Dominican nation without proper documentation. The irony of the pacific invasion narrative that informs these public discourses and policies is that it coexists with the active recruitment of Haitian laborers by Dominican employers in construction, domestic work, the sugar industry, and the informal economy (Castor 1978; CEFASA 2012; Corten et al. 1976; Lozano and Báez Evertsz 2013; Martínez 1995; Matibag 2003; Polanco 1994).

Though the pacific invasion has been part of a persistent anti-immigrant discourse, it is not the only way that Haitian-Dominican relations have been represented by the state or by private Dominicans. Even the anti-Haitian ideologue Balaguer (1983: 230) advocated "a friendship between both nations" and discussed the possibility of creating a democratic constitution shared by both Haiti and the Dominican Republic (220). The reality of a shared border, of a shared island, is undeniable and requires articulating affective ties between the people of both nations that are capable of sustaining a variety of political agendas.

For instance, Dominican scholarship defends the human and civil rights of people of Haitian descent. One example is the aforementioned book *La nueva inmigración* (2002), in which Silié et al. identify those sectors of the Dominican labor market most often occupied by workers of Haitian descent. They examined the conditions under which migrants are exploited because of their undocumented condition and to what degree they could be considered Dominican so as to be able to assert their right to proper documentation. Their argument focuses on Haitian descendants' civil rights. Along with other intellectuals and social activists, they emphasize how Haitians and Dominicans of Haitian descent acculturate to the cultural, social, economic, and political context of the Dominican Republic. These claims are important because otherwise, as one Dominican activist asserted, at any mention of Haitian descent conservative media outlets dismiss migrants' civil and human rights and the right to documentation for Dominicans of Haitian descent.[11] This dismissal often relies on the notions of inherent racial and ethnic difference.

For their study Silié et al. (2002) interviewed Haitians and Haitian-Dominicans about their linguistic and religious practices. They implicitly equated *dominicanidad* with Catholicism and the Spanish, while also identifying Haitianness with Creole, voudou, and *gagá*. The results of the survey indicate that "the majority of descendants of Haitians born in the Dominican Republic are mostly Catholic and that only a minority participates in the rites of voudou and the ceremonies of *gagá*" (164).

Gagá is a Haitian-Dominican spiritual practice that draws from Catholic and African traditions and also from the combined syncretic traditions of Haitians and Dominicans (Deive 1979; Matibag 2003). Researcher June C. Rosenberg (1979) asserts that *gagá* is a syncretic practice involving rituals of vodou, spiritism, and Catholicism. As a Haitian-Dominican celebration, it invokes spiritual forces from the Haitian and Dominican vodou pantheons in a three-day celebration that takes processions from one *batey* to the next.[12] According to Eugenio Matibag (2003: 15), it is "mostly Dominican-born revelers [who] dance their processions in and around the sugar refineries."

By arguing that a minority of the interviewees engage in Haitian and Haitian-Dominican religious practices, the study emphasizes how people of Haitian descent are incorporated into Dominican society. Unfortunately such framing strategically downplays Dominicans' participation in *gagás* and vodou practices and appears to purposely simplify the linguistic and cultural practices of people of Haitian descent, including Dominicans of Haitian descent, for the purpose of legitimizing their political claims.

In the twenty-first century neoliberal multicultural narratives underlie official state narratives of Haitian-Dominican relations. Haitian-Dominican collaboration has become the official slogan of both countries. Both states value and celebrate the cultural and historical differences of the neighbor. However, multiculturalist claims associated with neoliberal globalization do not entail a commitment to social justice or racial equity but rather silence how neoliberal economies produce surplus through the rearticulation of racial difference at the national and international levels (Puri 2004; Reyes-Santos 2008). Haitian and Dominican state officials involved in these efforts have mostly supported the economic development of the island through neoliberal policies and frequently ignore accusations of xenophobic animosity among the island's populations. For example, Haitian-Dominican efforts toward economic collaboration during the first three years of Hipólito Mejía's presidential term (2000–2004) were marked by a reliance on neoliberal strategies that posited the Dominican Republic as the bridge between Haiti and international finance institutions (Dupuy 2014). At the time Silié (2001: 5) pointed out, "Within the international community, President Mejía has eagerly promoted the need to support the development of Haiti through investment in development and, more specifically, with plans to turn the external debt of both countries into a direct investment that supports a bi-national program."

During the bicentennial celebration of the Haitian Revolution, Aristide thanked Mejía in Spanish for his support of Haiti and treatment of the island as "un matrimonio sin divorcio" (marriage without divorce; Vásquez 2004). Matibag (2003: 210) documents the ongoing discussion of a trilateral accord between the United States, Haiti, and the Dominican Republic to reduce the island nations' external debt. This discussion began in 1994, during Balaguer's last term as president, and continued into Leonel Fernández's term in 1996–2000. In 2000 an agreement of mutual cooperation was signed by the Association of Industries of Haiti and the Dominican Association of Free Trade Zones. By 2004 Dominican Grupo M had built a textile industrial park along the Haitian-Dominican border, in the Haitian town of Ouanaminthe/Juana Méndez, with the support of Dominican and Haitian business organizations and state officials as well as the United States. Grupo M quickly faced charges of labor rights violations and was accused of displacing Haitian peasants from their land. In 2011, meeting with Dominican, Haitian and U.S. state officials, as well as the Banco Interamericano de Desarrollo, Grupo M played a central role in discussions that laid out plans for further economic development in the town of Ouanaminthe ("Grupo M y Codevi" 2011).

All these efforts, undertaken by Dominican governments affiliated with different political parties, reiterate Mejía's representation of the Dominican Republic as an intermediary partner in transnational efforts led by the state, corporations, international aid agencies, or a combination of all of these. In the aftermath of the 2010 earthquake in Haiti, the Dominican Republic became the center of operations for a variety of international aid agencies. It also became the location for launching new economic enterprises in Haiti. In 2013 President Danilo Medina offered to collaborate with the Haitian government in reforestation efforts in order to address the ongoing environmental crisis in Haiti. In the context of neoliberal trade and aid, both countries partake of a state-sponsored marriage without divorce, seemingly respectful of each other's cultural and historical differences and economically sustained by neoliberal debt-relief projects (e.g., free trade zones). The states articulate a narrative of neoliberal multicultural kinship that appears to transcend colonial and elitist narratives of racial difference between Haiti and the Dominican Republic, in particular the narrative that undergirds the idea of a pacific invasion of Haitian migrants in the Dominican Republic. In the meantime Dominican, Haitian, and international corporations benefit from cheaper Haitian labor on both sides of the border.

Besides state initiatives to foster Haitian-Dominican collaborative projects, narratives of Haitian-Dominican solidarity exist around cross-cultural exchanges and social justice issues, such as the civil rights of Haitian migrants and Dominicans of Haitian descent, women's and LGBT rights, food sovereignty, labor struggles in free trade zones and the agricultural sector, and peasant struggles over land and sustainability. Dominican serial publications publish articles that assert shared religious, cultural, and class interests between Dominicans and people of Haitian descent. Two examples are "Gagá: Una expresión de vida que une dos culturas" (2003) by Margarita Quiroz and "Virgen de la Altagracia une a los pobres de Haití y República Dominicana" (2003) by Pedro Ruquoy. Through descriptions of Haitian-Dominican religious traditions and Catholic rituals in various interethnic communities, these articles dismantle discourses of cultural differences between Dominicans and Haitians and the respective blackening and whitening of these religious practices that are usually ascribed to one of the countries but not both. Kalalú, funded by Marilyn Gallardo, does similar work with children and teenagers, fostering an appreciation for both Dominican and Haitian dance and spiritual practices, as well as a sense of shared cultural heritage with other Antillean nations, while instilling pride in the children's Afro-Dominican heritage.[13]

In August 2005 the murder of three Haitians in the town of Haina, Dominican Republic, fomented the joint mobilization of the Haitian-Dominican Women's Movement (MUDHA) and Groupe d'Appui aux Rapatriés et Réfugiés (Support Group for Refugees and Repatriated Persons; GARR). In June 2013 representatives of the labor sector, Catholic and Christian institutions, and corporations, along with feminists, women's rights groups, peasants, Dominican migrant organizations in the United States and Puerto Rico, international aid organizations, and many others, signed the Compromiso Político y Social para un Nuevo Modelo de Gestión de las Migraciones de República Dominicana. This agreement seeks the implementation of already existing laws meant to regularize migration-related policies. In addition social movements, NGOs, and publications based in Haiti are active around issues of violence against people of Haitian descent on the island, workers' rights across the border, and environmental matters. The online publication *AlterPresse* has documented Haitian-Dominican collaboration around the issue of migration. In the article "Migration: Le GARR salue la decision de l'Eglise Catholique romaine" (2005) Lisane André congratulates the Catholic Church in both countries for simultaneously celebrating the Journée National des Migrants et Réfugiés (National Day of Immigrants and Refugees). *AlterPresse* has also covered cross-border efforts in its "Haiti/République Dominicaine" section, recognizing the shared ecological concerns of both countries. *AlterPresse* and another publication, *Haiti Progrés*, have demonstrated an ongoing engagement with labor struggles along the border, most explicitly related to the aforementioned neoliberal economic projects. *Haiti Progrés* has repeatedly reported on labor conflicts in Haiti's free trade zones, and *AlterPresse* has reported on the repression of both Haitian and Dominican workers at a public, soon to be privatized port in Santo Domingo. These publications maintain the existence of narratives of Haitian-Dominican relations that resist discourses of differentiation and are not necessarily shaped by neoliberal cooperation.

Within narratives of Haitian-Dominican solidarity it is crucial to recognize that women's and feminist movements, the LGBT movement, NGOs, and religious organizations have been at the forefront of new ways of imagining relations between the peoples of the island and the rest of the Caribbean. As I document some of these efforts, I try not to romanticize NGOs or deny that they can also be complicit with neoliberal agendas (Karim 2011). In attempts to retain scarce funding sources, NGOs often follow the dictates of foreign donors instead of addressing the needs of local communities or involving them in the process of addressing the issues that affect them the most, whether it is poverty, lack of water, earthquake relief, or limited or nonexistent educational facilities (Dupuy 2014; Schuller 2012) Sites where Haitian-Dominican solidarity is articulated are likely to be sites fraught with internal conflicts, competition for resources, and diverging agendas, as well as different ideas of what it means to articulate Haitian-Dominican solidarity networks. What is significant, however, is the articulation of narratives that tend to be ignored when *antihaitianismo* is the primary narrative of Haitian-Dominican relations expounded in scholarship and the media.

The Centro de Orientación e Investigación Integral in the Dominican Republic has an initiative for migrants' and refugees' rights in the Caribbean. It has created a report about the trafficking of women throughout the region, has produced a video campaign about HIV prevention meant to travel around the islands, and maintains ties to LGBT activists in Haiti. In June 2013 Amigos Siempre Amigos, a gay male organization in the Dominican Republic, hosted a reception for the Caribbean Forum for Liberation and Acceptance of Genders and Sexualities, attended by Caribbean activists and articulating a pan-Antillean vision for LGBT human rights.

La Colectiva Mujer y Salud has a long history of collaborating with colleagues in Haiti. They create educational materials in Spanish and Krèyol, cross the border to meet with women in Haiti working on gender violence, homophobia and transphobia, reproductive rights, and women's political participation. MUDHA is committed to the welfare of Haitian women and Dominican women of Haitian descent and their children, especially in Dominican *bateyes*. MUDHA addresses how women of Haitian descent along with men have participated in the economic structures of Dominican *bateyes*. Their work acknowledges that women of Haitian descent in the Dominican Republic enter an already gendered economy.[14]

La Confederación Nacional de Mujeres Campesinas (CONAMUCA) is another organization that focuses on the specific needs of women. They have built an educational retreat center in Miracielo, San Cristóbal, that offers internships, programs, and networks to address the realities of peasant women. They collaborate with Veterinarios sin Fronteras and Vía Campesina in Haitian-Dominican solidarity efforts over women's access to land, agricultural resources, food sovereignty initiatives, and protection from state policies that undermine women's ability to sustain themselves.

In its attempt to foster solidarity between Haitians and Dominicans, Centro Bonó, a Jesuit organization, has put forth *interculturalidad* as a model for interethnic relations. Centro Bonó organizes a variety of activities to enact this ideal for Haitian-Dominican relations. Its dossier of readings for a certificate on *interculturalidad* includes working definitions of the term as stated by Raúl Fornet Betancourt (2011, 2012). He defines *interculturalidad* as "a recuperation of the memories that narrate the open wounds produced by the imposition of a certain model of civilization" (2012: 188); it tries to create "a world whose realities do justice to cultural diversity with its memorial wisdom" (187). For Betancourt *interculturalidad* offers a vision of the world in opposition to neoliberalism, which can only understand subjects with respect to contracts made to mold people into efficient workers (187).

Interculturalidad emerges out of an ethical concern for the well-being of the other, deemed different from oneself.[15] It posits the notion that self and other change each other through quotidian encounters. Digna María Adames Núñez (2013) is one of the main proponents of Centro Bonó's migrants rights initiatives, and an avid advocate of Dominican youth of Haitian descent. She affirms that *"interculturalidad* seen this way wants to walk paths of creativity, of exchanges, conviviality, social articulation, celebration of what is beautiful, what is good, what is just, what humanizes all of us. It wants to solidify social relations and contribute to the well-being and knowledge of the other as a person with dignity, capable of transforming society in a positive fashion" (106).

Interculturalidad requires a willingness to transform power structures embedded in each person's psyche.[16] It also requires the will to learn about and with others, to enjoy one another, and to work through cultural misunderstandings and misconceptions. To accomplish these goals, Centro Bonó provides legal and logistical support and political education for labor organizers, migrants, and economically disadvantaged youth, as well as for youth involved in reconoci.do, the movement of Dominican youth of Haitian descent. It has created the game of Interculturalidad for community groups who want to create awareness and respect about cultural difference. Centro Bonó also organized a song contest to represent the political claims of reconoci.do that included Dominicans, Dominicans of Haitian descent, and Haitians in a well-attended celebration of interethnic solidarity.[17] In September 2013 Centro Bonó began building La Casa de la Interculturalidad, a space to host their Spanish, Krèyol, English, music, and theater classes in order to bring together Dominicans, Dominicans of Haitian descent, and Haitian migrants. Centro Bonó offers Krèyol language news and translations, food and medical supplies, and human resources to aid in reconstruction and relief efforts across the island.

Narratives of pacific invasion, acculturation, neoliberal multiculturalism, Haitian-Dominican solidarity, and *interculturalidad* negotiate tensions between national and transcolonial/transnational notions of kinship. The novels *Solo falta que llueva* and *The Farming of Bones* engage similar tensions. They enter a textual conversation that includes a long-standing tradition of Haitian and Dominican literature and historiography that has sought to represent the fraught, intimate nature of Haitian-Dominican relations, including authors such as Jacques

Roumain, Jacques Stephen Alexis, Jean Price-Mars, Guy Alexandre, Ramón Marrero Aristy, Juan Bosch, Andrés L. Mateo, César Nicolás Penson, and Freddy Prestol Castillo. I examine Estrella Veloz's and Danticat's novels as heirs to a historical negotiation of narratives that depict the Dominican Republic as a national family that confronts U.S. imperialist projects and as an emancipated, but grateful, child of Spain, with narratives that embed it within histories of transcolonial solidarity with Haiti. *Solo falta que llueva* and *The Farming of Bones* problematize representations of Haitian-Dominican relations as a marriage without divorce. The novels add another dimension to the nonliterary narratives previously discussed. They deploy the trope *como de la familia* (like family) to describe cross-class alliances among Dominicans, Haitians, and Dominicans of Haitian descent. In this way characters in each novel suggest the creation of a seemingly harmonious Dominican national family that must be protected from Haitian invaders. Conversely the novels also present a variety of Haitian-Dominican kinship ties that elide internal class, ethnic, racial hierarchies; the affective ties within a household serve to underscore similar power dynamics within national and transnational communities. The novels are textually aware of the complex, multiple historiographies of Haitian-Dominican relations that shape Dominican public discourse. Like the media and scholarly and political narratives I have presented, these literary narratives also present very intimate yet at times distant and suspicious hierarchical kinship relations between people of Haitian descent and Dominicans.

INTRAFAMILIAL VIOLENCE: HAITIAN-DOMINICAN RELATIONS IN *SOLO FALTA QUE LLUEVA*

The novel *Solo falta que llueva* reiterates the trope of the Haitian as invader that characterized mid-twentieth-century Dominican narratives of Haitian migration produced by the Trujillato. But it is a complex narrative of the national family in danger that incorporates Afro-Dominicanness and a critique of the working conditions faced by most Haitian migrants in the Dominican Republic. In a didactic, anti-imperialist tone that reminds the reader of *Over*, its narrator also denounces the exploitation of Dominican resources by transnational corporations. The national family must be protected from Haitian, North American, and European interests but must also show sympathy for Haitian migrants as siblings of the Haitian-Dominican family whose realities tend to be ignored by both states.

Similar to nationalist Trujillato narratives of the 1930s and 1940s, the novel assumes a nationalist position with regard to Haiti and the United States, although the usual narrative of the pacific invasion is transformed. In the novel the alleged Haitian invasion is imagined as an imperialist strategy of the United States, Canada, and France in the context of neoliberal globalization. The novel's formulation of an invasion is not simply fictional: on February 2, 2003, the newspaper *Hoy* published a legal discussion by various Dominican lawyers entitled "No son dominicanos." Various lawyers urged the country to limit migration and deny citizenship rights to Dominicans of Haitian descent in order to avoid the unification of the island by France, Canada, and the United States. The novel and these legal scholars were responding to French and U.S. proposals to liberalize trade between both countries and build free trade zones on their border, such as the one built by Grupo M in Juana Méndez.

The novel consists of a first-person narration by the main protagonist, a Dominican writer named Homero. The story takes place in the Dominican Republic in the early 2000s. At the beginning of the novel Homero accompanies a North American visitor, Giselle, on a road trip from the city of Santo Domingo to the countryside to visit her friend Rita Moinard. Upon their arrival they learn of Moinard's disappearance. Homero is intrigued and begins to investigate. As he gathers information about Moinard, he learns that she was collaborating with la Trilogía, a group whose purpose is to undertake the unification of the island as part of a larger plan by Haiti, the United States, Canada, and France. The group's membership is ambiguous throughout the novel, befitting a narrative about a conspiracy. The reader learns only that it is constituted by members of the aforementioned countries and that in the course of working with them, Moinard was assassinated. As he investigates Moinard's disappearance, Homero learns that the businessman Martín Marín, who had been investigating the group, is in an insane asylum, having seemingly fallen under a spell. Homero investigates the conspiracy and the fate of its victims and writes a report based on his information.

The narration takes a didactic tone that can be traced to the description on the book's back cover: "A political plot that recreates the debated theme of Haitian migration to the Dominican Republic, written without prejudices, with the convincing point of view of all of those involved." The back cover description of the award-winning journalist Estrella Veloz adds an aura of objectivity to the novel, which was sold as an unbiased narrative of Haitian-Dominican relations that gives equal weight to different points of view. It emphasizes Estrella Veloz's recognition by national and international forums, in particular for his journalistic work. His research on Haitians in the Dominican Republic has been published in various magazines and newspapers on the island since the 1990s.

One example is Estrella Veloz's article "Los haitianos, como las moscas, están donde quiera" (1999; Haitians, like flies, are everywhere), which made the front page of the magazine *Cañabrava*. It documents the abuses suffered by Haitian workers in the Dominican Republic, as well as Haitian-Dominican commercial exchanges that benefit various Dominican cities. However, his report takes a sensationalistic and derogatory tone when he asserts that Haitians reproduce like mice (9) and, like flies, can be found everywhere. The article points to the impoverished socioeconomic position of Haitians in the Dominican Republic while deploying dehumanizing metaphors to describe their reproductive and migratory practices. His voice becomes one among many in the Dominican media that routinely decry how Haitian women use Dominican hospitals and public services to give birth to their children. Although Estrella Veloz's intention is to call attention to the impoverished living conditions of the Haitians documented in his piece, his representation of Haitian women's reproductive needs echoes anti-Haitian narratives and social practices in the Dominican Republic.[18]

The publicity for the novel does not acknowledge its emphasis on the threat of a Haitian invasion. The magazine *Ahora*, in its section on recommended books, describes the novel in one sentence: "Rita Moinard is a character in *Sólo Falta que Llueva* who is witness to the existence of an organization called *La Trilogía*, whose fundamental mission is to organize its members so that they may infiltrate the state" ("Solo falta" 2004). Unlike the book cover, *Ahora* does not even reference a history of Haitian-Dominican relations. Other publications repeat the same sentence and add what seems to be the press release for the novel: "French citizen Rita Moinard's mysterious disappearance in Dominican territory, who it seems was swallowed by the earth, leads her intimate North American airhead friend and painter, Giselle Pritman, to undertake an investigation" ("Novela explora aspectos" 2004).

The dissonance between what is publicized about the novel and its actual content requires an examination of how the narrative of the pacific invasion is reconstructed from Homero's perspective. What is left unsaid? What are the silences and omissions that characterize the reviews of the novel? Parallels exist between the objectivity claims made for the novel's publicity and the didactic tone of the narrative. Homero undertakes a quasi-journalistic narrative with verifiable facts, which becomes a legitimate rewriting of the history of Haitian-Dominican relations, in a way that echoes the omniscient narrations of the nation in danger in both *Over* and *La Llamarada*. However, like the narrators in those novels, Homero's prejudices and assumptions lie beneath the surface.

At the beginning of the novel the story is presented as a historical narrative based on "facts from interviews, documents, testimonies, and letters, all from reliable sources" (Estrella Veloz 2004: 8). The reader does not know how Homero has gained access to these materials; however, a series of references to events that have shaped the representation of Haitian migrants in Dominican media since 2000 supports the purported veracity of the narrative and its relevance to concurrent discussions about Haitian-Dominican relations, CAFTA-DR, and the failed U.S. proposal for a free trade agreement of the Americas. These factual references include events such as the burning of a Dominican flag in a *gagá* ritual, discussions about the legal status of Dominicans of Haitian descent, and warnings about an ongoing unification of the island by the United States, France, and Canada.

Homero also speaks in the authoritative, omniscient first-person. However, his self-presentation as an objective source of historical truth is undermined by the novel's revelation of his privileged social position and point of view. This revelation appears in his depictions of working-class, black-identified, and female bodies. These subjects are members of the national family, *como de la familia*, but do not enjoy the same political agency as whiter, middle- and upper-class, male, heteronormative subjects.

For instance, his descriptions of cross-class relations elide the hierarchies of power at play within seemingly equal and reciprocal interactions between working-class and upper-middle-class Dominicans. In talking about Marín's wife, Tania, and the couple who would serve them at their property in the countryside, he does not recognize the position of power the landowners have over the peasants who work for them. Homero tells us, "The man in charge was an old peasant who had worked before with Tania's father, who had seen her being born and treated her like a daughter. His wife was also like a member of the family . . . always prepared [for Tania] her favorite dishes . . . a gesture that was reciprocated with gifts from the city" (25). *Como de la familia* is used to describe the proximity between Tania and her employees as a nonlabor relationship. The work of the peasants is not considered a part of a transaction but rather a gift, and Tania's "gifts from the city"—fabrics for the peasants to make dresses for wealthy women in town, including Tania—serve to further expand the idea of a familial relationship. Homero ignores the labor involved in the creation of the dresses and the evident need the peasant woman has to earn money in different ways, not only by working for Tania. By erasing the labor done by Dominican peasants and workers for landowners and businessmen, the novel is able to depict cross-class anti-Haitian alliances without considering the possibility of class conflict or Haitian-Dominican solidarity based on shared class interests. A sense of kinship is defined by the employers' and employees' *dominicanidad*, a national identity uncomplicated by class difference.

In addition blackness in the novel is mostly ascribed to non-Dominicans in a sympathetic but derogatory manner. When Homero describes Madame Pumba, a black Brazilian servant who had worked for Giselle, her skills as a cook are celebrated: "All those who tried her food would eagerly offer compliments to Madame Pumba . . . who would just respond in an outburst of laughter, showing her very white teeth which made her blackness stand out" (10). His comment reiterates the idea of *como de la familia* that characterizes servant-master relations in the novel. Homero describes a friendly relationship between her and her employers; however, his celebratory description of her body caricatures her blackness. Homero's condescending approach to her subjectivity signals her racial otherness.

Heteropatriarchal conventions of womanhood also shape the novel's portrayal of various female secondary characters, not only working-class Afro-descendent ones. When Homero interacts with Giselle, who is clearly an upper-class North American woman, he objectifies and infantilizes her. When she hears the news of the disappearance of Moinard and has to stay in a hotel with Homero while a storm passes, he says, "Giselle took her Martini glass again. . . . She lightly wet her lips, which in the lighting looked even more tempting. Her scared little face seemed to belong to a defenseless girl, almost about to cry" (38). In contrast with the Dominican peasant and Madame Pumba, Giselle is gendered by Homero as a sensual but helpless woman he needs to protect. The racial and class background of these women informs his representation of their gender difference. Nevertheless they are all seen in domestic spaces, and their subjectivities are only superficially explored in the narrative.

In contrast the novel presents working-class and upper-middle-class men in the midst of political turbulence relevant to the welfare of the nation. Homero's distinct descriptions of female and male characters of various class backgrounds are not coincidental. The fear of a Haitian invasion calls for the unity of all Dominicans, the national family, without regard to any preexisting class differences. The call for unity neutralizes potential challenges by working-class men to the status quo. Homero privileges his own perspective as an elite, whitened, and heteronormative man. His elitist biases are made evident in the relationships established among the masculine characters in the novel.

Interactions between the businessman Marín and a peasant named Eusebio Fuertes show how Haitian anti-Dominican and Haitian invasion projects are imagined in the text. Fuertes is the person who reveals to Marín the secret of la Trilogía. He works for Pastor, a Dominican of Haitian descent and the leader of the conspiracy. When Fuertes tells Marín about la Trilogía's plan to unite the Dominican Republic and Haiti, they become allies against what they believe to be an invasion of the country. In order to convince Marín of the urgency of the situation, Fuertes refers to nineteenth-century attempts to unify the island. He explains that the plot has not been revealed due to criticisms of Dominican racism toward Haitians: "[Haiti is] taking over the country, as part of a process coldly calculated since time immemorial, but nobody dares to say it out of fear of being called a racist or told that one has prehistoric notions about the territorial and cultural division of the nations" (84). Fuertes's statements link criticisms of racial discrimination and the twenty-first-century Haitian presence in the Dominican Republic to other moments that marked Haitian-Dominican relations, such as the 1822 unification, the 1844 Dominican independence from Haiti, and the 1937 massacre.

His version is confirmed, though complicated, by General Otilio Campos. Becoming another ally, Campos tells Marín that the conspiracy has been in progress since the late nineteenth century. According to him, it has not been stopped because it is in the agricultural and construction sectors' best interest to welcome migrant laborers. Campos recognizes the role played by Haitians in the Dominican economy and criticizes the economic interests that exploit them. However, despite his awareness of the economic factors that explain the presence of Haitians, he reiterates the narrative of the pacific invasion. He denounces planters and contractors as accomplices in the invasion. Campos legitimizes, from an official point of view, what Fuertes the peasant had confided to the businessman. Along with Fuertes and Marín, Campos articulates a narrative of Haitian invasion that replicates the fear of racial contamination that has historically permeated *trujillista* narratives about Haitian migrants.

Fuertes can differentiate Dominicans and Haitians only by relating the Haitians to Africa: "They cannot separate the call of the spirits of Africa from their perception of the relentless oppression that they have suffered for centuries" (83). According to him, Haitians learn to speak and eat like Dominicans, but, unlike real Dominicans, they will not be found in a Catholic church because of their African beliefs. Their African heritage is one Haitian quality that justifies resisting an invasion.

Marín himself, learning that a new immigration law will be implemented in the Dominican Republic, equates Haiti with Africa in a derogatory manner: "If things continue to be the way they are, we will suddenly become faggots and Africans—thought Marín, overwhelmed by hopelessness" (97). Once again the idea of an invasion is based on the notion that Dominicans must protect themselves from Haiti's African heritage and spiritual practices. Marín's vision of the result of the invasion reflects exclusionary nationalist discourses that reject Haitian blackness and non-gender-normative subjects, such as homosexual men. The national family would then be racially corrupted and unable to produce proper heteronormative citizens. Marín's despair sympathetically represents him as a character embodying the racist and heteropatriarchal discourses of the nation.

The narrator does not reject the implications of Fuertes's and Marín's anti-Haitian arguments but rather embraces them and presents the two men as heroes of the nation. Homero himself restates ideas espoused by Fuertes and Marín in his reflection on Haitian-Dominican cultural forms and organizations. Commenting on the rumor of a flag-burning incident at a *gagá* ritual, Homero disparagingly says, "The press published that the burning of a Dominican flag had occurred during a celebration of *gagá*, which is a parade of dance with drums, in which the participants *speak in tongues*, glossolalia is how it is called, and they fall like ripe *guanábanas* when the spirit rides them, making it necessary to give them a beating with a stick of pigeon peas to see if they will calm down, that it is enough and the poor soul cannot stand it anymore" (90). He mocks *gagá* rituals as a grotesque practice, unworthy of respectful attention. He also criticizes the alleged complicity of Haitian-Dominican organizations in the plot of invasion, and people who celebrate the shared Afro-Antillean cultural and spiritual heritages between Haiti and the Dominican Republic. For him any organization that attempts to build or sustain racial, cultural, filial, and communal kinship ties between Haiti and the Dominican Republic is an accomplice in the ongoing invasion.

His attitude is more fully understood when taking into account his avowal of a whitened *dominicanidad* that does not trace itself to Africa. Homero considers the ideas of Dominican intellectuals that document Afro-Antillean legacies to be vain efforts that serve only to further the interests of the invaders: "Various known intellectuals added themselves to the utopia, some inspired by what they called our true roots, which according to them came from the African continent" (100). He does not accept the unification of the island because of what he perceives as a natural racial difference between Haitians and Dominicans. Following the model previously presented in Dominican media, the narrative of the pacific invasion is restated in the novel through its narrator's devaluation of Haiti's blackness, a blackness proscribed by an imagined ideological and cultural proximity to Africa.

The novel's ending justifies Homero's fears and ties the ongoing perception of a Haitian invasion to a history of racialized conflict on the island. Homero hears the phrase "it only needs to rain" and "some gray clouds began to accumulate in the sky, signaling that it would in fact rain. The dice had been rolled" (136). It is significant that his fear of invasion is confirmed by the phrase "it only needs to rain" considering that, according to the novel, it was first uttered by the main schemer of the plot to unify the island: Mackandal. According to Homero, Mackandal realizes "it would not be easy, one just had to sow the seed. Afterward, in his own words, 'it only needs to rain'" (100). Mackandal, who is practically invisible in the narrative, as he was famed to be in real life, is depicted as a mischievous man with magical powers and the resources to get rid of those who put his goal at risk.

Mackandal is a historical reference to a Haitian slave made famous in the 1750s for poisoning planters in Haiti. He became a legend after people saw him escape the flames of colonial punishment in the form of an insect. Stories about him informed slave insurrections that resulted in the Haitian Revolution (Du Bois 2004: 50). In the novel his figuration in an antagonistic role highlights how narratives of the pacific invasion draw on colonial depictions of Haiti's antislavery revolutionary history. The idea of a pacific invasion renders impossible even the rhetorical state-sponsored marriage imagined by Mejía and Aristide. It (un)recognizes Haitians and Dominicans as siblings, the offspring of the same island, as Luperón imagined them to be back in the 1890s.

Despite Homero's *antihaitianismo* and disapproval of La Trilogia and their goals, he shares an anti-imperialist critique with them. In his description of the Dominican countryside, he critiques the presence of foreign economic investment on the island, such as the gold-mining company Barrick Gold: "We crossed the small town Maimón, whose inhabitants were proud of its gold mine, but [lived] with nonfunctioning traffic lights and houses made of wood, due to the lack of electricity, something very common to other small towns in the country where people still used kerosene lamps. It did not matter if they had an abundance of natural resources, whose exploitation benefited mostly foreign companies" (16). Homero discovers Moinard's explanation of La Trilogía's goals: that some Haitians and Dominicans are collaborating with the plot to unify the island to be able to resist, together, "the plans of imperialist and colonialist powers" (101). Though he shares an anti-imperial stance with La Trilogía and frames neoliberal transnational projects as imperialist schemes, Homero is not interested in their plan for Haitian-Dominican collaboration. He and Marín both dismiss an anti-imperialist agenda for collaboration due to a fear of racial contamination. I am not suggesting that political unification of the two countries is necessarily the only way a transcolonial/transnational anti-imperialist community should be built on the island; rather I call attention to how the idea of a pacific invasion does not recognize potential anti-imperialist solidarity ties between Haitians and Dominicans.

The novel offers a space to view a variety of discourses about Haitian-Dominicans in dialogue with each other and to examine their political implications. It speaks directly to the narrative of the pacific invasion, as well as to narratives of Haitian-Dominican collaboration sponsored by neoliberal states and solidarity efforts by grassroots organizers, cultural workers, and intellectuals. *Solo falta que llueva* exemplifies how notions of nationalist and transcolonial kinship, as well as historical disavowals of colonial/imperial kinship, are negotiated in a neoliberal context. Transcolonial and imperial kinship models are conflated in the novel when free trade agreements suddenly become the weapon of an involuntary unification of the island. Haiti then becomes an abusive partner, along with Canada, the United States, and France, of the Dominican Republic, but one still invested in an anti-imperial transcolonial agenda critical of North Atlantic paternalistic approaches to the island.

The novel also reconstitutes the national family as an entity deprived of internal racial, class, and gender conflict by deploying the trope *como de la familia*, while Homero's biases as an omniscient narrator reveal what must be silenced to assert the unity among all family members. Moreover the national family is in danger not only from North American and European imperialist plots but also from the complicity of

Dominicans and Haitians with transnational neoliberal projects that appear to deprive Dominicans of a better future. The novel envisions a nationalist critique of neoliberalism without demonstrating any hope for the nation.

LIKE A SISTER: HAITIAN-DOMINICAN RELATIONS
IN *THE FARMING OF BONES*

The state as a repressive and corrupt entity also appears as a trope in *The Farming of Bones.* In the novel Haiti and the Dominican Republic do not represent the interests of the poor, the working class, migrants, or women; it is *la familia* who sustains the most marginalized populations when the state has failed them.

Much has been said about the novel's women-centered recuperation of unofficial histories of the 1937 massacre, as well as how it blurs the racial and cultural distinctions between Haitians and Dominicans articulated by Trujillato intellectuals (Clitandre 2001; Francis 1999; Mata 2008; Shemak 2002). The novel also engages contemporary narratives of Haitian-Dominican solidarity even in the midst of such a violent manifestation of *antihaitianismo.* It remembers not only the massacre but also how Haitians, Dominicans, and Dominicans of Haitian descent have coexisted and shared kinship ties. It provides a narrative of Haitian-Dominican relations that does not solely rely on a critique of *antihaitianismo* but rather examines the basis of transcolonial kinship relations across the border. Class mediates Haitian-Dominican kinship throughout the novel.

Official Haitian and Dominican representations of the massacre underestimated how it literally and symbolically cut poor and dark-skinned Haitians and Dominicans from their communities and families on the Dominican side of the island. In *The Farming of Bones* the state-sanctioned metaphor of a marriage without divorce is not foreign to the amicable resolution of the massacre by the governments of the island. At the same time Haitians and Dominicans of Haitian descent are *como de la familia* in their relationships with Dominican employers, coworkers, romantic partners, and neighbors; they become kin across ethnic and class lines. As kin they find support and see their differences amplified within the context of the massacre and Trujillo's anti-Haitian discourse.

Mirroring *Over* and *Solo falta que llueva*, the novel reflects a concern with the U.S. occupation of both sides of the island and how the occupation informed the recruitment of Haitians to work on Dominican sugarcane fields and *centrales.* Once again critiques of U.S. political, economic, and military interests on the island are shared by Haitians and Dominicans. The novel's narrator, Amabelle, weaves together her personal experience of nationalist, Haitian-Dominican, and imperialist histories as she attempts to make sense of the violence, joys, pain, and feelings of belonging she has experienced on both sides of the border that divides the island.

Amabelle is a Haitian woman who was raised by an upper-middle-class Dominican family for whom she works as a housekeeper. Her parents drowned in the river that marks the border between Haiti and the Dominican Republic. Prior to their death she and her family lived in Haiti and participated in commercial exchanges across the border. When she was a child, Amabelle was taken as a servant by a Dominican, Doña Valencia, and her Spanish father. The novel introduces Amabelle as an adult who has fully undertaken her responsibilities at Doña Valencia's house. Amabelle considers the Dominican town called Alegría (Happiness) her home, a community constituted by Dominican and Haitian landowners, sugarcane cutters, servants, and artisans. She narrates the events surrounding the 1937 massacre and her consequent relocation to Haiti.

At the time of the massacre, Amabelle had been romantically involved with a Haitian sugarcane cutter, Sebastien, who migrated to the Dominican Republic during the 1916–34 U.S. occupation. Sebastien and his sister were executed by the Dominican army during the massacre. Amabelle escaped by going to Cap-Haitien, Haiti, with Sebastien's friend Yves. The years go by without many changes. She stays in Cap-Haitien with Yves's family, becomes a seamstress, and continues to suffer from the physical and emotional injuries received during her escape. In 1961 Trujillo is assassinated. Amabelle celebrates and returns for a day trip to Alegría, where she also looks for her childhood friend and mistress Doña Valencia. As night falls she returns to the Haitian side of the border and lies in the shallow river waiting for the dawn.

The uncertainty of rumors, some containing truth and others totally false, shapes the novel. No one is sure of what happens and why. At the beginning there are rumors of possible deportations and killings of Haitian migrants in the Dominican Republic. Some women tell Amabelle, "You heard the rumors? . . . They say anyone not in one of those Yanki cane mills will be sent back to Haiti" (Danticat 1998: 69). Even though these rumors are true, Amabelle and others do not take them seriously because there is no concrete evidence. In other moments in the novel, characters believe false rumors, such as when Amabelle visits Valencia in

1961, and Valencia doubts that she is truly Amabelle because she "spoke to many people who said they watched when she [Amabelle] was killed in La Romana" (294). For twenty-four years Doña Valencia believed the firsthand accounts that her servant was dead. Amabelle and Valencia recognize that their story is just one among many: "But as the señora [Valencia] had said, there are many stories. And mine too is only one" (305). Through Amabelle's retelling of different narratives surrounding the massacre, the novel creates a memory of what happened that relies on her personal fictional experience. It does not claim to represent a historical reality.

The formalistic structure of the novel reflects this mode of recounting the narrative as a form of personal testimony. *The Farming of Bones* incorporates chapters about her daily life in Alegría and Cap-Haitien. The chapters in boldface tell of her nights in Alegría when she could experience life without the constraints imposed by servitude. She spends the nights with Sebastien and/or dreaming of her parents and their death. After the massacre chapters in boldface reveal how Amabelle coped with the aftermath of the event. She reinvents Sebastien in her dreams. Through these fictionalized memories she lives with those who have died and processes what has happened. The novel's form permits a glimpse into Amabelle's emotional and spiritual experience of historical events.

The narrative structure does not seek resolution through a linear plot but rather mirrors Amabelle's sense of incompleteness for having lost her first family, her adoptive family (Francis 2010), and a potential family with Sebastien. Like *Solo falta que llueva*, Danticat's novel does not express the possibility of change or hope for a national or transcolonial/transnational project. Amabelle cannot imagine a different future because she sees herself as dead in life, not being able to fully move on after losing her loved ones. Having had no children, she cannot leave them her legacy, her memory, and the stories that have been silenced (Danticat 1998: 266). The novel itself becomes her attempt to leave her memory as an inheritance, a memory that many others want to see disappear.

Her memory speaks of the stories that do not fit within the conventional historical accounts of either the Dominican or Haitian nation-states. *The Farming of Bones* reproduces and rewrites existing narratives of the massacre. Despite claims to the contrary, it asserts that the Trujillo regime organized the massacre (Mateo 2004). Various characters critique the role played by U.S. economic interests in the Dominican Republic and Haiti in the exploitation of Haitian migrant labor in the

Dominican Republic and how the occupation government fostered Haitian migration to the neighboring country. The silent complicity of Haiti's presidents Sténio Joseph Vincent and Elie Lescot with the Dominican government is underscored.[19] And the kinship ties built among Haitians, Dominicans of Haitian descent, and Dominicans challenge the Trujillato's attempt to build strict racial distinctions between Haitians and Dominicans.

In *La République d'Haïti et la République Dominicaine* (1953), Jean Price-Mars discusses different versions of the massacre and how it was justified by the official account of rumors that some Haitians had been stealing cattle and chickens from Dominicans. Even Haiti's president Elie Lescot eventually accepted this version and did not pursue legal action against the Dominican Republic (Mateo 2004). According to this official version, it was a spontaneous uprising of enraged peasants. Price-Mars mocks this claim by challenging the idea that people at the border could differentiate between a Haitian and a Dominican stealing their livestock. According to him, and more recently Richard Lee Turits (2002; 138), people at the border speak both Haitian Krèyol and Spanish, cross the frontier frequently, and coexist in such a way that it is difficult to differentiate them.

The words of Valencia's husband, Señor Pico, a commander of the army, challenge these justifications for the massacre based on stories of chicken thefts or intrinsic cultural differences. Alluding to the murders and mass deportations of Haitians, he confirms the direct intervention of the Dominican state: "The operation would be quick and precise. To tell the truth, part of it had started" (Danticat 1998: 42). Later a Haitian peasant tells of how he was arrested for stealing his own chickens. If other characters believed the peasant, the official version upheld by both governments would not be tenable.

The novel assumes state complicity on both sides of the border in both the creation of the conditions that led to the massacre and its cover-up. *The Farming of Bones* criticizes the Haitian government for promoting migration and for justifying the massacre. Tibon, a Haitian migrant who accompanies Amabelle on their way to Haiti, affirms, "Poor people are sold to work in the cane field so our own country can be free of them" (178). His anger can be explained by the fact that U.S. authorities and corporations encouraged and, at times, also remunerated state officials and individuals involved in the recruitment of Haitian laborers for cane fields.[20] The narrative describes the lamentable process in which Haitian government officials collected and reshaped people's testimonies about the massacre. Yves says, "You tell the story, and then it's retold as they wish, written in words you do not understand, in a language that is theirs, and not yours" (246). The bureaucratic process does not represent the storytellers' experiences; instead the stories are co-opted by a state that colludes with the Dominican version of the events.

The various versions of the massacre that are represented point to the economic interests that shaped Haitian migration to the Dominican Republic and to the exploitation of Haitian workers. The 1937 massacre cannot be understood without placing it in the context of the internal changes in Haiti during and after the U.S. invasion. In the 1920s and 1930s U.S.-financed sugarcane plantations in Cuba and the Dominican Republic operated on cheap labor. The United States, the Dominican Republic, Haiti, and Cuba sponsored migratory movements whose destinations were *bateyes* in the Dominican Republic and Cuba (Castor 1978; Chinea 2005; Corten et al. 1976; Dupuy 2014; García Muñiz 2010; Inoa 1999; Roorda 1998). Migration relocated Haitians who were organizing against land dispossessions (Castor 1978); it eventually became a survival strategy for those who had lost their land in Haiti. Although migration was an official policy, it became problematic for Trujillo's government since Haitians who wandered across the border, worked and lived with Dominicans, or established their homes outside of the *bateyes* were viewed as a threat to the establishment of a clear frontier between the countries.

This novel alludes to the role played by U.S. capital in the exploitation of Haitian labor. U.S. supervisors and financial institutions managed the Dominican sugarcane industry. "How can the Yanki cane mills save anyone?" (Danticat 1998: 70), asks a Dominican woman of Haitian descent. She and her son do not have legal documentation because the *central* has kept their papers, tying them to the *batey*. When various characters explain their decision to migrate, the appropriation of land by U.S. investors is represented as a common reason for leaving Haiti. Sebastien's mother, Man Denise, laments that her son and daughter had to go to the Dominican Republic when the "Yankis" took their home and land to build a road (239).

By pointing to the histories of migration and the living conditions of people of Haitian descent in the Dominican Republic, the novel undermines the narrative of the pacific invasion, as well as any state responses to the experiences of Haitians, Dominicans of Haitian descent, and Dominicans during the massacre. The narration itself deconstructs derogatory discourses of difference because the narrator adeptly negotiates cultural registers across the border. Kinship relations across class, ethnic, and gender lines in the novel are not based on nationalist narratives but a quotidian experience of filial, communal, and cultural exchanges.

Throughout the narrative Amabelle has friendly and familial relationships with Dominicans, Haitians, and Haitian-Dominicans and communicates with them in their languages: Haitian Krèyol, Spanish, and even Alegrían Creole. Amabelle, Sebastien, Yves, Valencia, Tibon, and others share settings where Dominicans, Dominicans of Haitian descent, and Haitians coexist. For example, in her return to Haiti with Yves, Amabelle meets a Dominican woman who is looking for her Haitian boyfriend. At first Amabelle cannot identify the ethnicity of the woman and her sister because "those two seemed like they might be Dominicans—or a mix of Haitian and Dominican—in some cases it was hard to tell" (171). Her uncertainty points to an awareness that ethnic attributes and familial ties are shared by peoples from Haiti and the Dominican Republic.

Amabelle herself has a sister-like relationship with Valencia, despite being her servant. Valencia's treatment of Amabelle, however, reflects Valencia's position of power: "I thought of Señora Valencia, whom I had known since she was eleven years old. I had called her Señorita as she grew from a child into a young woman. . . . She on the other hand had always called me Amabelle" (63). Valencia warmly remembers having grown up with Amabelle, yet she does not reject her role of mistress of the house in their interactions. The kin relation of *hermanas de crianza* (sisters of the cradle) is overridden by the hierarchical rather than familial relationship between mistress and servant. Moreover when Valencia's dark-skinned baby girl is born, she laments what she perceives as her resemblance to Amabelle and her people. Valencia's own daughter brings into question her, and the Trujillato's, notion of what belonging to the Dominican national family entails. Class and race mediate the possibility of national and transnational kinship. Amabelle is *como de la familia*, but, next to her adoptive sister, her belonging to the affective unit requires her to assume a subordinate status to her whiter, richer, Spanish Dominican sibling.

Reimagining Haitian-Dominican Kinship

The Farming of Bones and *Solo falta que llueva* provide useful counterpoints to scholarly conversations about Haitian-Dominican relations. Matibag (2003: 4) theorizes the counterpoint as an approach to Haitian-Dominican relations that "accommodate[s] contradiction: fragmentation in unity, conflict in complementarity." Like Matibag's historical analysis of Haitian-Dominican relations from colonial times until 2003, analyzing *The Farming of Bones* reveals the "hidden linkages that have united [Haiti's and the Dominican Republic's] fates even when their animosity appeared at its most belligerent" (2). The metaphor *como de la familia* confirms and complicates his conceptualization of the counterpoint with respect to Haitian-Dominican historical relations.

Metaphors of family have characterized both national and transcolonial/transnational kinship narratives. The contradictions Matibag notes in his theorization of the counterpoint are possible due to contesting ideas of national and Haitian-Dominican kinship that are simultaneously in place. Kinship, notions of home, of belonging are at the center of the counterpoint that has characterized Haitian-Dominican relations.

The 1937 massacre is the paradigmatic moment of anti-Haitian violence cited by all academics, scholars, and political activists who study Haitian-Dominican relations on the island. *The Farming of Bones* suggests that, even in the massacre, *antihaitianismo* is not the only discourse that shaped notions of kinship, belonging, home, and solidarity among Haitians, Dominicans of Haitian descent, and Dominicans. Familial ties—whether by blood, interethnic marriage, or adoption—are realities that have created deep affective bonds among these populations in the past and the present.

Danticat's representation of those filial relations speaks to how Dominican youth of Haitian descent represent themselves as Dominicans and how other Dominicans support their struggles to assert their right to claim their Dominican nationality. Since 2010 every twelfth of the month, Dominicans of all backgrounds appear before the Presidential Palace to protest the frequent invalidation of identification documents of Dominicans of Haitian descent by the Junta Central Electoral. The slogan printed on T-shirts worn by members of the youth group reconoci.do tells us what we need to know about their sense of belonging to the Dominican Republic: "Yo soy de aquí" (I am from here). The land that received their parents or grandparents is the land that has nurtured them and their dreams. The T-shirt and the activism in support of reconoci.do speak to the possibility of an intercultural nationalism inclusive of the ethnic differences of national subjects.

Class, racial ideologies, and political interests shape kinship narratives. Sagás (2000) and Jarayam (2010) have explained that *antihaitianismo* does not target upper-class and middle-class Haitians in the Dominican Republic—such as investors, business people, students, or government officials—as it does poor and working Haitian migrants. Sagás correctly states that it is a discourse that, like anti-immigrant representations in the United States, seeks to divide working and poor people who in actuality share similar living conditions and demands for access to education, health care, land, and food. In *The Farming of Bones* class and race limit Amabelle's kinship ties with her adoptive sister, Valencia. But, as my analysis of narratives of Haitian-Dominican collaboration suggests, class-based concerns over land and labor rights for peasants and workers and intercultural efforts to valorize Haitian and Dominican cultural and spiritual heritages, including Afro- and indigenous based practices, also bring Haitian-Dominican communities together.

Now, in the early twenty-first century, organizations articulate ethnic, racial, and class-based kinship narratives among Haitians and Dominicans through their cultural, intellectual, and political work. Some examples are Guabancex, Kalalú Danza, and Batey Afro-Taíno, three groups that emphasize the indigenous and African legacies in the island; Centro Bonó's intercultural programs and its efforts to create better relations among Haitians, Dominicans, and Dominicans of Haitian descent; a variety of community organizations, including feminist and LGBT groups, that assert the human and civil rights of everyone regardless of their ethnic origin, gender, class, or sexual orientation; and cross-border efforts such as CONAMUCA, Vía Campesina and Veterinarios sin Fronteras (Veterinarians without Borders) that work in defense of the rights of laborers and agricultural workers. All of these projects sustain an *antillanista* and pan-American imagination of social struggles that can be traced back to Luperón's and Betances's transcolonial kinship narratives.

Moreover amicable relations between the Haitian and Dominican states are not new developments but rather characterize most of the island's history. If in the aftermath of the massacre both states colluded to ignore the violence enacted on poor Haitians and Dominicans, today both have failed to address the realities of thousands of migrants who remain undocumented in the Dominican Republic. The Ley General de Migración passed in 2004 has yet to be fully implemented. Thousands of Haitians who make it possible for the sugar industry to profit have changed the landscape of Santo Domingo. These migrants also provide all sorts of services in the informal economy, and then find themselves unable to regularize their status as migrants and workers. In old age, those who have contributed to the Dominican economy cannot claim the pensions that the government owes them. Their children born on the eastern side of the island cannot claim Dominican residency or citizenship.[21]

At the same time, during the presidential terms of Hipólito Mejía (2000–2004), Leonel Fernández-Reyna (1996–2000, 2004–12), and Danilo Medina (2012–present), a series of collaborative aid relief, environmental, and economic agreements have been reached between Haiti and the Dominican Republic, including the creation of a Comisión Mixta Bilateral. The commission's effectiveness is questionable, but it exists as an example of Haitian-Dominican state-sanctioned recognition of the shared interests of both nations.

Mejía posited the Dominican Republic as the bridge, the intermediary, between Haiti and international finance institutions (Dupuy 2014). The international response to the 2010 earthquake reflects the implementation of such plans. The headquarters of many aid agencies continue to be located in the Dominican Republic.[22] At the present moment the agencies continue to exert their influence on Haiti from the eastern side of the island. It still remains to be seen what the consequences will be for an even more impoverished and displaced Haitian population, and for Dominicans who, as of 2013, are facing higher consumer taxes, imports that threaten to displace a series of local agricultural products from the market, and ongoing restructuring adjustment programs. However, when examining such Haitian-Dominican collaborations as family relations, their internal power dynamics become evident. In this schema Haiti is *como de la familia* and still imagined as unfit to represent its own interests.

The trope *como de la familia* that appears in *Solo falta que llueva* and *The Farming of Bones* provides a lens through which to reexamine the variety of imaginings of Haitian-Dominican kinship and national kinship that permeate media, social justice organizing, and literature engaging cross-border relations on the island. Narratives of pacific invasion, acculturation, solidarity, and *interculturalidad* coexist in public discourse because Haitians, Dominicans, and Dominicans of Haitian descent constantly find themselves negotiating feelings of solidarity as well as suspicion in intimate, close quarters—whether in work spaces, familial or communal spaces, the market, government, or social justice organizing.

These novels complicate simplified narratives of Haitian-Dominican relations that ignore histories of kinship and solidarity among Dominicans, Haitians, and Dominicans of Haitian descent. Writing about *The Farming of Bones*, Donette Francis (1999) wonders if young Dominicans remember *el corte*—the massacre. The answer is yes, many do. They do in the continued struggles for human rights of Haitian migrants and reconoci.do's efforts to reclaim their documents as Dominican citizens of Haitian descent. Diasporic writers remember too. Along with other Caribbean diasporic writers, Danticat reexamines national and regional histories, where kinship ties and intimacy are reexamined through imaginative archives that tell untold stories, especially by women (Francis 2010).

During the past ten years cultural production on the island and by the diaspora has continued to offer new ways of thinking about Haitian-Dominican kinship. The pan-American circulation of media, films, and literature produced on the island and throughout colonial/imperial centers where Antilleans create new homes illustrates the varied character of narratives of Haitian-Dominican kinship. The 2012 film *El hoyo del diablo*, a horror flick directed by the Dominican Francis Disla on the island, depicts the granddaughter of a Dominican military general involved in the 1937 massacre. She is haunted by his spirit and the untold story of his participation. In March 2013, commemorating the 2010 earthquake in Haiti, the National Theater hosted a dance performance in solidarity with the continued efforts to rebuild Haiti. The film *Cristo Rey*, written and directed by the Dominican Leticia Tonos Paniagua and shown at the Toronto International Film Festival in September 2013, tells the love story of a Dominican woman and a young Dominican man of Haitian descent through a contemporary adaptation of *Romeo and Juliet*. Staying true to the Shakespearian tragedy, their love is rendered impossible when the male hero is assassinated by drug traffickers. The film publicly addresses the realities of Dominican-Haitian romantic and communal relationships and of undocumented Dominican youth of Haitian descent who find themselves at the mercy of police and migration officers.

Literature continues to engage the realities of Haitian-Dominican kinship, in particular the work of Dominican writers based in the United States. Angie Cruz's protagonists in *Let It Rain Coffee* (2005) are descendants of Chinese- and Haitian-Dominicans. The Colón family migrates to the United States, always aware of themselves as Dominicans of Chinese and Haitian descent (Chancy 2012). In the United States they create a family unit that includes a Salvadoran, Hush, and her baby, Consuelo, and they maintain their ties back on the island. Ana-Maurine Lara's *Erzulie's Skirt* (2006) narrates the love story between two Dominican women, one of Haitian descent. Their love enables them to build a family with their adoptive daughter, Yealidad. Together they survive economic hardship, xenophobia, and a tragic attempt to migrate to Puerto Rico by *yola*, a small boat, that leads to the death of their son. All these texts negotiate the representational challenge of addressing sameness and difference within pan-Antillean relations, without falling into the perils of discourses that devalue specific ethnic, racial, and national experiences. Romance, friendship, child rearing, and the creation of nonnormative families are tropes in these narratives that reimagine national and transnational kinship between Dominicans, Haitians, and Dominicans of Haitian descent. Imagining the intimacy of the household, these writers unravel racist, xenophobic, and heteropatriarchal ideas of marriage and family that have historically haunted both national and transcolonial kinship narratives. They illustrate the diversity of perspectives of Haitian-Dominican kinship that permeate Caribbean communities on the island and at home in colonial/imperial centers.

4 /   Family Secrets: Brotherhood, Passing, and the Dominican–Puerto Rican Family

In the nineteenth century secrecy was crucial for transcolonial conspiracies put forth by pro-independence revolutionaries seeking the constitution of an Antillean confederation (Arroyo 2013); it is also a crucial component in narratives of Dominican–Puerto Rican kinship. The metaphor of family secrets aptly describes how Dominican–Puerto Rican relations are formulated through cultural production. Representations of national and transcolonial/transnational families in Puerto Rico at times require a series of *secretos a voces*, secrets known but hidden in plain view. Whether Dominicans are seen as outsiders to the great Puerto Rican family or are imagined as integral components of Dominican–Puerto Rican extended families, secrets are what keep these transcolonial/transnational narratives of national kinship at play in Puerto Rican cultural practices.

Here I revisit an archive that, to some extent, has been previously analyzed by other scholars (Duany 2006; de Maeseneer 2002; Martínez–San Miguel 2003; Quintero Herencia 1996; Rosa Abreu 2002). In particular, following the analytical strategy deployed in the previous chapter, I build on Martínez–San Miguel's methodology to study how Puerto Ricans have imagined Dominican migrants and how Dominicans themselves have represented their experiences in Puerto Rico. Whereas Martínez–San Miguel seeks to understand how Cuban, Dominican, and Puerto Rican national and regional identities are transformed by migratory circuits in the Caribbean and New York City, by paying attention to metaphors and tropes of family secrets I explain the inverse feelings of empathy and rejection toward Dominicans that she documents in Puerto Rico. Pacini Hernández (2009) and Martínez–San Miguel have described Dominican–Puerto Rican relations as ambivalent. Cultural analysis suggests that a series of negations and secret complicities embedded in competing narratives of kinship between Dominicans and Puerto Ricans explains such ambivalence.

In this chapter I analyze the autobiography *Mona, canal de la muerte* (1995, Mona, Death Channel) by the Dominican Luis Freites, the iconic short story "Retrato del dominicano que pasó por puertorriqueño y emigró a mejor vida en Nueva York" (1995b, Portrait of the Dominican That Passed for Puerto Rican and Migrated to a Better Life in New York) by the Puerto Rican Magaly García Ramis, the television show *Entrando por la cocina* (1986–2002, Entering through the Kitchen), newspaper articles about Dominican migration, and ethnic/racial jokes about Dominicans in Puerto Rico. Each of these texts provides insight into the spoken and unspoken contours of kinship between Dominicans and Puerto Ricans. The autobiography and short story provide alternating views of brotherhood; the television show complicates these narratives of brotherhood by centering a female protagonist. The newspaper articles and jokes lay out the racial, class, and gender premises circumscribing narratives of national kinship and neoliberal transnational collaboration between Dominicans and Puerto Ricans.

Freites's autobiography provides a Dominican perspective on how kinship is built between Dominicans and Puerto Ricans on the island and the United States. The account suggests that transcolonial solidarity is possible only when these populations find each other as migrants in New York City. In this context brotherhood acts as a metaphor for Dominican–Puerto Rican relations.

García Ramis's short story allows the reader to experience the ambivalent nature of Puerto Rican relations on the island. It tells the story of a group of Puerto Rican males who help their Dominican friend to pass as one of their own so that he can migrate to New York. But the story reveals that the racial and ethnic marginalization of Dominicans is not limited simply to imagining Puerto Ricans as whiter, more educated, modern Antilleans. It suggests that Puerto Rican Afro-diasporic, male, heteronormative, and working-class aesthetics associated with rap and hip hop culture can also be deployed to marginalize Dominicans. The secret complicity constructed with the Puerto Rican guys comes at the expense of the Dominican Asdrúbal's own, ethnic-specific understanding and performance of blackness and masculinity.

The television comedy *Entrando por la cocina* complicates these previous narratives of male brotherhood by introducing a Dominican female character, Altagracia, to commercial Puerto Rican television. The show features a Dominican–Puerto Rican extended family and marriage that reveals its secrets and airs the dirty laundry of Dominican–Puerto Rican communities to a public that can identify with, or at least recognize, the show's interethnic working-class characters. The show's humor makes reference to Puerto Rican transnational/transcolonial, cross-cultural, working-class survival strategies.

To understand how Dominicans are excluded or incorporated into *la gran familia puertorriqueña*, it is necessary to engage the dual reality of Puerto Ricans as Antilleans as well as citizens of the United States. Migrating to Puerto Rico, Dominicans seek wages in U.S. dollars to send remittances home and hopefully acquire the documentation—U.S. residency or citizenship—that will allow them to travel freely between Puerto Rico and the Dominican Republic, and Puerto Rico and the U.S. mainland. Many hope to either migrate to the U.S. mainland or to benefit from the higher standard of living in Puerto Rico, while remaining in a geographical, cultural, and linguistic setting that is more familiar to them as people from the Caribbean (Duany 2011; Duany et al. 1995; Rey 1999–2000). Puerto Rico then becomes a bridge between the Dominican Republic and the United States and enables many Dominicans to sustain long-standing economic, familial, and cultural ties in all of these locations, what some have called the "transnational village" (Duany 2011; Levitt 2001). In this transnational village, Dominican migrants must negotiate Puerto Ricans' perceptions of them as blacker, underdeveloped, non-U.S.-born, Antillean neighbors (Duany 2011; Duany et a1. 1995; Martínez–San Miguel 2003; Reyes-Santos 2008).

Puerto Ricans: Antilleans and U.S. Citizens

Puerto Rico is an unincorporated territory of the United States. Its political status, since 1952, is as an *Estado Libre Asociado* (free associated state). Puerto Ricans are U.S. citizens and elect their own governor, legislature, and mayors. The island's laws are subject to veto by the U.S. Congress, and its commerce is controlled by the United States. Unlike U.S. states, Puerto Ricans on the island do not vote for the president and do not have voting representatives in Congress. As a political entity, the island represents the United States, though the state, administered by local politicians, claims to represent a national collective culturally defined as Puerto Rican, not American. I echo Jorge Duany's (2007: 52) analysis that there must be a necessary distinction between cultural and political nationalisms in order to understand Puerto Rican politics and notions of identity.

It is possible for these two forms of nationalism to be simultaneously operationalized, as has historically been the case in the Dominican Republic. But in the case of Puerto Rico, cultural nationalism does not imply political nationalism. For many Puerto Ricans, cultural nationalism has thrived, both on the island and in the U.S. Puerto Rican diaspora communities (Duany 2007; Flores 2009). This is regardless of voting patterns that speak to divided opinions on the nation's political status vis-à-vis the United States.[1]

Debates about the political status of the island have historically been informed by the implementation of an industrial economic development program, in place since the late 1940s, which sought to modernize and industrialize the island. This program, known as Manos a la Obra (Operation Bootstrap), provided incentives to U.S. corporations to invest in Puerto Rico, which included exemption of tax duties, government subsidies for infrastructure on the island, and reduced labor costs. Puerto Rico became a showcase and model of development for Third World elites and was promoted as a friendly alternative to the Soviet and Cuban models (Briggs 2002; Grosfoguel 2003: 57). Historians and economists have argued that Puerto Rico was the testing ground for the conditions that characterize late twentieth-century models of economic development throughout the globe: export-processing activities, U.S. hegemony, crippling of local agricultural and industrial projects, cuts in government spending, and the proletarianization of rural and female subjects (Briggs 2002: 195; Maldonado Denis 1976: 28; Ríos 1995: 142).

The recent migration of Dominicans to Puerto Rico is related to the implementation of similar economic policies in the Dominican Republic. Dominican migration to Puerto Rico and the U.S. mainland increased significantly after the 1961 assassination of Trujillo and the 1965 U.S. invasion of the Dominican Republic (Duany et a1. 1995; Martínez–San Miguel 2003: 152; Torres-Saillant and Hernández 1998).[2] The 1965 U.S. immigration law promoted the distribution of larger numbers of visas to Dominicans, who took advantage of the opportunity to migrate to the United States in significant numbers in order to escape unemployment or underemployment and political repression. Since the economic model supported by the United States and international aid agencies for Third World countries required political stability, researchers have suggested that the United States allowed the entrance of large numbers of

Dominicans so as to contain political dissidence (Torres-Saillant and Hernández 1998: 38–39).

The economic crisis and political repression associated with President Balaguer's implementation of International Monetary Fund and other financial restructuring policies between 1983 and 1996 served as a catalyst for undocumented migration from the Dominican labor sectors to Puerto Rico (Graziano 2013; Martínez–San Miguel 2003; Silié et al. 2002). The Dominican Republic's economic destitution, coupled with limited access to visas, increased undocumented maritime migration to Puerto Rico, across the Mona Channel that separates the two islands (Graziano 2013; Silié et al. 2002). A U.S. amnesty issued in 1986 allowed undocumented migrants in the country before 1982 to acquire legal documentation, including Dominican migrants (Duany et al. 1995; Martínez–San Miguel 2003). The implementation of neoliberal policies in the Dominican Republic since the 1970s has also propelled Dominican migrations to the U.S. mainland and Europe. In these cases Puerto Rico may sometimes serve as a stepping stone and safe haven on the journey to mainland dreams.

Since the 1970s there have been great transformations in the Puerto Rican economy. The elimination of tax exemptions, such as Sección 936 in 1996, impacted U.S. industries that profitted from them. The extension of the U.S. federal minimum wage to the island led to the flight of investment capital to other locations (Davis and Rivera-Batiz 2006: 290). As a result industries that were in Puerto Rico moved to other locations, such as the Dominican Republic and Central America, in order to employ cheaper labor. A trademark of neoliberal globalization, the privatization of public utilities, such as water, electricity, and the telephone company, and the accompanying reductions in government and the public welfare services have increased the cost of living on the island and have decreased the expendable income of the working and middle classes. In the 1980s and 1990s Puerto Rico's main employers were the multinational commerce and service sectors and, most extensively, the local government (see Ríos 1995). Now, in the early twenty-first century, hundreds of locally owned small businesses have suffered the onslaught of U.S. megastores (Walmart, Kmart, Home Depot, etc.) that have been established throughout the island. Downtowns that used to be commercially vibrant have become deserted. Between 2009 and 2010 more than ten thousand state employees found themselves unemployed. This was a result of two government actions: Governor Luis Fortuño declared a state of fiscal emergency through executive orders OE-2009-001 and

OE-2009-004, and Puerto Rican legislators passed Ley 7, approving a drastic reduction of government jobs.

The service sector on the island, as in the United States, has become a source of mostly part-time employment for an impoverished workforce that does not receive benefits such as health care. Puerto Rican economic and living conditions resemble those of poor communities on the U.S. mainland, with increasing unemployment and declining social security benefits and government subsidies for education, nutrition, and housing for low-income families (Fujiwara 2008). Many people are also working in the informal economies, where workers (known as *chiriperos*) do not appear in government statistics; they do not report their means or their earnings, though many do pay taxes (Duany et al. 1995). Dominicans in particular are often found on the streets, repairing cars, selling ice cream or home-made food, cleaning houses, in construction, and picking coffee beans. These are a few of many occupations devoid of social prestige and benefits such as pensions, health care, or retirement (Duany 2011: 207; Graziano 2013; Duany et al. 1995). For instance, most coffee plantations offer meager wages (US$100–150 per week) to Dominican migrants, many of whom risk deportation if they attempt to leave the plantation site (Graziano 2013: 93). Many Dominican migrants stay because, in spite of that risk, their earnings in U.S. dollars allow them to send remittances home.

Duany (2003: 6) has calculated that at the beginning of the twenty-first century there were between 90,000 and 120,000 Dominicans in Puerto Rico; they have become the largest migrant population on the island (Duany 2011). The president of the Comité Dominicano de los Derechos Humanos (Dominican Human Rights Committee) in Puerto Rico, José Rodriguez, stated in 2013 that the figure was as high as 400,000. It is estimated that at least half of the Dominican migrant population is undocumented.

Dominican migrants must incorporate themselves into a Puerto Rican economy where the working poor are constantly struggling to make ends meet. They must reconcile their everyday realities with the promises of the American Dream. As Dominicans and Puerto Ricans encounter each other in deteriorating socioeconomic circumstances, Puerto Ricans displace their own unsteady notions about blackness onto the recent arrivals. Dominicans in these instances are imagined as blacker than Puerto Ricans (Dinzey Flores 2013; Duany 2011; Martínez–San Miguel 2003; Rivero 2005).

Y tu abuela, ¿dónde está? Race, Nation, and the Secrets of the Great Puerto Rican Family

One of the secrets of the great Puerto Rican family is its own blackness. But it is a *secreto a voces*, known and celebrated through rap and *reggaetón* (Dinzey-Flores 2013; Domino Rudolph 2011) and *bomba* and *plena* performances. Despite being indexed in the realm of cultural expression, blackness is silenced in historical narratives and political, educational, and cultural policies (Dávila 1997; Godreau et al. 2008; Rodríguez-Silva 2012; Suárez Findlay 1999). It is hidden in family genealogies plagued by Spanish great-grandfathers and possibly a Taíno grandmother, and revealed again whenever Puerto Ricans ask one another, "Y tu abuela, ¿dónde está?" (And, your grandma, where is she?),[3] a prompt that asks interlocutors to recognize their black ancestors.

Discourses on *mestizaje* in Puerto Rico produce the whitening and blackening of the great Puerto Rican family. This family is discursively constituted by the romantic and sexual relations—coercive and consensual—between Spanish, Native, and African populations. *Blanqueamiento* (whitening) is possible "by marrying lighter-skinned individuals to gain social status and supposedly dilute, through mixture, the 'African blood' of the next generation" (Godreau et al. 2008: 117). Whitening is seen as a desirable process because it is an attempt to erase the social stigma associated with blackness: backwardness, uncleanliness, criminality, and a lack of intelligence (Godreau et al. 2008; Massó Vázquez 2013; Rivero 2005; Zenón Cruz 1975). At the same time, racism is not an issue that is widely discussed or publicly recognized on the island.

In Puerto Rico the lack of state-sponsored exclusionary policies based on race has permitted a limited recognition of African ancestry in narratives of the great Puerto Rican family, as much as it has informed a dominant narrative of racial democracy. The cultural imagination of *puertorriqueñidad* disseminated by the state-sponsored Instituto de Cultura Puertorriqueña (ICP; Institute of Puerto Rican Culture) historically consisted of the Hispanicization of the demographic and cultural components of the nation through *mestizaje*, which erases racial distinctions between the island's inhabitants. Arlene Dávila (1997: 71), in her anthropological study *Sponsored Identities: Cultural Politics in Puerto Rico*, highlights how in the history of the ICP the national subject has been the light-skinned Hispanic *jíbaro* from the mountains, marked with "a tinge of Indian heritage." Dávila argues that the standards imposed in the last decades of the twentieth century by the ICP to authenticate any cultural group reinforce Hispanicized notions of traditional Puerto Rican cultural practices, while limiting Afro–Puerto Rican practices to very specific zones, such as the town of Loíza and the coast. Black populations and *jíbaros* of the central mountain range (Godreau et al. 2008) are kept as secret members of the Puerto Rican family whose visibility would undo this whitened, spatial representation of the island. The other secret that holds together the metaphorical great Puerto Rican family is that class and space can not only whiten but also blacken Puerto Ricans.

In her sociological study "La gran familia puertorriqueña a 'ej prieta de beldá'" (The Grande Puerto Rican Family "Is Really Black"), Arlene Torres (1994: 289) argues that references to class are employed in Puerto Rico to euphemistically talk about race and, at the same time, deny racist practices: "The cultural mapping of the landscape in Puerto Rico is critical because it is racialized and class based." Torres explains how people from the capital, San Juan, are considered to be more educated than people from the rest of the island, and, in general, people from the interior are considered to be more educated than those from the coast. These regional distinctions are racialized: "'Jíbaros,' country peasants, reside in the rural areas, and darker-skinned people live on the coast" (295). Residential areas in particular towns follow a similar logic:

> Most Puerto Ricans, particularly those who do not reside in the area, believe that poor, dispossessed, and dark-skinned Puerto Ricans reside in *arrabales*, sectors of towns or villages with substandard housing, and in *caseríos*, public housing complexes. Puerto Ricans quickly associate the name of an *urbanización* [suburb] with the class status of the people who reside there. . . . The people there are not categorized as *gente negra*, black people. The residents of *urbanizaciones* are perceived to be socioeconomically better off, better educated, and *más culto* [more refined] than residents in *caseríos*. In fact, the working poor in the *urbanizaciones* are not always economically better off than those living in *caseríos*. However, their social status is higher precisely because they are located in a particular sociogeographical space. (296)

This *secreto a voces*—the association of socioeconomic standing with spatiality—shapes how Puerto Ricans imagine nationals in racialized terms. In spite of the continued affirmation of the three *raíces* (roots) of the Puerto Rican family, as well as the common praise of Puerto Rico's modernization and higher standard of living when compared to other

Caribbean territories, references to class status might be used to refer to the marginality of nationals and nonnationals in nonracial terms, while being a crucial aspect of the racialization process. Poverty becomes a racial marker of blackness. These class and racial dynamics are reproduced by the implementation of neoliberal policies.

For instance, Zaire Dinzey-Flores (2013: 147) argues that since the 1990s the neoliberal privatization of public housing complexes (*residenciales públicos*) and the never-ending spread of gated communities have furthered racial and class exclusions in Puerto Rico and limited the possibility of nonfamilial as well as cross-class kinship ties that tend to characterize cities. In other words, the myth of the Puerto Rican family united across class differences has been dismantled by the construction of residential spaces. Gates were built around public housing complexes, and the police proceeded to occupy them in a widely and dramatically publicized anticrime campaign called Mano Dura by the governor at the time, Pedro Roselló. In the meantime middle- and upper-class communities became gated communities that purported to keep residents safe from the *ola criminal* (criminal wave) by passing rules such as restricting who could walk on their streets. Residents of *caseríos* were then "locked in, locked out" to prevent the contamination of spaces imagined as whiter and wealthier. In this way poor and dark-skinned people in Puerto Rico are criminalized (Dinzey-Flores 2013: 153; Godreau 2008).

The *secreto a voces* that threatens the cohesion of the great Puerto Rican family also shapes public narratives of Dominican–Puerto Rican relations. Dominicans, regardless of skin color, are perceived as similar to dark-skinned Puerto Ricans and are "often seen as lawless and poor and contaminating the island" (Dinzey-Flores 2013: 138). Nonetheless neoliberal kinship narratives ignore these perceptions of Dominican migrants.

The Extended Families of Neoliberal Globalization

Transnational kinship narratives of Dominican–Puerto Rican relations are conveniently deployed in neoliberal free trade agreements and require that all participants collaborate in the U.S.-led war on drugs and war on terror. Puerto Rico's economic indicators—high debt rates, dependency on federal aid, and a failing service economy (Dinzey-Flores 2013: 22)—may suggest that the development model has not succeeded. Yet the modernization of Puerto Rico under U.S. rule turned the island into the international community's ideal model for CAFTA-DR, an agreement endorsed by the U.S. president George W. Bush on August

2, 2005. This modeling mirrors earlier moments in Puerto Rican history, such as the 1950s, when Puerto Ricans shared the bureaucratic and technological know-how of the United States with other Latin American nations and newly independent Caribbean nations through the Punto 4 program (Alvarez Curbelo and Rodríguez Castro 1993).[4] In the context of CAFTA, Puerto Rico was then positioned to be the emissary to the rest of the region, espousing U.S. free market rhetoric. Soon after CAFTA was approved by the U.S. Congress, Puerto Rico's governor Aníbal Acevedo Vilá went to the Dominican Republic to lobby for its acceptance. Costa Rica, Nicaragua, and the Dominican Republic were the only countries that had not yet signed (Hernández Cabiya 2005: 93). Puerto Rico's involvement in the negotiations could be read as an act of good faith. After all, CAFTA-DR, the war on drugs, and the war on terror appear to address urgent questions of economic development and public safety. Since the implementation of Department of Homeland Security protocols after the 2001 attack on the Twin Towers in New York City, the Puerto Rican government, the U.S. Coast Guard, and the Dominican Coast Guard have collaborated to police maritime transit through the Mona Channel under the rubric of the long-standing war on drugs and now the war on terror (Graziano 2013). These surveillance strategies that seek to deter drug traffickers and potential terrorists are a requirement of any commercial agreement between the United States and the Dominican Republic, as well as their intermediary, the Puerto Rican government.

And they are not the only contemporary projects that have envisioned Puerto Rico as an intermediary between its sibling, the Dominican Republic, and the imperial parental figure of the United States. For example, the late Puerto Rican political analyst Juan Manuel García Passalacqua (1993) imagined Puerto Rico as the mediator/interlocutor between the Caribbean and the United States while the region was being integrated into a globalized economy. According to him, a Puerto Rican Free Associated Republic sharing national defense with the United States, but autonomous in every other matter, would make possible his vision of Puerto Rico as the leader and spokesperson of the region: "Our long democratic and electoral tradition, our relatively developed infrastructure, and the advantages enjoyed as a result of a more vigorous economic growth, would turn the *Free Associated Republic of Puerto Rico* into the region's center of gravity " (135). Moreover, since the 1990s the government of the island has fostered commercial ties with its neighbor. This has led to an increase in daily ferry trips between the two territories.

Every year hundreds of Puerto Ricans take advantage of the financial differentials enabled by neoliberal globalization, which has increased the possibility of owning property and time shares in tourist towns such as Punta Cana, and of travel to visit the Dominican Republic's renowned all-inclusive tourist resorts.

However, these circumstances rely on downplaying the fact of Puerto Ricans' U.S. citizenship and the fact that Puerto Ricans are in a slightly privileged position in any agreement with the Dominican Republic. Unlike most Dominicans, Puerto Ricans can travel to the United States without a visa and to the Dominican Republic with a tourist visa easily purchased at the airport for US$10. Moreover the U.S. Department of Homeland Security and Puerto Rican law enforcement agencies criminalize undocumented Dominican migrants as potential drug traffickers and terrorists (Graziano 2013). This is one of the *secreto a voces* of neoliberalism. Another is that Puerto Ricans—through political, economic, social, and cultural practices that identify the island as a modern, developed, industrial, consumer society—are whitened compared with other Antilleans by their U.S. citizenship. These are the secrets that hamper the imagination of an extended Dominican–Puerto Rican family within neoliberalism and naturalize the exploitation of undocumented Dominican workers who often, especially in the construction sector, are not paid their earned wages. These same secrets underscore the racial discrimination and criminalization of Dominicans living in a deteriorating neoliberal Puerto Rican economy (Graziano 2013).

National Kinship: Migrants and Criminals

If Dominicans are understood to be criminals, then any ethical concern for their well-being is overridden by media concerns with public safety.[5] Representations of the population as undocumented migrants, invaders, and poor people ignore that middle- and upper-class Puerto Ricans profit from the fact that Dominicans, specifically undocumented migrants, tend to be paid less than Puerto Ricans, and as laborers in the informal economy they do not receive social security, health care, and other related benefits (Graziano 2013; Nina-Estrella forthcoming). They also provide services for Puerto Rican working and middle classes, business owners, or consumers who are also trying to survive the onslaught of neoliberalization and the failure of development.

A quick overview of the newspaper *El Mundo* at the Lázaro library at University of Puerto Rico, Río Piedras, provides insight into the public representation of poor Dominicans as criminals who cannot be fully integrated into the Puerto Rican family. Articles published during the 1960s, 1970s, and 1980s defend the legal rights of these migrants and support their claims for political asylum. This is evidenced in articles such as Germán E. Ornes's "Espera decisión de Washington sea inicio de nuevo trato para exiliados dominicanos" (It is hoped that Washington's decision will result in better treatment for exiled Dominicans; 1961); Bienvenido Ortiz Otero's "Decreta libertad 5 dominicanos entraron ilegalmente a la Isla" (Freedom granted to five Dominicans who entered the island illegally; 1978); Fidel Rodríguez Alicea's "Indocumentados huyen de gobierno de Balaguer" (Undocumented flee Balaguer's regime; 1986); and "Dominicanos en Puerto Rico viajan a votar" (Dominicans in Puerto Rico travel to vote; 1986). These articles collectively show sympathy for and solidarity with Dominicans and recognize their ties to their homeland.

In the 1980s, when neoliberal policies were consolidated in Puerto Rico and the Dominican Republic, representations of Dominican migrants as invaders increased. As Yeidi M. Rivero (2005), Duany (1990), and Martínez–San Miguel (2003) suggest, between the 1980s and 1990s Dominicans became "the new limit against which the most recent coordinates of Puerto Ricans' cultural and racial identity were negotiated" (Martínez–San Miguel 2003: 154). On January 3, 1987, the newspaper *Nuevo Amanecer*, under the sensationalist headline "Dominicanos invaden a Puerto Rico" (Dominicans invade Puerto Rico), reported that between 1982 and 1985 undocumented migration by boat from the Dominican Republic had increased 400 to 500 percent. The article compares Dominican migration to Puerto Rico and Haitian migration to Florida, affirming that the former is a more significant situation and therefore must be treated as an urgent matter. According to the author, Dominicans integrate easily into Puerto Rican society and are always willing to accept the jobs rejected by Puerto Ricans; they do janitorial work and domestic tasks and frequently act as strikebreakers in factories. Even then the article surmises that many Dominicans cannot find work and are forced to become purse stealers, thieves, and prostitutes, increasing the already high index of criminality on the island.

Dominicans are perceived as hard-working people willing to take the worst jobs in order to integrate themselves into Puerto Rican society. However, their willingness to work less well-remunerated jobs also marks them as rivals of Puerto Rican workers. Those who cannot be absorbed by the local economy are imagined as criminals who contribute to the criminalized landscape of the nation. Their criminalization is gendered.

The article suggests that men commit petty crimes and women engage in sex work, which in turn worsens an existing problem of criminality in the island. Simultaneous representations of Dominicans as hard workers, strike breakers, and criminals exemplify the ambiguity embedded in popular and media representations. As Martínez–San Miguel (2003) eloquently explains, feelings of sympathy and hostility toward Dominicans coexist in a national landscape. Those ambivalent attitudes (Pacini Hernández 2009) characterize Dominican–Puerto Rican interethnic relations in the context of a shrinking labor market and the criminalization of poverty on the island.

This ambivalence is grounded in narratives of national kinship of the great Puerto Rican family that exclude Dominicans as poor, criminalized, racialized migrants. But these narratives originally targeted poor Puerto Ricans. The racialization and criminalization of poor, black-identified communities in Puerto Rico informs discourses on Dominican migrants. For instance, the article "Arrestan a 60 indocumentados" (Sixty undocumented [people] were arrested) provided by the Agencia EFE to *El Mundo* (March 11, 1988) describes how state agencies undertook an operation in "the state's housing projects in San Juan and other places of high criminal activity" in order to capture undocumented migrants. Most of those arrested were of Dominican descent. It is significant that the article criminalizes the places where the migrants were found. As Dinzey-Flores (2013) and Torres (1998) argue, the criminalization of public housing projects is informed by a racialized understanding of their inhabitants.

The graphic image accompanying the article clearly racializes the bodies of Dominican migrants by caricaturizing them. The caricature wrongly imagines that most migrants are male; it includes only one woman in a group of five migrants. In contrast a 1987 survey showed that three out of five Dominicans living in Santurce, a prominent Dominican community in San Juan, were women. A 2009 Puerto Rico Community Survey documented that 55.3 percent of Dominicans on the island are women (Duany 2011; also see Angueira 1990). The caricature also refers to common media coverage that depicts men in public housing projects engaged in criminal activities, often drug-related. The Dominican finds himself or herself racialized by criminalization as an undocumented migrant as well as in relation to the racialization of the impoverished Puerto Rican communities receiving him or her. A 2011 report by the U.S. Department of Justice, as well as a 2010–11 Amnesty International report, noted that Dominicans and Puerto Ricans of Dominican descent are systematically discriminated against by the Puerto Rican police. The police frequently profile these populations and subject them to racist and xenophobic comments and even physical violence and mistreatment. In 2010 a petition was presented at the Human Rights Commission of the Organization of American States to investigate the continued police harassment of a Dominican community in the town of Toa Baja, Puerto Rico (U.S. Department of Justice 2011).

One of the family secrets unraveled by Freites, García Ramis, and the TV show *Entrando por la cocina* is how the shared racialization and criminalization of poor Puerto Ricans and Dominicans produces a complicity fraught with tension, what Ramón López calls an "intervened solidarity" (cited in Martínez–San Miguel 2003: 114; 1998: 151). This complicity enables Dominican–Puerto Rican kinship—extended families not necessarily sanctioned by, and even working against, the neoliberal transnational logic of the state. But it is a complicity interrupted by the racist and xenophobic logic of the ethnic jokes that are constantly articulated on the island. These jokes distinguish Puerto Ricans from their presumably backward, less intelligent Dominican siblings.

Secreto a voces: Dominican–Puerto Rican Complicity and the Ethnic Joke

> *Why do Dominicans place a quarter on their ears?*
> *To listen to Fifty Cents.*
> *Why do they do the same with a ketchup bottle?*
> *To listen to salsa.*
> *Why do they put the computer by the window?*
> *To search for Windows.*
> HEARD IN CIDRA, PUERTO RICO, DECEMBER 24, 2004

Among Puerto Ricans, humor—most explicitly, ethnic jokes—acts as a discursive site for communities to negotiate their tense, complex, relationships with Dominican migrants. Ethnic jokes construct a border between Dominicans and Puerto Ricans that is clearly hostile, articulates a vulnerable Puerto Rican sense of superiority over Dominicans, and attempts to signal who belongs to the Puerto Rican family and who does not (Martínez–San Miguel 2003; Quintero Herencia 1996). The jokes cited above, which I overheard at a family Christmas gathering, serve as an example of the common tropes found in representations of Dominicans. They were elaborated in a competition between cousins and uncles, in which the goal was to come up with the best jokes about Dominicans as poorer, less educated, less developed, and consequently blacker than Puerto Ricans. This competition, taking place in a small mountain town, among all Puerto Rican family members, is not extraordinary but part of the fabric of everyday interactions between Puerto Ricans, constructing a Puerto Rican community by sharing anti-Dominican sentiments (Martínez–San Miguel 2003: 153).

To belong to a Puerto Rican community requires being willing to temporarily forget, ignore, hide—in other words, to keep as a secret—friends, neighbors, and relatives of Dominican descent or one's own Dominican ancestry. At that same Christmas gathering were people who, in a different context, fondly talked about their Dominican best friend or cousin. Besides the *secreto a voces* of its blackness and class conflict, the great Puerto Rican family keeps its members of Dominican descent near yet outside itself, through the vehicle of the ethnic joke. Belonging to a dominant, mainstream Puerto Rican community requires sharing the laughter of the ethnic joke. And, as Martínez–San Miguel (2003: 157) points out, laughter is not a light matter; rather it manifests the ways Puerto Ricans rethink their understanding of who they are as people, and their national identity, through their engagement with Dominican migrants and their cultural practices.

Ethnic jokes about Dominicans circulate widely through social interactions in family gatherings, schools, work spaces, and public spaces and through popular culture on the island. They reiterate representations of Dominicans in terms of poverty and a lack of education and technological knowledge (Martínez–San Miguel 2003; Quintero Herencia 1996), though their humoristic structure opens the possibility of showing sympathy for the migrant. The joke that introduces this section illustrates one of the most common structures of ethnic jokes. The question-and-answer structure prompts tentative responses from an audience that keeps reproducing the classed assumptions behind the ethnic joke. The Dominican is imagined as a subject who, unlike Puerto Ricans, does not understand technological artifacts or lacks the ability to think like most people. It exaggerates differences between Dominicans and Puerto Ricans as people who, sharing the same urban spaces in San Juan, cannot be easily differentiated from one another (Martínez–San Miguel 2003: 156). Moreover these jokes trivialize Puerto Ricans' national identity by equating it with the island's consumer culture.

Puerto Ricans in the United States also assert their belonging to a Puerto Rican community by articulating anti-Dominican ideas through the ethnic joke. This is important for a community whose

puertorriqueñidad is constantly questioned by Puerto Rican government agencies and traditionalist sectors that represent island-based
Puerto Ricans as more authentic than those on the mainland (Duany
2002; Flores 2009). Puerto Rican transnational communities are articulated through the Internet, where ethnic jokes about Dominicans appeal
to geographically dispersed audiences. For instance, the email "Teléfono
dominicano con cámara" (Dominican phone with camera) sent to Puerto
Ricans located on the island and in the United States in 2004, reads:

> TELEFONO CON CAMARA INTEGRADA
> OHPEROBUENO EISTE MODELO ESTA EN ESPECIAI POR
> LA MODDICA SUMA DE TRES PESO CON CUATTRO CEINTA-
> VOS DOMINICAINOS . . . NO DEJE PASAI ESTA OFERTA TU.

> TELEPHONE WITH INTEGRATED CAMERA.
> OH WELL, YOU KNOW. THIS MODEL IS A DEAL FOR
> THE SMALL AMOUNT OF THREE DOMINICAN PESOS AND
> FOUR CENTS. DON'T LET THIS OFFER GO BY, YOU.[6]

The misspelling of words, a subverted syntactical structure, the addition
of *i*'s to various words, and the use of the phrase "oh pero bueno" without spaces between words reflect stereotypical portrayals of Dominicans
as uneducated and common parodic exaggerations of Dominican eth-
nolinguistic attributes. The price of the phone, 3.04 Dominican pesos,
further insinuates Dominicans' poverty.

The accompanying photograph of the Dominican camera–cell phone
shows a landline phone with a 35mm camera duct-taped to the talking piece.
The visual image signals mainstream conceptualizations of the Dominican
Republic, and therefore Dominicans, as underdeveloped. One could read a
certain sense of ingenuity in the creation of a Dominican camera-phone,
though the parody of Dominican speech (and illiteracy) places the expected
Puerto Rican reader in a superior position. The ethnic joke works under the
assumption that the economic limitations that would motivate Dominicans to undertake such makeshift projects are not experienced by Puerto
Ricans. It exaggerates economic differences between both populations.
Puerto Ricans' U.S. citizenship is imagined as a guarantee of their ability
to consume modern products. The ethnic joke asserts representations of the
nation that imagine Puerto Rico as more developed than other Caribbean
territories due to its political relationship with the United States.

It would be incorrect, however, to assume that the prejudices and
assumptions that form the basis of this kind of humor always preclude

expressions of solidarity. As the joke competition wound down, some of the same people who just minutes before had been making jokes affirmed their friendship with Dominican coworkers, neighbors, and family. Others demonstrated their empathy for the economic circumstances that underlie Dominican migration, in particular the crossing of the dangerous maritime passage, el Canal de la Mona, which separates the two islands. Others drew parallels between their own experience of migration to the United States and those of Dominican migrants to Puerto Rico. Puerto Ricans who have migrated are aware of the fact that the same or similar jokes are said about Puerto Ricans in the United States and about other low-income migrants throughout the world. Dominicans, in this sense, are understood as Antillean relatives who share histories of migration, a cultural heritage, and communal spaces with Puerto Ricans.

These interpersonal and cybernetic interactions reveal one of the secrets of the Dominican–Puerto Rican family: that many Puerto Ricans know in their flesh the kind of poverty and marginalization ascribed to Dominicans through ethnic jokes and recognize the racism and xenophobia behind them. As I discovered trying to track down who had sent me this email from the island, the violence exerted by the joke was recognized, even if quietly, by other Puerto Ricans. In response to my query, I received two emails claiming that I was racist for even mentioning the email, which we had all received simultaneously. And I never received anything like it ever again. It became clear very quickly that I had broken an implicit understanding among my Puerto Rican peers that allowed us to participate in a racist and xenophobic email exchange as long as it went unrecognized. I had not participated in the usual "silencing of race" (Rodríguez 2013). These interactions also suggest that Puerto Ricans of Dominican descent at times must keep their Dominican ancestry as a *secreto* and silence themselves as their Puerto Rican counterparts use humor that excludes them and their parents from the Puerto Rican national family. This awareness points to the narratives of Dominican–Puerto Rican complicity that follow.

The Secrets of the Dominican–Puerto Rican Family

So far this chapter has provided some examples of how national and transnational kinship narratives between Dominicans and Puerto Ricans emerge in the public sphere in Puerto Rico. The review of newspaper articles and ethnic jokes gives us a glimpse into the *secretos a voces* embedded in the metaphor of the great Puerto Rican family. These *secretos* underlie the affective ties between national subjects, as well as in transnational projects that characterize Dominican–Puerto Rican relations in a neoliberal Caribbean: CAFTA-DR, the war on drugs, and the war on terror. The *secretos* of Puerto Ricans' blackness and poverty—and of Dominicans' experience of racist, xenophobic, and economic violence—are made evident and require that we interrogate simplified narratives of a cohesive national family and Dominican–Puerto Rican collaboration.

The interplay between national and transcolonial/transnational kinship narratives in literature and on television impacts how working-class Dominicans and Puerto Ricans appear to be in secret complicity with one another. The ambivalence that, other scholars argue (Pacini-Hernández 2009; Martínez-San Miguel 2003), characterizes Dominican–Puerto Rican relations is grounded in these constantly competing and co-constitutive narratives. What *Mona, canal de la muerte,* "Retrato del dominicano que pasó por puertorriqueño," and *Entrando por la cocina* unravel is that, in spite of the racial and xenophobic violence of anti-Dominican expressions such as the ethnic joke, Dominican–Puerto Rican solidarity is often an act of transcolonial mutual recognition between racialized and criminalized working peoples on the island. In the texts discussed here, at times such solidarity requires complicity in interethnic efforts that challenge U.S. immigration policies, such as the *matrimonio de conveniencia* that helps a Puerto Rican get U.S. citizenship for a Dominican or when Dominicans pass for Puerto Rican with fake or purchased documents, often with the help of friends willing to teach them how to perform *puertorriqueñidad.* At other times it is a quotidian complicity represented by chosen extended families that emerges in everyday efforts to make ends meet.

Brotherhood, marriage, and family appear once again, as they have throughout the texts analyzed in this book, as metaphors that describe affective ties between Antilleans. And in every instance secrets must be kept. Sometimes those secrets sustain both Dominicans and Puerto Ricans—and their interethnic families and communities—in the face of racial, class, gender, and state violence. Often the family's *secreto a voces* is the marginality of the Dominican in relationship to his or her Puerto Rican *pana* (friend), romantic partner, or neighbor. All those family secrets enable working-class Dominicans and Puerto Ricans to negotiate their survival in a neoliberal economy that continues to fail on its promises of U.S. capitalist development.

Mona, canal de la muerte: Brotherhood on the Island and New York City

With his autobiography *Mona, canal de la muerte* (1995), Luis Freites joined other Dominican authors in Puerto Rico, the Dominican Republic, and the U.S. mainland who have articulated a vision of Dominican–Puerto Rican relations shaped by their shared migratory experiences. The critical texts, *Mirada en tránsito* (1999) by Eugenio García Cuevas and *Puerto Rico y Santo Domingo también son* (1999) by Miguel Angel Fornerín, document points of contact between Puerto Rico and the Dominican Republic in terms of their history, culture, social dynamics, and population movements.[7] Cuevas discusses the violence of the ethnic joke, as well as instances of solidarity between Dominicans and Puerto Ricans sharing communal spaces in San Juan. Fornerín recognizes the ties existing between Dominican and Puerto Rican literary traditions and represents himself as someone who inhabits and celebrates both cultural spaces (Martínez–San Miguel 2003: 194).

The Dominican novels *Marina de la Cruz* (1994) by Félix Darío Mendoza, *Viajes suicidas* (1996) by José Francisco Cheas, and *Mar de sangre* (1996) by Elba Domenech Soto explicitly describe terrifying maritime migration attempts and tend to be based on facts or someone's real-life experience (Torres-Saillant et al. 2004: 27–28).[8] *Puerto Rico: Una ruta incierta al norte, la travesía en yola* (1993) by Raúl Martínez Rosario is another autobiography. Like *Mona, canal de la muerte,* it tells the story of a Dominican man who travels to Puerto Rico by *yola*, lives in the metropolitan area, and finds a way to migrate to the U.S. mainland. Eventually, like Freites, he returns to the Dominican Republic. Together these authors are concerned with the kinship ties that are broken or created between Dominicans, and Dominicans and Puerto Ricans, brought together by migration.

Mona, canal de la muerte is a remarkable example because it illustrates some of the secrets that make Dominican–Puerto Rican solidarity (im)possible. The narrative is organized in three sections: the first describes how people migrate from coastal towns in the Dominican Republic to Puerto Rico; the second tells the experience of the narrator in Puerto Rico; the third concentrates on his stay in New York and final return to the Dominican Republic. Freites's first-person construction of a migrant subjectivity highlights the violence the narrator is subjected to as an undocumented worker. His personal experience is meant to speak to a Latin American audience, but especially a Dominican one. The narrator places his own personal story alongside anecdotes about other Dominicans who have attempted to migrate or have migrated to Puerto Rico. He provides extensive evidence as justification for his eventual return to the Dominican Republic, arguing that what he and other migrants suffer is not worth leaving their country of origin.

The narrator's point of entrance in Puerto Rico enables him to quickly learn one of the secrets that sustains the national family: the common practice of offering an underpaid job, devoid of social prestige and benefits, to an undocumented migrant. This secret allows Puerto Ricans to reduce their living and business expenses at the expense of Dominican migrants. In Barrio Obrero, Puerto Rico, the narrator enters the workforce as the janitor at a local bar. He writes, "Someone had to do this work and the most appropriate person was someone who needed to work, who did not have any other possibilities, like an undocumented foreigner" (Freites 1995: 46). At first he is grateful to have a job, and he presumes solidarity with his Puerto Rican employer. Eventually, though, he realizes that his salary covers only rent and food, condemning him to live "in misery and poverty" (46). While his employer takes advantage of his condition as an undocumented migrant, the police are a constant threat to his stay in Puerto Rico; to avoid deportation, he has to hide whenever they come to the bar. Eventually he decides to leave his job and has to accept that his supervisor will not pay him for his last week of work. As the Comité Dominicano de Derechos Humanos and Frank Graziano (2013) have documented, these experiences are representative of what many undocumented migrants live through. Because the narrator is a migrant, he is criminalized, which renders him a nonsubject within the scope of civil law in Puerto Rico. This criminalization extends into the realm of labor, at work and at home, and limits any potential solidarity between the narrator and the Puerto Ricans he encounters. Under these conditions marriage, brotherhood, and an extended family with Puerto Ricans is possible only when he migrates to New York.

Luckily, marrying a Dominican woman in Puerto Rico eventually enables him to acquire U.S. citizenship and migrate to New York. He falls in love with Stefanía, who had obtained her legal documents to stay in Puerto Rico by paying a Puerto Rican man to marry her.[9] Stefanía's secret indirectly enables the narrator to pursue the American Dream in New York, along with Puerto Ricans. After marrying his beloved Stefanía, he acquires the legal documentation needed to apply to better jobs and stop hiding from the police. But he soon realizes that in Puerto Rico his documented status does not bring him better economic opportunities. Though he has gained legal entry into the Puerto Rican family, he has not been accepted as someone with the same rights and skills as Puerto Ricans. His experience is not exceptional. The project Voces con Eco has documented that anti-Dominican discrimination prevails in working-class, urban, Dominican–Puerto Rican communities in San Juan (Nina-Estrella forthcoming). It includes interviews with fifteen Puerto Ricans and two Dominican community leaders. Their answers, as well as Ruth Nina-Estrella's discussion of what interviewers encountered through the project, confirm that the narrator's experiences mirror how other Dominicans continue to face discrimination and mistreatment every day. The racist, xenophobic, and classist narratives that describe Dominicans as invaders, criminals, unskilled, dirty, and poorer than, blacker than, and not as smart or modern as locals naturalize his exploitation and discrimination as an outsider to the Puerto Rican family. The great Puerto Rican family pushes him out of its limits until he decides to move to New York with Stefanía. He hopes to find better opportunities there.

What he finds in New York are not necessarily better working conditions but rather a transcolonial community of African Americans and Latin Americans, including Puerto Ricans, tied by a shared experience of racism and labor exploitation. If in Puerto Rico he remains an outsider to the Puerto Rican national family, in New York City he lives on the margins of a U.S. society that profits from the labor of racial minorities and migrants (Grosfoguel 2003). The American Dream is unraveled by its well-known, yet hidden, secrets: non-Anglo Americans, including U.S. citizens and documented and undocumented migrants, are often faced with insurmountable obstacles to its realization.

In New York City the narrator finds himself once again in the less well-remunerated service sector of the economy, as many Dominicans have before him (Duany 2011; Hernández 2002). He can find only janitorial work, therefore joining the same economic sector he inhabited in Puerto Rico. At first it seems ideal because he does not need to communicate in English to work. However, the racist violence he experiences in the work space colors his everyday life: "My immediate supervisor was happy screaming at his subordinates, including myself. This man felt pleasure in humiliating the workers, especially blacks and Latin Americans, screaming at us and calling us names charged with racism" (Freites 1995: 72). The work space becomes a site where different Latin Americans interact with each other and with the local African American population. As a result of their shared experiences, they develop solidarity bonds with one another. These are the sites from which transcolonial/ transnational cultural production emerges.

Rap and hip hop came out of the encounter between African Americans, Puerto Ricans, Dominicans, and Jamaicans (Flores 2000; Rivera 2009). *Reggaetón*, identified mostly as Puerto Rican, has been transformed by encounters between Dominicans and Puerto Ricans both in the United States and on the island (Pacini-Hernández 2010). All of these Afro-diasporic musical forms have been a manifestation of shared experiences, exchanges, and solidarities among mostly working-class communities and residents of public housing projects on the island and the mainland—all who must endure the burden of racism and criminalization. The narrator's solidarity mirrors these transcolonial/transnational processes of encounter, cultural exchanges, and mutual recognition. Dominican migrants find themselves at home and in community and, in this case, develop a sense of transcolonial brotherhood with fellow minorities in the United States. There they share a process of racialization through their participation in the lower strata of U.S. socioeconomic hierarchies.

The narrator's extended Dominican–Puerto Rican family is a response to the interethnic experiences arising out of U.S. racism and economic hardship. He becomes the close friend of a Puerto Rican, Joel, and his family. In New York both "were foreigners. He, despite his North American citizenship, suffered the same disdain directed toward Latin Americans" (Freites 1995: 78). When Joel's son is wrongfully charged by the police and ends up in prison, the narrator accompanies his friend through the pain of losing his son to a criminal justice system that targets poor, urban, African American, and Latino populations (Davis 2005). Though Puerto Ricans are born U.S. citizens, the narrator concludes that they, like him, are racialized and treated like foreigners. Of course his status as a documented migrant generates parallels to the experiences of Puerto Ricans and African Americans, differently than was the case when he was undocumented and subject to potential deportation.

Once the dirty little secrets of a capitalist neoliberal U.S. society and, by extension, Puerto Rican society are revealed, the narrator loses hope of achieving the American Dream. Exclusionary anti-Dominican ideas of national kinship limit his economic and social possibilities in Puerto Rico, as he simultaneously experiences mistreatment and exploitation by Puerto Ricans. U.S. racism appears to condemn him to a life of constant struggle and humiliations. The anecdote about Joel's son and his imprisonment exemplifies for the narrator an intergenerational experience of racist, xenophobic, and economic violence. Both scenarios render migrants and their children as outsiders of the Puerto Rican national family and the U.S. melting pot, in contrast to the myths that allegedly create a unified national community out of many different people.

Fifteen years after their arrival in the United States, the narrator and Stefanía decide to return to the Dominican Republic. In the end, "the golden dream of migration through the Mona Channel" (96) remains unaccomplished. Only his experience of transcolonial brotherhood remains as a positive memory and experience of belonging, home, and kinship with Puerto Rican men. It is this brotherhood that motivates him to speak to other Latin American migrants, not only Dominicans, about his dangerous and dire experiences of migration to Puerto Rico and the U.S. mainland. He renames the Mona Channel the "Death Channel" as a way to deter others from going through a maritime passage that takes its survivors to a place where, as the short story "Retrato del dominicano" also suggests, they will be marginalized as foreigners and Dominicans.

"Retrato del dominicano": Brotherhood and Passing

In both *Mona, canal de la muerte* and "Retrato del dominicano," written by the Puerto Rican Magaly García Ramis (1995b), transcolonial brotherhood requires complicity between Dominicans and Puerto Ricans. While Joel and the narrator of *Mona, canal de la muerte* are in solidarity with one another in the face of U.S. racism, the act of passing for Puerto Rican requires the Dominican Asdrúbal to trust his islander Puerto Rican friends, or *panas* (bros), in "Retrato del dominicano." This complicity is also represented in other Puerto Rican literary texts about Dominican migration, such as the play *Indocumentados: El otro merengue* (1989) by José Luis Ramos Escobar and, more recently, the novel *Cualquier miércoles soy tuya* (2004) by Mayra Santos-Febres. In *Indocumentados* the Dominican Gregorio passes for a Puerto Rican by buying documents from a Puerto Rican woman whose son has died. He becomes Luis Jiménez. In *Cualquier miécoles soy tuya*, Tadeo, a Dominican of Haitian descent, is unwillingly embedded in a complicated web that involves Puerto Rican drug dealers, corrupt government officials, and a Puerto Rican journalist, friend, and coworker at a motel. Blackmailed to help a drug ring and their accomplices in government, and in desperate need to sustain his elderly mother back in the Dominican Republic, undocumented Tadeo tries to pass for Puerto Rican in a flight to Miami. In both cases the Dominicans pay a high price for their secret, illegal incorporation into a Puerto Rican community. Jiménez

(Gregorio), must join Puerto Ricans as they crack jokes about Dominicans in order to authenticate his performance of *puertorriqueñidad*, losing his connection to his real identity, his community, and eventually his life (Martínez–San Miguel 2001: 103). Tadeo ends up in a federal prison and can no longer help his mother. As soon as he is released, he will be deported.[10]

In "Retrato del dominicano," the Dominican protagonist Asdrúbal also loses, or at least must pretend to lose, aspects of his identity by adopting his Puerto Rican friends' postures and attitudes. He must effectively perform the narrative of belonging to the Puerto Rican nation in order to migrate to New York City. Transcolonial brotherhood here is only possible because of Asdrúbal's performance of a *puertorriqueñidad* that allows his Puerto Rican friends, and airport officers, to read him as kin. The story situates Asdrúbal in Santurce, a Dominican enclave in San Juan. He plans to migrate to New York without legal documentation. His Puerto Rican friends—the "muchachos" (guys) of the neighborhood's high school—teach him how to pass as a Puerto Rican at the airport. They also help him obtain false identification and the right attire, which they believe will allow him to deceive the immigration officer. The story ends when the Puerto Ricans snap a photograph of Asdrúbal, just after the airport immigration officer allows him to continue to the plane. While illustrating how the secret of passing requires Asdrúbal to painfully shed cultural markers of his *dominicanidad*, the short story undermines narratives that portray the Puerto Rican family as whiter, demonstrating the exaggerated racial and economic differences between Dominicans and Puerto Ricans.

Martínez–San Miguel (2003: 173) writes that "this short story could have a double reading: one that explores and reconstructs a Puerto Rican national identity in contradistinction to a Dominican one, and another that problematizes the utopia of the profound Caribbean solidarity invoked by the text." The story speaks to this ambivalence—the simultaneous feelings of sympathy and hostility—that characterize Puerto Rican representations of Dominicans through the ethnic joke, literature, and discussions about the origins and production of *reggaetón* (Martínez–San Miguel 2003; Pacini-Hernández 2009; Reyes-Santos 2008). If one follows the logic of the ethnic joke, the idea of a Dominican passing for Puerto Rican seems almost impossible. The ethnic joke imagines Dominicans representing everything Puerto Ricans are not: underdeveloped, poor, and ignorant. As a consequence the picaresque-like (de Maeseneer 2002) phrase "Retrato del dominicano que pasó por puertorriqueño" could be read as a function of the absurdity of such an idea and the consequent laughter produced by its impossibility. However, the phrase might also highlight the incredible amount of skill and guile an individual requires to successfully perform the deception. An audience familiar with the ethnic joke may read the title in both these ways, engaging in the usual mockery of the migrant, while recognizing his or her resourcefulness.

This potential double reading is informed by the Puerto Rican characters' affirmation of an Afro-diasporic, working-class, masculine, urban national identity that can accommodate, though imperfectly, transcolonial brotherly ties with Dominicans. If we understand Asdrúbal to be subjected to the violent mockery of the Puerto Ricans for his Dominican ethnic specificity, it is not because of an idea of national kinship that silences, rejects, or tries to whiten Puerto Ricans' blackness. In this case the Puerto Rican *panas* mock Asdrúbal's specifically Dominican embodiment of blackness and masculinity. Their sense of belonging to a Puerto Rican national family is marked by their embodiment of transnational/transcolonial Afro-diasporic cultural practices, such as hip hop, circulated by Puerto Ricans in their back-and-forth movement between the island and the mainland. Here a hegemonic notion of black, working-class manhood in Puerto Rico intervenes in Puerto Rican–Dominican complicity and solidarity.

As Martínez-San Miguel (2003: 173) asserts, the story seems to be a recipe for how to become Puerto Rican—not a whitened Puerto Rican, but definitely a heteronormative, masculine man. Some of the advice given by the Puerto Ricans in the story include "Don't walk so erect, as if someone put a stick up your ass. Let yourself go, you know, brother, loosen your shoulders. . . . And don't open your eyes so much. You Dominicans look around sometimes like you're scared, with eyes like frozen fish. . . . That name Asdrúbal is ridiculous. . . . You have to have a name from here, with an ID, just in case, brother, you have to call yourself Luis, José, Willie, Ilving, whatever you want. And you have to get a stylish haircut, change that haircut" (García Ramis 1995b: 108–9). The story is a recipe for a particular *puertorriqueñidad*: working-class, urban, youthful, and masculine. The recipe is the product of a particular class and gendered experience that is, to some extent, shared by the Puerto Ricans and Asdrúbal, but mostly by a Puerto Rican understanding of black aesthetics and Hispanicization of U.S. cultural practices such as naming. Asdrúbal becomes Willie, short for the Anglo-American William, in order to pass for Puerto Rican. He is also supposed to mimic a looser walk that reminds the reader of African American and Puerto Rican urban youth culture of the time.

Through these jokes about Asdrúbal, it becomes immediately clear that the extended Dominican–Puerto Rican family is a brotherhood. Women have no space in it. Asdrúbal must perform a Puerto Rican masculinity by showing his Puerto Rican friends that, like them, he too can objectify women on the street. Passing requires not only accepting Puerto Ricans' jokes about Dominicans but also following ethnic-specific gender conventions: "Don't look around so much, you see? Puerto Rican men don't look around, except far away, unless a good-looking female goes by or just any female, you see? But, among *machos*, one does not look at other *machos*, one looks to the distance. That's it, turn the head towards where I am talking, but look far away" (108–9). The Puerto Ricans affirm their own masculinity while questioning Asdrúbal's. Their camaraderie depends on sharing a masculinity that turns women into the object of their gaze. They mock him because his gaze does not follow their heteronormative standards for Puerto Rican men. Transcolonial brotherhood and national kinship, though differently manifested, are articulated mostly at the expense of women and require conformity with heteronormative gender norms.

On the other hand, the same male characters that might ascribe *puertorriqueñidad* to U.S. names have no particular political allegiance to the nation-state. They challenge the boundaries that define U.S. citizenship and the great Puerto Rican family through their secret complicity with the Dominican. When the immigration official asks Asdrúbal-Willie where is he from, his friends take a picture from the gate.

> At that precise moment Willie heard people calling him and turned around to see the guys standing outside with a camera, screaming at him—Smile for the picture of the graduating class.—And, at the same time, Willie, smiling at the guys, told the immigration officer—From Pueltojrico (Puerto Rico)—and bid farewell waving his arm. The Mister told him—thanks, go ahead—and he turned around, and walked slightly hunched, dragging his feet as if nothing mattered to him. He took out a five-toothed pick and passed it through his high-top fade as he walked down the corridor on his way to the Jumbo Jet that took him to New York. (112)

His performance of *puertorriqueñidad* becomes complete when his *panas* take a fictional class photograph. In this moment he is connected to a Puerto Rican community. The immigration official—marked by the

Anglicism "Míster" as either an Anglo-American or simply a representative of the United States—accepts Willie's performance without asking for his fake identification card. The photograph memorializes the visual image that allows him to pass for Puerto Rican in front of the state representative. But this image also captures an Afro-diasporic imagination of *puertorriqueñidad* built through the interactions of African Americans, Puerto Ricans and other Antilleans in New York City, and Puerto Rican communities on the island (Domino Rudolph 2011; Flores 2000; Rivera 2009).

As we can see with Asdrúbal-Willie's new Puerto Rican haircut, the story defines *puertorriqueñidad* through references to local articulations of masculinity informed by exchanges between urban youth cultures on the island and in the continental United States. Asdrúbal's *pelo malo*, cut in a high top fade, is a signifier of a 1980s hair style associated with black-identified men on the island and in the United States. His hair, skin color, and performance of young urban working-class masculinity suggest a performance of *puertorriqueñidad* that would be read more in terms of blackness than whiteness within Puerto Rico's racial spectrum. The Puerto Ricans make him look like one of them even as they themselves participate in an Afro-diasporic urban youth culture in the making.

This is not surprising if we consider that Dominicans have made their home in transnational communities—such as Santurce, Barrio Loíza, Barrio Gandul, Capetillo, and Seboruco—marked by their black history. Asdrúbal-Willie enters into Dominican–Puerto Rican kinship relations in the context of Santurce, a community with a specific Afro-diasporic history. It is where *cimarrones* (maroons), blacks who had escaped slavery, built autonomous communities under Spanish colonial rule. Santurce is where migrants and black-identified peoples have coexisted and engaged in transnational cultural exchanges throughout the twentieth and now twenty-first century (Berríos Miranda and Dudley 2008; Duany 2003). In "La migración caribeña en Puerto Rico," Jorge Duany (2003: 7) writes, "In Santurce and Río Piedras, Dominicans tend to live in neighborhoods with high concentrations of poor people, blacks and foreigners." Duany's depiction of Santurce's racial, ethnic, and class demographics reflects not only the area's history but also the color-based social hierarchies that hinder the social mobility of non-white-identified peoples in Puerto Rico.

Raquel Rivera argues that "the socioeconomic conditions of working class Puerto Ricans lead them to identify with black working-class music such as rap" (cited in Domino Rudolph 2011: 34) and its associated aesthetic practices. Rap is a genre that denounces working-class Puerto Ricans' historical racialization and criminalization on the island and the U.S. mainland. The working-class Puerto Rican guys in García Ramis's story are clearly identifying with rap and hip hop–related aesthetic practices and expect Asdrúbal-Willie to do the same. In order to pass for Puerto Rican, he must embody the black heritage and masculinity informed by the aesthetic premises of rap and hip hop culture. This version of *puertorriqueñidad* is a secret that elite, whitened narratives of the great Puerto Rican family wish to silence. But it is a secret public enough to allow Asdrúbal to migrate to New York City as Willie.

The male characters of the story espouse a transcolonial brotherhood that supports Puerto Ricans' narratives of belonging to a Puerto Rican family, while undermining Asdrúbal's ability to affirm his identification with Dominican communities. The secret complicity constructed with the Puerto Rican guys comes at the expense of Asdrúbal's own, ethnic-specific understanding and performance of blackness and masculinity. To some extent we could say that Puerto Ricans' performance of an Afro-diasporic blackness can also become hegemonic and exclusionary of others,[11] in particular Dominicans, as they build Dominican–Puerto Rican kin relations and collaborations, secrets and complicity, both in Puerto Rican and U.S. mainland communities.[12]

This marginalization of Asdrúbal's Dominican embodiment of a black masculinity speaks to a reality Pacini Hernández (2009) has documented—and I have noted elsewhere (Reyes-Santos 2008)—with regard to the participation of Dominicans in the musical genre *reggaetón* on the island and abroad. *Reggaetón* is a more recent transformation of the rhythms and practices associated with rap and hip hop (see Rivera et al. 2009. The presence of Dominicans in *reggaetón*, including the renowned production duo Luny Tunes (Francisco Saldaña [Luny] and Víctor Cabrera [Tunes]), tends to be silenced in public discourse, even while Dominicans and Puerto Ricans continue to collaborate in the development of the genre, such as its most recent uproot, *bachatón*, a combination of Dominican *bachata* and *reggaetón* (Pacini Hernández 2009, 2010).

Reading this short story with an Afro-diasporic lens offers an approach to Dominican–Puerto Rican relations that engages national and colonial/imperial kinship narratives built not on whitening but on working-class, black-identified practices. If Puerto Ricans are not supposed to be as black as Dominicans, then this story of passing cracks open the secrets of definitions of the national family that attempt to whiten it vis-à-vis Dominicans. Dominican–Puerto Rican complicity and brotherhood emerge from a similar economic, racial, and gender experience and from their defiance of the state, its narratives of national kinship, and Puerto Rico's required loyalty to its imperial adoptive parent, the United States. It is a complicity consolidated through the imposition of an Afro-diasporic Puerto Rican–identified masculine aesthetic sensibility that becomes hegemonic in the story and is built at the expense of Asdrúbal's own ethnic and gender specificity.

But Asdrúbal is not simply a victim of his friends' norms. He also wants to pass and will do what it takes to succeed. One of the secrets of transcolonial brotherhood presented here is that Dominicans must pretend to subordinate themselves to the Puerto Ricans' representation of who they are and should be. Using humor to describe the process of assimilating, Asdrúbal plays a joke on his difference and also on the Puerto Ricans. Martínez–San Miguel (2003: 174) correctly calls attention to the story's representation of the effects of U.S. colonialism on what have become signifiers of *puertorriqueñidad* (e.g., names like Willie and Ilving). Their Puerto Rican name for Asdrúbal, Willie Rosario, ironically shows the constitution of *puertorriqueñidad* by the guys, who claim Hispanicized versions of U.S. names as their own. The Puerto Rican nation they envision has been politically and culturally informed by the United States; it is not an independent political entity like the Dominican Republic. This reality explains why Dominican men in the story question the masculinity and arrogance of the Puerto Rican guys in the context of a dependent relationship with the United States. Asdrúbal's Dominican business partner, with whom he operates a hot dog cart, Diosdado, tells him, "We walk very erect, because we are sons of a republic. Those from here are not. A labor leader told me that a while ago. The Puerto Ricans, those guys from the barrio, walk a little hunched over, and like dragging their feet, as if they did not care about anything and it is because they are already citizens and don't worry about the future" (García Ramis 1995b: 108). The Puerto Rican guys make fun of Asdrúbal's masculinity because of his demeanor, but Diosdado critiques their masculinity as a lack of pride and complacency born of their colonial relationship with the United States. Diosdado associates political independence with masculinity. For him, Puerto Rican men cannot claim to be complete men without Puerto Rico's independence from the United States.

In the story the Dominicans mock Puerto Rican men's ethnic difference and their U.S. citizenship. But the Dominicans' point of view remains marginal; it is a secret used to protect them from the Puerto Rican men who could betray them to the authorities. Their legal status puts them in a vulnerable position with respect to their Puerto Rican friends. None of the Dominicans make fun of Puerto Ricans in their presence. In this way Dominican migrants' agency is not lost but rather embedded within humor and secrets.

The famous Puerto Rican TV show *Entrando por la cocina* picks up on this aspect of Puerto Rican–Dominican relations. It inserts an outspoken Dominican female protagonist, named Altagracia, into mainstream television. Her refusal to accept being called a *sirvienta* (servant) instead of an *empleada doméstica* (domestic worker) calls public attention to the power relations that inform the intimate space of middle-class Puerto Rican households in San Juan, where Dominican women fill a significant labor niche (Nina-Estrella forthcoming). Though she is a caricature of a Dominican woman, unlike the narrator in *Mona, canal de la muerte* and Asdrúbal, Altagracia is not quiet. She is imagined as a potential national subject, the engine of an active working-class Dominican–Puerto Rican extended family. In *Entrando por la cocina* the *secreto a voces* of Dominican–Puerto Rican working-class complicities is made visible.

Entrando por la Cocina: Marriage and the Dominican–Puerto Rican Family

Entrando por la cocina aired at noon, five days a week, for sixteen years, from 1986 to 2002, as part of the hour-long *El Show del Mediodía*.[13] It was a ten-minute comedic sketch that took place between live cooking classes, interviews with local celebrities, and music. *El Show del Mediodía* and *Entrando por la cocina* were produced by the Puerto Rican Luis Vigoreaux Lorenzana. Each episode followed TV sitcom structure: order, break in the social order, and resolution that restores social relations. The working-class characters of the show, including Altagracia (Yasmín Mejía), are constantly trying to better their economic conditions by breaking social conventions and expectations, only to find themselves in the same place.

Altagracia is a domestic worker for the upper-middle-class Don Luisito, played by Luis Vigoreaux, who plays version of himself as a light-skinned, urban male playboy and entrepreneur. Altagracia's Dominican origin is emphasized through various cultural and linguistic traits. She bears the name of the patron virgin of the Dominican Republic and speaks with an exaggerated Dominican, country, *cibaeño*-like accent, calls on la Virgen de la Altagracia when something unexpected or outrageous happens, listens to Dominican merengue, and repeats

FIGURE 1. Altagracia (Yasmín Mejías), protagonist of *Entrando por la cocina*. Photo by Buenas Nuevas, June 6, 2013. Accessed August 25, 2014. http:// www.buenasnuevaspr.com/2013/06/portada-yasmin-mejias-agradecida-de. html. Courtesy of buenasnuevaspr.com.

common Dominican linguistic attributes such as the phrase "oh pero bueno." The show incorporates parodic representations of her accent and jokes about her inability to say certain words or understand business concepts used by the more educated Don Luisito. Her pronunciation of words such as *patentizar* (to create a patent) constantly mark her difference as a working-class Dominican migrant. Common stereotypes are reproduced through linguistic difference. In Puerto Rico the "linguistic identification of a speaker as Dominican already entails within the listener the preconceived notion of a less educated, poor immigrant" (Suárez Büdenbender 2013: 130). Such linguistic prejudices lead to the association of Altagracia as a light-skinned Dominican character with all the racialized ideas about poor Dominicans being blacker than Puerto Ricans (Duany 2011; Reyes-Santos 2008).

While the show turns a Dominican female character into a living stereotype of her people, it inserts her into a community constituted by her Puerto Rican working-class friends. Every episode consists of various friends visiting Altagracia while her boss is at work. Her friends include two Puerto Rican domestic workers, Enriqueta (Carmen Nydia Velázquez) and Cari (Walleska Seda); her boyfriend, Tato (Pedro Juan Texidor), who is a Puerto Rican mechanic; a flamboyant gym trainer named Guille (Víctor Alicea); Policarpio (Shorty Castro), a handyman; and various domestic workers. Each one has an outfit, hairdo, phrase, and/or musical number that highlights their ethnic, gender, class, racial, and sexual difference. If Altagracia stands in as a caricature of Dominicans,[14] her friends are stereotypical representations of working-class Puerto Ricans.

Altagracia and her friends are all those people who are not supposed to be seen entering through the front door of a respectable middle-class household but rather *por la cocina* (through the kitchen). The kitchen door is meant to invisibilize those who make middle-class life in Puerto Rico possible, during a period (the 1990s) when the news, media, and other popular sitcoms, such as *Mi familia*, were constantly referring to the island's economic decline (Rivero 2005).[15] The show makes Altagracia's limited socioeconomic mobility visible and symptomatic of a neoliberal labor market. This market keeps generating the growth of suburbs, gated communities, and, as Altagracia remarks, "más casas, más casas" (more houses, more houses), while she cannot afford to buy "a casita" (a cottage) to share with Tato. Though the show ended in 2002, its appeal is intergenerational.

Entrando por la cocina was embedded in a television market that had historically negotiated the incorporation of migrants, in particular Cuban migrants, and black-identified populations into Puerto Rican society (Rivero 2005). Yeidi M. Rivero's groundbreaking *Tuning Out Blackness* discusses how the 1980s show *Los suegros* (The In-laws) exemplified how post-1959 Cuban migrants were reconfigured as white- and middle-class-identified members of the Puerto Rican family. The sitcom tells the story of a CubaRican family brought together by marriage. The in-laws, a Puerto Rican and a Cuban couple, must face their prejudices about one another in order to accept the marriage between their children. Whereas in the 1960s Cuban migrants were the imagined outsiders, by the 1980s Cubans appeared on the locally produced situation comedy *Los suegros* as ambivalently welcomed members of the Puerto Rican family (Rivero 2005: 21). By then Dominicans were considered the darker and poorer newcomers to Puerto Rican society. While Cubans become incorporated as in-laws into Puerto Rican television's imagination of the great Puerto Rican family, Dominicans have not received the same treatment. As the first TV show with a Dominican character as its protagonist, *Entrando por la cocina* illustrates that Dominicans are incorporated into the Puerto Rican imagination of the island as underprivileged siblings, unable to catch up with the island's modernization, unlike their Cuban counterparts.

A similar class experience among Dominican migrants and working-class Puerto Ricans informs how they build transcolonial kinship ties through metaphors of marriage, brotherhood, and family. But unlike "Retrato del dominicano" and *Mona, canal de la muerte*, in the TV show brotherhood is not the primordial metaphor for Dominican–Puerto Rican kinship. Neither is sisterhood. Nor do marriages of convenience or narratives of passing figure into the show's metaphors of Dominican–Puerto Rican complicity. Marriage does emerge as a trope, but it is not associated with the need to acquire legal documentation or the desire to migrate to the U.S. mainland; instead it appears as the consummation of a Dominican–Puerto Rican family that wishes to grow roots on the island itself in order to produce new national subjects. Tato and Altagracia's romantic relationship is central to each of the episodes. Every weekday at noon, Tato enters through the front door—as opposed to the back door—and into the house's living room to the tune of a romantic song. He embraces Altagracia and showers her with compliments. This is one of the iconic moments of each episode.

As a metaphor for Dominican–Puerto Rican relations, their marriage has been a success among the show's fans and has been crucial for the show's development as well as for its offshoot in private performances and theater performances and, more recently, its comeback as a musical. The musical celebrated Altagracia and Tato's fictional twenty-fifth silver wedding anniversary to packed audiences in Bellas Artes, one of Puerto Rico's most important cultural venues, in 2012.

Nonetheless Tato and Altagracia do belong to a larger family, though it is not the nuclear family structure that has historically characterized the institutionalization of marriage by the state in the U.S. mainland and Puerto Rico (Suárez Findlay 1999). Their extended family is built on working-class Dominican–Puerto Rican kinship ties that provide them with emotional sustenance and with material help when needed. It is an extended family that resembles the kinship networks that tend to be constituted by non-blood-related people in urban centers (Dinzey-Flores 2013). All episodes take place in the intimacy of Don Luisito's house, where Altagracia lives and where all of her friends encounter each other. The constant goings and comings of Guille, Enriqueta, Cari, Tato, Policarpio, and the rest resemble those of extended family structures whereby members help each other deal with quotidian struggles to access economic and social resources (Suárez Findlay 1999).

This extended family is as important as the romantic relationship between Altagracia and Tato. If Tato's entrance is iconic, Guille's entrance through the house's kitchen door is one of the most memorable moments of 1990s Puerto Rican television. Every time Guille comes to visit his *amiguita* (very dear friend) he is introduced by his rendition of the Puerto Rican singer Chayanne's "Si quieres bailar," as well as his sensual dances—including his notorious "booty shakes." As an effeminate man, apparently gay but closeted, Guille is one of Altagracia's accomplices in shaking up Don Luis's white-identified, middle-class, gender-normative, Puerto Rican, urban, patriarchal male social norms.

If there is something that produces cohesion among them it is their irreverent treatment of Don Luisito's rules and any social convention meant to curtail their mobility and visibility. The domestic workers and other friends of Altagracia use any door they like to enter the house. Don Luis accuses them of "entertain[ing] themselves there all day" (Vigoreaux 2012c) while he is away. Whenever they can, Altagracia's friends eat and drink from Don Luis's fridge. Along with her, they fulfill their duties minimally, and any reason to take a break is a good one, such as in the episode "Asiento de cuero," when Altagracia and her neighbor comment on how the weather makes work impossible. Altagracia says, "It is cloudy. . . . One cannot wash dishes, wash the garage, do anything" (Vigoreaux 2012a). Her friends also give her rides, share urgent news with her, and help her clean the house after Don Luis's parties. This is the secret complicity shared between members of Altagracia's Dominican–Puerto Rican family. It is a *secreto* that is not a secret once the show portrays its subversive possibilities through the transcolonial affective bonds built between the Puerto Rican characters and Altagracia.

The reality of discrimination against Dominicans is also portrayed in the show. Don Luis embodies a narrative of national kinship that imagines Dominicans as permanent outsiders. He does not hesitate to voice his doubts about Altagracia's intellectual capacity. In the episode "El sandwich," when she asks what it means to patent a product, he replies, "You do not have the brain for that" (Vigoreaux 2012c), dismissing her question. Unfortunately the script makes it seem as if Don Luis is right. She spends the rest of the episode unsuccessfully trying to say the word *patentizar*. Each attempt becomes a prompt for the laughter of a mostly Puerto Rican audience. We could assume that the ethnic joke simply unifies Puerto Ricans against the Dominican, but the overarching narrative of a working-class, Dominican–Puerto Rican extended family complicates such a reading. Her Puerto Rican friends cannot say the word either. Therefore Don Luisito's prejudice applies to poor and working Puerto Ricans as well. This shared class experience explains the Dominican–Puerto Rican kinship in the show. Demeaning, con-descending representations of working-class Dominicans and Puerto Ricans by middle- and upper-class Puerto Ricans allow Altagracia and their friends to find common ground.

These transcolonial kinship relations are, however, constantly betrayed as multiple characters make fun of Altagracia's lack of education and presumed lack of intelligence, sometimes out of economic self-interest. Guille asks her, "What do you have in your brain? *Mangú*?" (Vigoreaux 2012a). He uses markers of *dominicanidad*, such as a traditional Domini-can dish, *mangú*, to crack jokes at her expense. Altagracia also makes fun of him, but, contrary to what neoliberal advocates wanted us to believe in the 1990s and today, the playing field is not level. She has more to lose when his jokes reproduce widespread ideas about the Dominican popu-lation in the island. The stakes are also higher for her because Guille can appeal to his *puertorriqueñidad* and male privilege to benefit from interactions with Don Luis. At different moments he activates national and patriarchal kinship narratives that distance him from Altagracia and place his loyalties with the boss, the normative citizen.

When Don Luis is present or involved in any matter from which eco-nomic profit can be gained, Guille suddenly becomes manly and willing to ignore his friend's needs and dreams. For Don Luis he develops the persona of a womanizer, with plenty of female lovers. When Don Luis invites a baseball recruiter to the house, Guille and Tato pretend to be the players that Don Luis has bragged about (Vigoreaux 2012b). They and Altagracia hope that the recruiter will be the ticket to another life, the life of millionaires. For Altagracia and Tato, this is an opportunity that may allow them to buy their *casita*. As they try to reach some kind of agreement, Guille takes the recruiter aside and tells him that Tato is an effeminate man who would paint his nails in the locker room, using homophobia to secure a deal. He succeeds until his flamboyant charac-ter betrays him, and in the end no one gets hired by the team. Guille's homosexuality is another *secreto a voces* that is meant to explain how he belongs with the other marginalized characters. But the secret also allows him to mobilize his male and ethnic privilege and to betray those with whom he shares an experience of exclusion from heteropatriarchal, whitened, middle- and upper-class representations of the national fam-ily. Such betrayals are never fully successful. He cannot deny his authen-tic self, especially around his extended family. Every time he attempts to do so, he is forgiven for his transgression and reintegrated into the community. Each episode interrupts the expected social order and then ends by restoring order through the reconstitution of kinship ties. The Dominican–Puerto Rican family secrets continue to sustain the inter-ethnic, working-class community construed within the show as they face external and internal power dynamics.

Secretos a Voces of Dominican–Puerto Rican Kinship Narratives

Family secrets are a useful trope for understanding cultural repre-sentations of Dominican–Puerto Rican relations. These secrets con-tain insights into Puerto Ricans' ambivalence toward Dominicans, an ambivalence grounded in narratives of national kinship of the great Puerto Rican family that exclude Dominicans as poor, criminalized, racialized migrants but that also originally targeted poor Puerto Ricans. Anti-Dominican discourses such as those in media, ethnic jokes, and literature attempt to keep the realities of poor and dark-skinned Puerto Ricans a secret in order to sustain claims of a united national family. But these claims do not succeed. Across a range of narratives Dominican and Puerto Rican characters interrogate and dismantle Puerto Ricans' collusion with the neoliberal agendas embedded in the war on drugs and the war on terror, which criminalize Dominican migrants. Dominicans register their awareness of Puerto Ricans who may at times act like loyal Antillean siblings and at other times disown them.

Puerto Ricans and Dominicans recognize shared class and racial expe-riences. The campaign Santurce no se vende (Santurce is not for sale), undertaken in 2003 by various community groups, is an example of soli-darity born of mutual recognition. The campaign entailed the collabora-tion of the Coalición para la Defensa de Santurce (Coalition in Defense of Santurce), which is composed by Comité de Derechos Humanos Domini-cano (Committee of Dominican Human Rights), the Junta de Acción Comunitaria San Mateo de los Cangrejos (Community Action Council of San Mateo de los Cangrejos), Pro Rescate del Viejo San Juan (Pro-Rescue of Old San Juan), and Movimiento de Unidad Obrera Dominicana (Move-ment of Dominican Workers Unity), among other groups ("Santurce no se vende" n.d.). The community struggled against the development efforts of a state-sponsored private enterprise and the attempted gentrification of the neighborhood. Many residents had been asked to relocate or to sell their properties for prices that would not allow them to afford another residence (Rosario 2003: 13). The campaign publicly advocated for a project more inclusive of the community's needs (Vázquez Zapata 2003: 4). Santurce no se vende is an example of interethnic collaboration in a place that has been historically stigmatized as a black neighborhood—more recently as a Dominican one—and that has been negatively impacted by government projects that privilege the interests of corporate business.

Since 2006 the project Voces con Eco (Nina-Estrella forthcoming) has created intercultural dialogues and education programs that bring together Dominicans and Puerto Ricans in the barrio Capetillo in Río Piedras, Puerto Rico.[16] The goals are to undo stereotypes that divide the community; make Dominicans' experiences visible to the rest of the community; and provide artistic means of expression for Dominican youth and Puerto Rican youth of Dominican descent. Voces con Eco has produced photo exhibits and a documentary titled *Ojos que no ven* (Eyes That Do Not See) based on the material collected with the community. As in the Dominican Republic, intercultural education efforts are a strategy to improve relationships between migrant families and locals. This project utilizes an intercultural framework in order to work toward incorporating Puerto Ricans of Dominican descent into the national family.

Santurce no se vende and Voces con Eco are examples of a public Dominican–Puerto Rican struggle. But solidarity efforts often require Dominicans and Puerto Ricans to be secretive. Secrecy is not only central to narratives of Puerto Rican national kinship but is also an integral component of narratives about Dominican–Puerto Rican solidarity. Working-class Dominicans and Puerto Ricans become accomplices in narratives of transcolonial solidarity where they defy the neoliberal state's status quo by employing survival strategies in order to improve their marginal conditions. Dominican–Puerto Rican brotherly ties that sustain the possibility of Dominicans passing for Puerto Ricans and Dominican–Puerto Rican extended families that challenge the limits imposed on their physical and social mobility are some of the secrets that characterize survival strategies by both populations in a neoliberal economy.

Analyzing how cultural productions use metaphors of brotherhood, family, and marriage to narrate Dominican–Puerto Rican relations requires us to ask what is at stake when we choose to keep certain secrets for the sake of national and transcolonial/transnational families, especially those families we create in dire circumstances. It asks us to be mindful of the violence, abuses, and hierarchies that we tend to ignore or silence (Rodríguez 2013) in order to sustain a variety of chosen families throughout the Caribbean and its diasporas. These families continue to transform each other as they encounter one another through the migratory circuits that characterize the neoliberal Caribbean.

On the Decolonial Affective Matrix

Utilizing the decolonial affective matrix to explore narratives of kinship in the Caribbean provides new insight into the study of Dominican–Puerto Rican relations. It makes visible how Dominican's integration into a neoliberal Puerto Rican society is informed by various narratives of filial, romantic, and sexual relations; how Puerto Ricans see themselves as whitened by the legacy of *la madre patria*, Spain, and by their U.S. citizenship (colonial/ imperial kinship); how they often imagine themselves as a racially mixed family whose blackness is not as black as Dominican's (national kinship); and by working-class pan-Antillean complicity and solidarity (transcolonial kinship). Transcolonial brotherhoods appear in defiance of the United States, its racist and xenophobic histories and immigration policies. Colonial/imperial kinship is complicated by these brotherhoods, as well as by national kinship narratives based on Afro-diasporic, urban youth cultures.

Class, race, national identity, gender, and sexuality are crucial analytical sites for scholars studying narratives of Dominican–Puerto Rican relations. These identifications can propel or deter kinship ties. Puerto Ricans and Dominicans, like Haitians and Dominicans, can be *como de la familia* (like family) as members of a transcolonial/transnational family whose rights are circumscribed by class, racial, ethnic, gender, and sexual location in social hierarchies. Working-class national kinship does not necessarily require the exclusion of Altagracia as a Dominican migrant. And, as "Retrato del dominicano" suggests, exclusionary ideas of national kinship are not only white-identified in Puerto Rico. Puerto Ricans' embodiment of black-identified aesthetics may entail a silencing of Dominicans' own experience of their African heritage. In *Mona, canal de la muerte*, Dominican–Puerto Rican kinship is possible only when both communities share the experience of migration in New York City.

As Antilleans have known since the nineteenth century, in New York City and other metropolitan centers, transcolonial solidarities are built that are at times impossible—or difficult to accomplish—back at home (Arroyo 2013; Flores 2009; Martínez–San Miguel 2003; Rivera-Velázquez 2008). *Our Caribbean Kin* provides several narratives about the kinds of kinship possibilities historically available to Antilleans on the islands, but also as they migrate across islands or north. Some of the pitfalls and potentials ascribed here to transcolonial/transnational, national, and colonial/ imperial kinship narratives provide a compass for contemporary efforts to build political solidarity among Antillean populations, Afro-diasporic communities, and all those we may consider to be our people.

Coda: On Kinship and Solidarity

The notion of a decolonial affective matrix acknowledges that historically Antilleans have found a multiplicity of ways to explain who we understand our kin to be, in other words, how we represent our political alliances and solidarities. While claiming certain kinds of families, Antilleans have had to reckon with a variety of political demands that at times lead us to privilege either transcolonial, national, or colonial kinship models and to articulate narratives of brotherhood, marriage, and family that combine these models to different degrees.

At the Transnational Black Feminist Retreat organized by the Dominican American author Ana-Maurine Lara in the Dominican Republic in March 2013, the decolonial affective matrix was at play in interactions between participants from the United States, Haiti, Puerto Rico, Jamaica, Cuba, and the Dominican Republic. As black-identified feminists, participants were deeply invested in the creation of transcolonial kin networks. The sea that could be seen every day from their dorms in Miracielo reminded participants of their shared transatlantic and Caribbean histories, of past and present water crossings.

The organization that provided housing for the retreat in the rural community of Miracielo, La Confederación Nacional de Mujeres Campesinas (CONAMUCA), works with rural women who advocate for land rights and the right to produce their own food in the Dominican Republic, Haiti, and many other countries. The retreat center is named after Mamá Tingó, a woman killed in 1974 as she attempted to defend the rights of hundreds of peasants who were being displaced from the land they had worked for generations. A mural of Mamá Tingó reminds guests of the spirit of struggle that drives CONAMUCA's work in the Dominican Republic and in their international efforts with organizations such as Vía Campesina. Their work exemplifies contemporary manifestations of transcolonial solidarity in the region.

The retreat participants spent the week talking with CONAMUCA leaders; activists of the Haitian-Dominican Women's Movement (MUDHA); La Colectiva Mujer y Salud, an organization that defends the human and civil rights of lesbian, transsexual, and heterosexual women; and members of reconoci.do, a group of Dominican youth of Haitian descent. They also took a historical tour of the first *ingenio* (sugar factory) of the Americas at Boca de Nigua led by the anthropologist Fátima Portorreal; visited a community center and ecological park (CEDOPAZ) in San Cristóbal (led by its founder, Erasmo Lara), where they danced to the sacred beat of palos drums; and toured the *ilé* (religious house of santería practitioners) of Cuban iya Abbebe Ochún. After consulting CONAMUCA leaders, the retreat's participants left the organization a mural depicting three women whose legacy they had felt throughout their week together: Ana María, a leader of an eighteenth-century insurrection against Spanish colonials in Boca de Nigua; Sonia Pierre, the founder of MUDHA; and Mamá Tingó. The mural also includes the image of a young woman, a representative of the ongoing and future struggles.

The narrative that accompanies the mural states:

This mural represents the women's struggle in the Dominican
Republic. Ana María represents the first example of Afro-descendant
struggle for our people's liberty and self-determination. She led the
rebellion against the Spanish *colonizers* in 1796 at Boca de Nigua
and established a cooperative government in the region. Her spirit
of perseverance continues in the work we see in Mama Tingo's life,
her sacrifice for the cause, her love for the land, and the women and
men who work it. We see that commitment and will in Sonia Pierre
and her work at the *bateyes* with women of Haitian descent in the
Dominican Republic. . . . The young woman in the *conuco* represents all of the women who continue to fight for a future and for the
land that they live in. Her attentive look shows us her intention to be
aware of the realities that surround her and to act responsibly in the
face of injustice. This young woman reminds us of the present and

future generations that fight to affirm their rights for life, land, food sovereignty, and remembering their history.

For the retreat's participants, Tingó, Pierre, and Ana María are predecessors that inspire Dominican struggles for land rights and food sovereignty, against racism, sexism, and colonialism, migrants' rights and the rights of their children, as well as their own attempts to address racial, economic, and gender violence in other places. The mural illustrates how participants saw themselves sharing kinship ties with all the people who had graciously hosted them and those predecessors who motivate their quotidian struggles for social justice.

Invoking these legacies of resistance, the mural synthesizes the desire for transcolonial kinship among self-identified Afro-descendant feminists at the retreat, including gay-identified men and lesbian, straight, and queer-identified women. It was not an attempt to erase the class, national, and ethnic differences articulated among retreat participants and those who graciously hosted them. Those differences were hard to forget as people shared their experiences with one another. They required participants to constantly engage and question their understanding of how blackness and feminism are articulated across national boundaries. This was illustrated in endless conversations about the meaning of blackness in the Dominican Republic and the United States and the perception that Dominicans do not accept their blackness just because it is not manifested in terms legible to North American interlocutors. Those conversations demonstrated that national differences and colonial/imperial privilege continue to challenge decolonial solidarity efforts among Antilleans and Afro-diasporic communities.

What has inspired this book is a desire to examine the affective ties and the notions of belonging that sustain Antilleans as we attempt to create a world that transcends our colonial and capitalist histories of racial, gender, and economic injustice. I have sought to explain how narratives of kinship can move us to be ethically concerned for one another in spite of our differences, or not. The decolonial affective matrix describes the three main narrative models—transcolonial, national, and colonial—that have characterized how we Antilleans imagine how we must care for one another. The matrix poses an alternative to existing approaches to colonialism/imperialism, nationalism, transcolonial realities in the Caribbean and elsewhere. Metaphors of kinship are a productive site of inquiry to assess the political potential of decolonial intellectual and

FIGURE 2. *Las Mujeres de la Tierra*. Mural. Art design by Latasha Diggs. Painted by Transnational Black Feminist Retreat Participants. CONAMUCA, Miracielo, Dominican Republic. Photo by Dana Asbury. March 17, 2013. Courtesy of Dana Asbury.

political solidarity projects invested in addressing the colonial histories that shape our world.

Our Caribbean Kin provides several narratives about the kinds of political communities historically available to Antilleans on the island and also as they migrate across islands or north. Some of the pitfalls and potentials ascribed here to transcolonial/transnational, national, and colonial/imperial kinship narratives provide a compass for contemporary efforts to build political solidarity among Antillean populations, Afro-diasporic communities, and all those we may consider to be our people. But first we must not be afraid of airing our dirty laundry, uncovering our ugly truths and internal silences, as Antilleans.

I hope that, just as I have been inspired by solidarity efforts with people in the United States, Asia, the Caribbean, and Latin America, others will find in this book something useful to their own attempts at conceptualizing political alliances. As fellow scholars attempt to theorize North-South feminist and queer projects, Native and Afro-diasporic communities, antiracist movements, alliances between whites and people of color in the United States, working-class and middle-class people, heterosexuals and queer people, and others, paying attention to kinship metaphors as well as representations of empathy, sympathy, love, and compatibility may shed light on the preconceptions we have of who are "our people" (Hames-García 2011), who are those with whom we are in solidarity, ethically moved to accept their struggles as our own.[1]

Notes

Introduction

1. Feminist and queer studies scholarship in particular has motivated this inquiry into kinship among Antilleans. See Allen 2011; Brennan 2004; Cabezas 2009; Decena 2011; Edmondson 1999; Francis 2010; Janer 2005; Mayes 2014; Rivera-Velázquez 2008; Williams 2013. I must thank Minnie-Bruce Pratt and M. Jacqui Alexander, facilitators of the 2009 Transnational Queer Studies Summer Institute held by the Future of Minority Studies Consortium at Cornell University, for their questions. They helped me realize that kinship was the motor behind this project.

2. See Hames-García's discussion of solidarity in *Identity Complex* (2011) and Lugones's theorization of coalitions in *Pilgrimages/Peregrinajes* (2003).

3. The concept of chosen families, derived from queer activism and scholarship (Weston 1991), informs how I think about choice in the construction of kinship networks. Instead of assuming that blood ties and notions of territorial and cultural belonging are naturally what explain kin relations, I emphasize how Antilleans choose to imagine all kinds of families and communities that complicate Eurocentric ideals of family.

4. Cabezas (2009) has shown the need to engage how Antilleans choose to describe kin relations as we address questions of colonialism, imperialism, and neoliberal globalization. By paying attention to the affective bonds that emerge between locals and tourists in the Dominican Republic and Cuba, Cabezas complicates simplistic narratives of oppression and victimization, or celebration of such encounters, especially for women in the tourism industry.

5. Another productive example of how "part of the family" works to describe employer-employee relations is Stoler's (2002) discussion of how Javanese domestic workers were represented by their Dutch employers before the occupation of Japan and the independence of Indonesia from the Netherlands. Her discussion centers on colonizer-colonized relations and how, by claiming filial ties with their domestic

workers, employers elided deep power dynamics and inequalities. At the same time, the notion "part of the family" signals how employers and employees, colonials and locals, shared intimate spaces and activities in their quotidian life.

6. Transnationalism has been useful to describe the processes of circular migration, economic and cultural remittances, and political and cultural identities of Dominicans and Puerto Ricans (Duany 2011; Grasmuck and Pessar 1991). My use of the term is meant to engage a reconfiguration of power relations between the North and the South, evident in neoliberal discourses since the 1970s. I do not aim to highlight, as other scholars have, how migrants and their children continue to relate to their homeland and identify with it after years living abroad.

7. All translations are mine, unless otherwise noted.

8. The Federation of the West Indies led a very short life, from 1958 to 1962. See Dash 1981, 1998; García Muñiz and Giovanetti 2003; King 2001; Stephens 2005.

9. This proposal is in conversation with Arroyo's (2013) discussion of the affective politics of freemasonry in the Antilles, including Betances's writings.

10. See Arroyo (2013) and Mayes (2014) for related discussions about political pragmatism in Caribbean regionalist and nationalist thought.

11. Fátima Portorreal, personal conversations with author, October 2013–March 2014.

12. The Dominican studies scholar Ramona Hernández prompted me to rethink my initial dismissive critique of nationalism and to assess its political value for Caribbean communities. Personal conversations, June–July 2010.

13. See Bergeron (2004: 20) for a related discussion about colonial paternalism.

14. For pertinent histories of neoliberalism and development theory, see Appelbaum and Robinson 2003; Harvey 2003; Bergeron 2004; Benjamin 2007; Escobar 1995; Petras 2000; Trouillot 2003.

15. I must recognize a conversation with Shalini Puri about the value of fieldwork and ethnographic approaches for literary analysis (February 2011, Yale University).

16. For similar interventions, see editorial 2013; Reyes-Santos 2013a; "Rubbing Shoulders" 2014. Moreover the journal Black Scholar will publish in 2015 a volume dedicated to complicating mainstream representations of Dominican antiblack racism as an exceptional case in the Caribbean.

17. Personal conversation with IACHR official, March 2014.

18. Candelario's (2007) research speaks to these moments of encounter between Dominicans, African Americans, and other Latin American/U.S. Latino populations in New York City and Washington DC. She argues that in both locations Dominicans differentiate themselves from African Americans, without necessarily denying their own blackness but rather by affirming their ethnic specificity. She also documents the historical collaboration of Dominicans and African Americans in struggles against segregation and antiblack racism in DC. According to Torres-Saillant (2000), these encounters have transformed young, second-generation Dominicans' articulation of racial identities and embodiment of their black heritages.

19. Ileana Rodríguez helped me see that the book does, to some extent, "air the dirty laundry" of intra-Caribbean relations. Personal conversation, April 2014.

20. For more information about the summit's proceedings and interviews with participants, see www.caribe-america.blogspot.com and https://www.youtube.com/user/irmaryblogspot.

1 / The Emancipated Sons

Preliminary versions of parts of this chapter have been published by *Callaloo* (2013) and *Estudios Sociales* (2013).

1. See introduction for a broader discussion of the term transcolonial kinship.

2. The upcoming digital collection of historical documents about women's political activism in the Dominican Republic led by Ginetta Candelario, April Mayes, and Elizabeth Manley will provide easier access to primary sources that will give us an even deeper understanding of the role of women in *antillanista* and nationalist struggles, in particular those organized in Puerto Plata.

3. The ongoing publication of Betances's oeuvre by Félix Ojeda Reyes and Paul Estrade will be the most complete compilation of his writings.

4. For other important contributions to antislavery struggles of the time by Haitian intellectuals, see Firmin (1884) 2003.

5. For the influence of Latin American, French, and British political thought on *antillanismo*, see Ojeda Reyes and Estrade 2000.

6. For a historical study of Betances's diplomatic work in Paris, see Gónzalez Vales 1978; Ojeda-Reyes 1984.

7. His brother Adolfo Betances and nephew Felipe Betances lived in Jacmel, Haiti, as Betances's 1895 will attests (2008: 188); it seems that they settled there in the 1870s.

8. See scholarship about Luperón: Hernández Flores 1983; Rodríguez Demorizi 1975; Castro Ventura 2002; Tolentino Dipp 1977a, 1977b.

9. Mella (2013) is another important intervention in this conversation that complicates the historical discourses on the Dominican independence from Haiti in 1844.

10. My participation in ceremonial spaces—*velaciones, palos*, initiations—in the Dominican Republic allowed me to witness concrete indigenous contributions to Dominican spiritual and cultural traditions. Taíno cultural recuperation efforts led by Jorge Estevez, Ana-Maurine Lara, Irka Mateo, and the group Guabancex in the Dominican Republic ask scholars to seriously engage black and indigenous cross-fertilizations in the Antilles.

11. For a short discussion of proposals to create a Haitian-Dominican Confederation during the War of Restoration, see Cordero Michel 1998.

12. For Haitian-Dominican collaborations, see Hernández Flores 1983.

13. I must acknowledge Prof. Ramona Hernández for calling my attention to this passage.

14. See Miguel (2005: 82–84) for a discussion of how notions of civilization and barbarism informed Dominican nationalist discourses.

15. See Candelario (2007) for a discussion of how an Indo-Hispanic notion of identity informed twentieth-century ideas about *dominicanidad* that seek to recognize race mixture while affirming the cultural specificity of the Dominican Republic vis-à-vis Haiti and the United States.

16. Ferreira da Silva (2007), Stoler (2002), and Lugones (2007) have produced insightful commentaries on the historical construction of European and non-European women as legal subjects, wives, and mothers in Europe and in European and U.S. colonial regimes. Briggs's (2002) study of the disciplining of gender and sexuality and women's reproduction in Puerto Rico in the early twentieth century is a remarkable contribution to the study of how women were incorporated as colonial subjects by U.S. imperial projects.

17. See Roy-Féquière (2004) and Janer (2005) on gender and nationalist narratives.

18. See introduction.

19. See Arroyo (2013) and Mayes (2014) for related discussions about political pragmatism in Caribbean regionalist and nationalist thought.

20. Johnson (2012) discusses transcolonial collaborations and reverberations of the Haitian Revolution throughout the circum-Caribbean region.

21. For instance, see Brathwaite 2009; Ramphal 2009.

2 / Wife, Food, and a Bed of His Own

1. See Chantalle Verna's forthcoming book *Haiti and the Uses of America: Rapprochement Culturel with the United States, 1930–1950* (Cornell University Press) for a pertinent discussion of the Good Neighbor Policy and pan-Americanism in Haiti.

2. See Sommer's (1988) discussion of the characterization of the petit-bourgeois in *Over*.

3. A decade or two later, the Haitian writers Jacques Roumain (1944) and Jacques Stephen Alexis (1955) also documented these realities as they imagined Haitians finding themselves away from home in Cuban and Dominican cane fields. Their novels, *Gouverneurs de la rosée* and *Compére, General Soleil*, respectively, are beautifully crafted texts about these intra-Caribbean encounters prompted by the U.S. occupation and their consequences.

4. The republication of *Over* in 1963 speaks to another moment of nation building: the end of the dictatorship and the election of Juan Bosch. This new regime sought to undertake an agrarian reform in light of its reformist social-democrat tendencies. See Sommer 1988.

5. In Puerto Rico the writings of Antonio Pedreira, Margot Arce, René Márquez, Julia de Burgos, and Abelardo Díaz Alfaro were also added to the canon. In the Dominican Republic the canon includes Freddy Prestol Castillo, Virgilio Díaz Grullón, Sócrates Nolasco, Franklin Mieses Burgos, and Aída Cartagena Portalatín.

6. Sugar production was transformed by people from Hispaniola who moved to Puerto Rico beginning in the nineteenth century, and by Puerto Ricans who relocated and invested in the Dominican Republic in the twentieth century (García Muñiz 2010; Geggus 2001). For example, a Puerto Rican corporation led by the Serrallés family was responsible for introducing the *vales* that produced widespread labor strikes in the 1920s in Dominican *centrales*; *vales* were a form of payment that could be used only in *central*-owned businesses (Inoa 1999: 11).

7. See Rodríguez Castro (1993) for a discussion about how the Ateneo's 1940 Forum negotiated the interests of Puerto Rican government officials and intellectuals invested in the incorporation of Puerto Rico within Western culture and the modernization of Puerto Rico through its affiliation with the United States.

8. For this reason Negrón-Muntaner and Grosfoguel (1997) have coined the term *ethnonation* to refer to Puerto Rico's cultural, historical, and racial specificity in spite of its political relationship with the United States.

9. By the 1950s Puerto Ricans' nationalist affirmations of their cultural differences from the United States, like their use of Spanish, were no longer considered a threat to the island's colonial relationship with the United States but rather were understood as an asset that turned the island into the ideal bridge between the United States and Latin America (Urrutia 1993).

10. The *jornalero* system (1849–73) was created by the Spanish colonial government to supply haciendas with workers. To avoid ending up in prison *jornaleros* had to always carry a notebook detailing where and for whom they worked. *Agregados* shared their harvest with the *hacendado* in exchange for land on which to live and to grow food staples. Both kinds of workers tended to end up indebted to the *hacendado* and therefore had a difficult time leaving. The promise of paying the *hacendado* for any advances, seed, or agricultural tools with the next harvest would keep them in the same place.

11. Poets like Luis Palés Matos, who sought to assert the black heritage of Puerto Ricans and other Antilleans, in a somewhat caricatured manner, were recognized by critics like Margot Arce but were not fully incorporated into the vision of this generation (Janer 2005; Roy-Féquière 2004).

12. Forty years after its publication, Laguerre articulated contours of this *antillanista*, transcolonial vision of Puerto Rico as a member of a broader Antillean community constituted by the cross-cultural exchanges of indigenous, African, and Hispanic populations.

13. For a rich ecological reading of *La Llamarada* and discussion of how Laguerre's commitment to protect Puerto Rico's natural resources was an extension of his nationalist project, see Paravisini-Gebert (2008).

14. See chapter 1.

15. See chapter 1.

16. I employ the term *criollo* in the chapter to refer to a local landowner class that traces its roots back to Europe.

17. See Corten et al. (1976) and Corten (1976) for clear, enlightening analyses of the sugar industry in the Dominican Republic and its reliance on Haitian laborers during the early and mid-twentieth century.

18. According to Price-Mars (1953), there were twelve thousand dead; Larrier (2001) affirms there were twenty thousand; and Simpson (1940) five thousand. The historian Bernardo Vega (1995) has concluded that there were five thousand to six thousand victims.

19. Candelario (2007) has argued that during the occupation and the Trujillato an Indo-Hispanic identity was constructed to differentiate Dominicans from both Haitians and Americans. Hispanic cultural attributes were emphasized in contrast to Haitians' French legacy and U.S. Anglo-Saxon heritage. Indigeneity provided nationalists with a rhetorical device that allowed them to claim their right of political sovereignty and also described the particular racial mixture and miscegenation processes that characterized Dominicans. She also traces how these ideas about the nation were reproduced by the government, cultural institutions, and scholarship.

20. For a similar discussion of Dominican racial and ethnic identities, see Candelario 2007.

21. This ending suits the economic projects of the Trujillo regime and permits the incorporation of Marrero Aristy, a former communist activist, within the government. As Sommer (1988) asserts, though the novel could be read as a criticism of Trujillo's policies with regard to Haitian migrants and communism, its ending leaves a vacuum of leadership that could be filled by the Benefactor of the Fatherland, Trujillo. He would purportedly protect the national landscape against U.S. economic interests and foster productive spaces where Dominican men and women could properly produce whitened citizens. However, the novel's attention to the most marginal

populations in the *batey* and with the struggles of working peoples may explain why it was republished at another moment of nation building, when the populist Juan Bosch was elected president after Trujillo's assassination.

22. See chapter 1.

23. The Dominican Studies scholar Ramona Hernández prompted me to rethink my initial dismissive critique of nationalism and to assess its political value for Caribbean communities. Personal conversations, June–July 2010.

3 / Like Family

1. I observed the graffiti in November 2012, after moving to the area.

2. I do not mean to underestimate transnationalism as an analytical paradigm that has been useful to describe the processes of circular migration, economic and cultural remittances, and political and cultural identities of Dominicans and Puerto Ricans (Duany 2011; Grasmuck and Pessar 1991). My use of the term is meant to engage a reconfiguration of power relations between the North and the South since the 1970s by neoliberal discourses, not to highlight, as other scholars have, how migrants and their children continue to relate to their homeland and identify with it after years living abroad. Lionnet (2000) has coined the term *transcolonial* to describe horizontal, South-South relations between people still experiencing legacies of colonial subordination; I use here as well to denote decolonial projects that challenge racism and other forms of social oppression inherited from European colonialism across national boundaries. Transnational, for Lionnet, privileges North-South relations shaped by the mobility of capital, neoliberal states, and international aid agencies.

3. Petras's (2000) critique of NGOs in Latin America, Schuller's (2012) ethnographic study of NGOs in Haiti, and Karim's (2011) indictment of NGO-sponsored microfinance in Bangladesh, as well as Dupuy's (2010) recent NACLA report, *Disaster Capitalism*, require that we ask difficult questions about NGOs and their complicity with imperial and paternalist systems of governance.

4. See Reyes-Santos 2013b.

5. The United States invaded the island numerous times throughout the twentieth century. They invaded the Dominican Republic in 1916 and occupied the country until 1924 and invaded again in 1965. They invaded Haiti in 1915 and occupied it until 1934; they invaded again in 1991 and 2004.

6. For similar interventions, see the editorial in *Revista Estudios Sociales* (2013: 5); Reyes-Santos (2013a); and "Rubbing Shoulders" (2014). The journal *Black Scholar* will soon publish a volume dedicated to complicating mainstream representations of Dominican antiblack racism as an exceptional case in the Caribbean.

7. For a discussion of Haitian migrants' contribution to a variety of economic sectors in the Dominican Republic, including the production of sugar cane, rice, coffee, and plantains, see CEFASA 2012.

8. The website http://www.reconoci.do documents current struggles of Dominicans of Haitian descent for legal recognition of their birth certificates and right to proper legal identification documents.

9. Balaguer was president during and after the Trujillo dictatorship. His terms were 1960–62, 1966–78, and 1986–96.

10. See chapters 1 and 2; Horn 2014; Mayes 2014; Martínez Vergne 2005.

11. Personal conversation, Centro Bonó, February 2013.

12. Personal observation, *gagá* in San Pedro de Macorís *bateyes*, March 2013.

13. Personal conversations with Marily Gallardo, March 2013 and May 2013.

14. For discussions on the particular position of Caribbean women in local economies, see World Bank 2002; Kempadoo 2004; Cabezas 2009.

15. For another discussion of *interculturalidad* pertinent to education in Latin America, see Taboada and Reding Blase 2011.

16. Conversation with author, September 2012.

17. Participant observation, January–May 2013.

18. Centro Bonó has tried to target this issue with journalists through workshops with media. Participant observation, November 2012.

19. See Mateo (2004) for an illuminating discussion of how the Haitian and Dominican states handled the aftermath of the massacre.

20. For discussions of population control, labor, and migration policies during the U.S. occupations of the Dominican Republic and Haiti, see Castor 1978; Dupuy 2014; García Muñiz 2010; Mayes 2014; Roorda 1998.

21. From a discussion (January 2013) at "Análisis de coyuntura" (Conjunctural Analysis), a monthly open forum at Centro Bonó in the Dominican Republic. The goals of the event are to debate matters of social and political significance. Scholars, government officials, and social justice organizations are invited to share their points of view on an issue. Between fifty and two hundred people attend, on average.

22. For a historical narrative of how international aid for Haiti has been incorporated into the Dominican Republic since the 1990s, see Dupuy 2014. Corten (2013) includes contributions by Guy Alexandre, Wilfredo Lozano, Rubén Silié, Báez Everst, and Laennec Hurbon that further elaborate on this recent history.

4 / Family Secrets

1. For this reason Negrón-Muntaner and Grosfoguel (1997) have coined the term *ethnonation* to refer to Puerto Rico's understanding of its cultural, historical, and racial specificity in spite of its political relationship with the United States.

2. For a discussion of the political and economic factors influencing Dominican migration to the United States, see Torres-Saillant and Hernández 1998

3. This questions draws from the famous poem by Puerto Rican Fortunato Vizcarrondo, "¿Y tu agüela, a'onde ejta?" (1942; Rivero 2005). The poetic voice asks a white-identified Puerto Rican to recognize his black ancestors, including his black grandmother in the kitchen.

4. Ileana Rodríguez, telephone conversation, May 2014.

5. In the Brazilian context, Ferreira da Silva (2007: 441) documents how black-identified Brazilians—"black, *mestiço*, and *blackened* white Brazilians"—are racialized through the trope of illegality tied to the category of "the poor." Criminal activities associated with poverty rather than race are invoked to justify police violence in shantytowns. The poor can then be violently persecuted by the police because their assumed criminal activities, and blackness, deem them non- or less human, and therefore not protected by any discourse of civil or human rights; a "logic of obliteration" applies to them; their lives are deemed expendable.

6. "Oh well, you know" is my translation of the phrase "oh pero bueno," which characterizes Puerto Rican depictions of Dominican slang.

7. In 2008 Cuevas published a short story collection titled *Sujetos y predicados* in which various stories also narrate the experiences of Dominican migrants in Puerto Rico.

8. These fears are replicated in the Dominican press, where stories of shipwrecks and editorials concerned with the large outbound undocumented migration of Dominicans are frequently found. Some examples of media coverage are de Miguel 2004; "Ex cónsul" (2002); "Investigan a militares" (2004). See Graziano (2013) for a discussion of how these representations of migration in media impact potential migrants.

9. The *matrimonio de conveniencia* is a performance of affect between a Puerto Rican and a Dominican that secretly benefits both parties: the Dominican gains the right to residency and citizenship after proving, in a series of interviews and documents, that the marriage is legitimate; the Puerto Rican profits from the money exchange (Graziano 2013). As Graziano describes in his study of undocumented Dominican migration to Puerto Rico, this kind of marriage does not preclude love or a sexual relationship. At times it is arranged with a Puerto Rican friend, a Puerto Rican of Dominican descent, or Dominicans who are already U.S. citizens. It can be the result of a community effort to help bring someone from the Dominican Republic or to prevent losing someone who is already in Puerto Rico. Often couples maintain their friendship or relationship, even after the marriage has been accepted as legitimate. This is true even when partners have another family back in the Dominican Republic.

10. Two other well-documented examples of Puerto Rican literary texts about Dominican migration are Gratacós Wys 1998; Vega 1983.

11. Thanks to Ana-Maurine Lara for feedback that helped me better state these conclusions.

12. Candelario's (2007) research speaks to these moments of encounter between Dominicans, African Americans, and other Latin American and U.S. Latino populations in New York City and Washington, DC. She argues that in both locations Dominicans differentiate themselves from African Americans, without necessarily denying their own blackness but rather by affirming their ethnic specificity. She also documents the historical collaboration of Dominicans and African Americans in struggles against segregation and antiblack racism in DC. According to Torres-Saillant (2004) these encounters have transformed young, second-generation Dominicans' articulation of racial identities and embodiment of their black heritages.

13. The popularity of the show has risen to transnational Christian networks where Altagracia's character is frequently featured. Moreover Yasmín Mejía, the actress who plays Altagracia, is a household name in Puerto Rico, recognized for her famous character as well as for her election to the Puerto Rican Legislature (2000–2004).

14. For a discussion of Dominican stereotypes in Puerto Rican TV shows, see Rosa Abreu 2002.

15. *Mi familia* is a Puerto Rican sitcom modeled after the U.S. black-oriented comedies *The Jeffersons* and *The Cosby Show* that ran between 1994 and 2003. As Rivero (2005: 152) documents, it was a show about a lower-middle-class black family that foregrounded their *puertorriqueñidad* rather than their blackness.

16. Personal conversation with Ruth Nina-Estrella, July 2014.

Coda

1. Throughout the years, finding myself in conversation with people such as Michael Hames-García, María Lugones, Chandra Mohanty, Chuong-Dai Vo, Ernesto Martínez, Steve Theodore, Jacqui Alexander, David Vázquez, Shari Hundhorf, Yuderkys Espinoza, Digna María Adames, Nadia Ellis, Ana-Maurine Lara, and Celiany Rivera-Velázquez has been illuminating as I develop a model to understand the relevance of affective ties for solidarity movements across colonial/imperial and national lines in the Caribbean.

References

Acosta, M. 1976. "Azúcar e inmigración haitiana." In *Azúcar y Política en la República Dominicana*, edited by André Corten. Santo Domingo: Taller.

Adames Núñez, Digna María. 2013. "Interculturalidad como horizonte y praxis." *Estudios Sociales* 41, no. 154: 87–107.

"A fondo del tráfico humano." 2005. Special report. *El Nuevo Día* (Guaynabo, PR), May 8.

Alcántara Almánzar, José. 1984. *Narrativa y sociedad en Hispanoamérica*. Santo Domingo: Instituto Tecnológico de Santo Domingo.

Alexander, M. Jacqui. 2005. *Pedagogies of Crossing: Meditations on Feminism, Sexual Politics, Memory, and the Sacred*. Durham, NC: Duke University Press.

Alexandre, Guy. 2013. "Algunos aspectos de evolución del Estado dominicano entre 1918 y 2011: Materiales para un análisis." In *Haiti y República Dominicana: Miradas desde el siglo XXI*, edited by André Corten. Port-au-Prince: C3 Éditions.

Alexis, Jacques Stéphen. 1955. *Compère Général Soleil*. Paris: Gallimard.

Allen, Jafari S. 2011. *¡Venceremos? The Erotics of Black Self-Making in Cuba*. Durham, NC: Duke University Press.

Alvárez Castellano, Francisco. 2004. "Deshaitianizar el país." *Hoy* (Santo Domingo) 22: 76.

Alvarez Curbelo, Silvia. 1993. "La conflictividad en el discurso politico de Luis Muñoz Marín: 1926–1936." *In Del nacionalismo al populismo: Cultura y política en Puerto Rico*. Río Piedras: Universidad de Puerto Rico.

Alvarez-Curbelo, Silvia, and María Elena Rodríguez-Castro, eds. 1993. *Del nacionalismo al populismo: Cultura y política en Puerto Rico*. Río Piedras: Universidad de Puerto Rico.

Anderson, Benedict R. 1991. *Imagined Communities: Reflections on the Origin and Spread of Nationalism.* London: Verso.

André, Lisane. 2005. "Migration: Le GARR salue la decision de l'Eglise Catholique romaine." AlterPresse, September 2. Accessed October 31, 2005. http://www.alterpresse.org/article.php3?id_article=3196#.U3bZoS9Wo7A.

Andújar, Carlos. 2011. *La presencia negra en Santo Domingo.* Santo Domingo: Letra Gráfica.

Angueira, Luisa. 1990. "La migración de mujeres dominicanas hacia Puerto Rico." In *Los dominicanos en Puerto Rico: Migracion en la semi-periferia,* edited by Jorge Duany. San Juan: Ediciones Huracán.

Aponte Ramos, Lola. 2003. "Enrique Laguerre y la memoriosa construcción del blanquito en *La Llamarada.*" *Revista Iberoamericana* 69: 895–908.

Appelbaum, Richard P., and William I. Robinson, eds. 2005. *Critical Globalization Studies.* New York: Routledge.

Applebaum, Nancy, Anne S. Macpherson, and Karin Alejandra Rosemblatt. 2003. Introduction to *Race and Nation in Modern Latin America.* Chapel Hill: University of North Carolina Press.

Arnedo-Gómez, Miguel. 2006. *Writing Rumba: The Afrocubanista Movement in Poetry.* Charlottesville: University of Virginia Press.

"Arrestan a 60 indocumentados." 1988. *El Mundo,* March 11.

Arroyo, Jossiana. 2013. *Writing Secrecy in Caribbean Freemasonry.* New York: Palgrave Macmillan.

Ascención, Joaquín. 2004. "Convencidos de la trama para matar ilegales." *El Vocero* (San Juan), August 24.

Associated Press. 2009. "Dominicans in Beach Gear Demand Access to Beaches." Posted by Lizabeth Paravisini-Gebert, October 11. Accessed March 15, 2013. http://repeatingislands.com/2009/10/11/dominicans-in-beach-gear-demand-access-to-beaches/.

Azcona, Manuel. 2001. "Calderón dice que su gestión ayudará a inmigrantes de RD." *El Nuevo Día,* December 8.

Báez Fumero, José Juan. 1999. "Enrique A. Laguerre: Arte y Teoría." *Horizontes: Revista de la Universidad Católica De Puerto Rico,* no. 81: 133–57.

Balaguer, Joaquín. 1983. *La isla al revés: Haití y el destino dominicano.* Santo Domingo: Fundación José Antonio Caro.

Barnes, Natasha. 2006. *Cultural Conundrums: Gender, Race, Nation, and the Making of Caribbean Cultural Politics.* Ann Arbor: University of Michigan Press.

Belén Cambeira, Alán. 2001. "La denuncia socio-política en la novela *Over* del escritor dominicano Ramón Marrero Aristy." *CLA Journal* 45: 243–52.

Benítez Nazario, Jorge. 2001. *Reflexiones en torno a la cultura política de los puertorriqueños.* San Juan: Instituto de Cultura Puertorriqueña.

Benítez Rojo, Antonio. 1996. *The Repeating Island.* Translated by James Maraniss. Durham, NC: Duke University Press.

Benjamin, Bret. 2007. *Invested Interests: Capital, Culture, and the World Bank.* Minneapolis: University of Minnesota Press.

Bergeron, Suzanne. 2003. "Challenging the World Bank's Narrative of Inclusion." In *World Bank Literature*, edited by Amitava Kumar. Minneapolis: University of Minnesota Press.

———. 2004. *Fragments of Development: Nation, Gender, and the Space of Modernity.* Ann Arbor: University of Michigan Press.

Bernabé, Jean, Patrick Chamoiseau, and Raphael Confiant. 1993. *Eloge de la Créolité / In Praise of Creoleness.* Bilingual edition translated by M. B. Taleb-Khyar. Paris: Gallimard.

Berríos-Miranda, Marisol, and Shannon Dudley. 2008. "El Gran Combo, Cortijo, and the Musical Geography of Cangrejos/Santurce, Puerto Rico." *Caribbean Studies* 36, no. 2: 21–151.

Betances, Ramón E. 2001a. "La abolición de la esclavitud en Puerto Rico y el gobierno radical y monárquico de España." In *Las Antillas para los antillanos*, edited by Angel Rama. San Juan: ICP.

———. 2001b. "Alejandro Petión." In *Las Antillas para los antillanos*, edited by Angel Rama. San Juan: ICP.

———. 2001c. "Los detractores de la raza negra y de la República de Haití." In *Las Antillas para los antillanos*, edited by Angel Rama. San Juan: ICP.

———. 2008. "A Demetria Betances Alacán." In *Ramón Emeterio Betances: Obras Completas*, vol. 2. San Juan: Puerto.

Bibliografía haitiana en la República Dominicana. 1994. Río Piedras: Facultad de Humanidades, Departamento de Historia, Universidad de Puerto Rico, Recinto de Río Piedras.

Blanco, Tomás. 1981. *El prejuicio racial en Puerto Rico.* 7th ed. Río Piedras: Huracán.

Bonó, Francisco. 1939. "Letter to Luperón." In *Notas autobiográfricas y apuntes históricos*, vol. 3. 2nd ed. Santiago: El Diario.

Brathwaite, G. C. 2009. "Political Symbolism and the Spirit of CARICOM: Is It Fantasy?" June 13. Accessed May 5, 2010. http://www.normangirvan.info/political-symbolism-and-the-spirit-of-caricom-is-it-fantasy-george-c-brathwaite.

Brau, Salvador. 1986. Prologue to *El Gíbaro.* Hato Rey: Cultural Puertorriqueña.

Brennan, Denise. 2004. *What's Love Got to Do with It? Transnational Desires and Sex Tourism in the Dominican Republic.* Durham, NC: Duke University Press.

Briggs, Laura. 2002. *Reproducing Empire: Race, Sex, Science, and U.S. Imperialism in Puerto Rico.* Berkeley: University of California Press.

Buscaglia-Salgado, José F. 2003. *Undoing Empire: Race and Nation in the Mulatto Caribbean.* Minneapolis: University of Minnesota Press.

Cabezas, Amalia. 1999. "Women's Work Is Never Done: Sex Tourism in Sosúa, the Dominican Republic." In *Sun, Sex, and Gold: Tourism and Sex Work in the Caribbean*, edited by Kamala Kempadoo. Lanham, MD: Rowman and Littlefield.

————. 2009. *Economies of Desire.* Philadelphia: Temple University Press.

"CAFTA Facts: The Case for CAFTA." 2005. *CAFTA Policy Brief.* Office of the United States Trade Representative.

Calle 13. 2012. *Latinoamérica.* Music video. Accessed April 10, 2013. http://vimeo.com/29729951.

Calvo, Luz, and Catriona Rueda Esquibel. 2012. "Our Queer Kin." In *Gay Latino Studies: A Critical Reader,* edited by Michael Roy Hames-García and Ernesto Javier Martínez. Durham, NC: Duke University Press.

Candelario, Ginetta. 2007. *Black behind the Ears.* Durham, NC: Duke University Press.

Castor, Suzy. 1978. *La ocupación norteamericana de Haití y sus consecuencias 1915–34.* Habana: Casa de las Américas.

Castro, Juan E. de. 2002. *Mestizo Nations: Culture, Race, and Conformity in Latin American Literature.* Tucson: University of Arizona Press.

Castro Ventura, Santiago. 2002. *Andanzas Patrióticas de Luperón.* Santo Domingo: Manatí.

CEFASA. 2012. *Condición y aportes de la mano de obra de origen haitiano a la economía dominicana.* Santiago: Premium.

Chancy, Myriam J. A. 2012. *From Sugar to Revolution: Women's Visions of Haiti, Cuba, and the Dominican Republic.* Waterloo, Canada: Wilfrid Laurier University Press.

Charters, Mallay. 1998. "Edwidge Danticat: A Bitter Legacy Revisited." *Publishers Weekly* 245: 42–43.

Cheas, J. F. 1996. *Viajes Suicidas.* Miami: Lily.

Chinea, Jorge Luis. 2005. *Race and Labor in the Hispanic Caribbean.* Gainesville: University Press of Florida.

Civolani, Katerina. 2013. "'Vidas Suspendidas': Efectos de la resolución 012–07 sobre la población dominicana de ascendencia haitiana." *Estudios Sociales* 41, no. 154: 69–86.

Clarke, Kamari Maxine, and Deborah A. Thomas. 2006. *Globalization and Race.* Durham, NC: Duke University Press.

Clitandre, Nadège. 2001. "Body and Voice as Sites of Oppression: The Psychological Conditions of the Displaced Post-colonial Haitian Subject in Edwidge Danticat's 'The Farming of Bones.'" *Journal of Haitian Studies* 7.2: 28–49.

"Comisión Mixta Bilateral es insuficiente." 2012. *Boletín Informativo Comisión Mixta Bilateral* 1 (January–February): 1–2. Centro Bonó, Santo Domingo.

Las Constituciones de Haití. 1968. Composition by Luis Mariñas Otero. Madrid: Cultura Hispánica.

"Constituyen el Centro Domínico-Haitiano." 1983. *El Sol* 12: 23.

Cordero Michel, Emilio. 1998. "República Dominicana, cuna del antillanismo." Paper presented at the Cuarto Encuentro del Seminario Internacional

Identidad Cultural y Sociedad en las Antillas Hispanoparlantes, July 5–7, Santiago de Cuba. Accessed January 27, 2010. http://clio.academiahistoria.org.do/trabajos/clio165/Clio_2003_No_165-12. pdf.

Corten, André, ed. 1976. *Azúcar y política en la República Dominicana*. 2nd ed. Santo Domingo: Taller.

———, dir. 2013. *Haiti y República Dominicana: Miradas desde el siglo XXI*. Port-au-Prince: C3 Éditions.

Corten, André, Mercedes Acosta, and Isis Duarte. 1976. "Las relaciones de producción en la economía azucarera dominicana." In *Azúcar y Política en la República Dominicana*, edited by André Corten. Santo Domingo: Taller.

Corten, André, and Isis Duarte. 1995. "Five Hundred Thousand Haitians in the Dominican Republic." *Latin American Perspectives*, no. 3: 94.

Costa, Marithelma. 2004. "*La Llamarada* de Enrique Laguerre: Una novela de la tierra." In *Actas del XIV Congreso de la Asociación Internacional de Hispanistas*, vol. 4. Newark, DE: Juan de la Cuesta.

Cruz, Angie. 2005. *Let It Rain Coffee*. New York: Simon & Schuster.

Danticat, Edwidge. 1998. *The Farming of Bones*. New York: Soho.

Dash, J. 1981. *Literature and Ideology in Haiti, 1915–1961*. Totowa, NJ: Barnes & Noble Books.

———. 1998. *The Other America: Caribbean Literature in a New World Context*. Charlottesville: University Press of Virginia.

Dávila, Arlene. 1997. *Sponsored Identities: Cultural Politics in Puerto Rico*. Philadelphia: Temple University Press.

Davis, Angela Y. 2005. *Abolition Democracy: Beyond Empire, Prisons, and Torture*. New York: Seven Stories Press.

Davis, Martha Ellen. 2004. *La Ruta hacia Liborio*. Santo Domingo: Manatí.

Davis, Steven J., and Luis A. Rivera-Batiz. 2006. "The Climate for Business Development and Employment Growth." In *The Economy of Puerto Rico: Restoring Growth*, edited by Susan Margaret Collins, Barry Bosworth, and Miguel A. Soto-Class. Washington, DC: Brookings Institution Press.

Decena, Carlos Ulises. 2011. *Tacit Subjects: Belonging and Same-Sex Desire among Dominican Immigrant Men*. Durham, NC: Duke University Press Books.

Deive, Carlos E. 1979. *Vodú y magia en Santo Domingo*. Santo Domingo: Museo del Hombre Dominicano.

de Maeseneer, Rita. 2002. "Sobre dominicanos y puertorriqueños: movimiento perpetuo?" *Centro* 14: 53–66.

de Miguel, Diana. 2004. "Xenofobia políciaca amenaza a los emigrados dominicanos en Puerto Rico." *Diario Libre*, February 17.

Derby, Lauren Hutchinson. 2009. *The Dictator's Seduction: Politics and the Popular Imagination in the Era of Trujillo*. Durham, NC: Duke University Press.

Derby, Lauren Hutchinson, Eric Paul Roorda, and Raymundo González. 2014.

The Dominican Republic Reader: History, Culture, Politics. Durham, NC: Duke University Press.

Dinzey-Flores, Zaire Z. 2013. *Locked In, Locked Out: Gated Communities in a Puerto Rican City.* Philadelphia: University of Pennsylvania Press.

Domenech Soto, Elba. 1996. *Mar de Sangre.* Santo Domingo: Taller.

"Dominicanos en Puerto Rico viajan a votar." 1986. *El Mundo* (San Juan), May 16.

"Dominicanos invaden a Puerto Rico." 1987. *Nuevo Amanecer,* January 3.

Domino Rudolph, Jennifer. 2011. "Pidieron Cacao: Latinidad and Black Identity in the Reggaetón of Don Omar." *Centro Journal* 23, no. 1: 31–53.

Duany, Jorge, ed. 1990. *Los dominicanos en Puerto Rico: Migración en la semiperiferia.* Río Piedras: Huracán.

———. 2002. *The Puerto Rican Nation on the Move: Identities on the Island and in the United States.* Chapel Hill: University of North Carolina Press.

———. 2003. "La migración caribeña hacia Puerto Rico: Su impacto demográfico, socioeconómico y cultural." *Revista del Instituto de Cultura Puertorriqueña* 4: 3–13.

———. 2006. "Racializing Ethnicity in the Spanish-Speaking Caribbean." *Journal of Latin American and Caribbean Ethnic Studies* 1, no. 2: 231–48.

———. 2007. "Nation and Migration: Rethinking Puerto Rican Identity in a Transnational Context." In *None of the Above: Puerto Ricans in the Global Era,* edited by Frances Negrón-Muntaner. New York: Palgrave Macmillan.

———. 2011. *Blurred Borders: Transnational Migration between the Hispanic Caribbean and the United States.* Chapel Hill: University of North Carolina Press.

Duany, Jorge, Luisa Hernández Angueira, and César A. Rey. 1995. *El Barrio Gandul: Economía subterránea y migración indocumentada en Puerto Rico.* San Juan: Universidad del Sagrado Corazón.

Duarte, Isis. 1976. "Las relaciones de producción en la economía azucarera dominicana." In *Azúcar y Política en la República Dominicana,* edited by André Corten. Santo Domingo: Taller.

Du Bois, Laurent. 2004. *Avengers of the New World.* Cambridge, MA: Belknap Press of Harvard University Press.

Dupuy, Alex. 2010. "Disaster Capitalism to the Rescue: The International Community and Haiti after the Earthquake (Report: Haiti)." *NACLA Report on the Americas,* no. 4: 14.

———. 2014. *Haiti Essays on the Politics and Economics of Underdevelopment, 1804–2013.* Hoboken, NJ: Taylor and Francis.

Dussel, Enrique D. 2011. *El pensamiento pilosófico latinoamericano, del Caribe y "latino" (1300–2000): Historia, corrientes, temas y filósofos.* México, DF: Siglo XXI.

Editorial. 2013. *Revista Estudios Sociales* 41, no. 154: 5–9.

Edmondson, Belinda. 1999. *Making Men.* Durham, NC: Duke University Press.

Ellis, Nadia. 2011. "Out and Bad: Toward a Queer Performance Hermeneutic in Jamaican Dancehall." *Small Axe: A Caribbean Journal of Criticism*, 7–23.

Escobar, Arturo. 1995. *Encountering Development: The Making and Unmaking of the Third World*. Princeton, NJ: Princeton University Press.

———. 2006. "Revisioning Latin American and Caribbean Studies: A Geopolitics of Knowledge Approach." *LASA Forum* 37: 11–13.

Estívaliz, Iaki. 2004. "Inmigración ofrece nuevo servicio." *El Vocero* (San Juan), August 24.

Estrade, Paul. 2000. "Un gran amigo de Francia." In *Pasión por la libertad*, edited by Félix Ojeda Reyes and Paul Estrade. San Juan: University of Puerto Rico Press.

Estrella Veloz, Santiago. 1999. "Los haitianos, como las moscas, están donde quiera." *Cañabrava*, June, 8–9.

———. 2004. *Solo falta que llueva*. Santo Domingo: Collado.

Etienne, Yolette. 2001. "Jumping over Fire." In *Walking on Fire: Haitian Women's Stories of Survival and Resistance*, edited by Beverly Bell. Ithaca, NY: Cornell University Press.

"Ex cónsul propone contratos temporales." 2002. *El Caribe*, February 26.

Fernández Olmos, Margarite. 1978. "El haitiano en la literatura dominicana." *Studies in Afro-Hispanic Literature* 3: 231–43.

Fernández Olmos, Margarite, and Lizabeth Paravisini-Gebert. 2003. *Creole Religions of the Caribbean: An Introduction from Vodou and Santería to Obeah and Espiritismo*. New York: New York University Press.

Fernández-Valledor, Roberto. 1999. "Caña, café y tabaco en tres novelas de Enrique A. Laguerre: Su realidad social." *Atenea* 19: 23–49.

Ferrao, Luis Angel. 1993. "Nacionalismo, hispanismo y élite intelectual en el Puerto Rico de los años treinta." In *Del nacionalismo al populismo: Cultura y política en Puerto Rico*, edited by Silvia Alvarez-Curbelo and María Elena Rodríguez-Castro. Río Piedras: Universidad de Puerto Rico.

Ferreira da Silva, Denise. 2001. "Towards a Critique of the Socio-logos of Justice: The *Analytics of Raciality* and the Production of Universality." *Social Identities* 7: 421–54.

———. 2005. "'Bahia P lo Negro': Can the Subaltern (Subject of Raciality) Speak?" *Ethnicities* 5: 320–42.

———. 2007. *Toward a Global Idea of Race*. Minneapolis: University of Minnesota Press.

Ferrer, Ada. 2009. "Speaking of Haiti: Slavery, Revolution, and Freedom in Cuban Slave Testimony." In *The World of the Haitian Revolution*, edited by David Geggus and Norman Fiering. Bloomington: Indiana University Press.

Ferrer Gutiérrez, Virgilio. 1940. *Luperón: Brida y Espuela*. Habana: Carasa y Compañía.

Firmin, Antenor. (1884) 2003. *De l'égalité des races humaines: Anthropologie positive*. Paris: Harmattan.

Fischer, Sybille. 2004. *Modernity Disavowed: Haiti and the Cultures of Slavery in the Age of Revolution*. Durham, NC: Duke University Press.

Flores, Juan. 2000. *From Bomba to Hip Hop: Puerto Rican Culture and Latino Identity*. New York: Columbia University Press.

———. 2009. *The Diaspora Strikes Back: Caribeño Tales of Learning and Turning*. New York: Routledge.

Fornerín, Miguel Angel. 1999. *Puerto Rico y Santo Domingo también son*. San Juan: Isla Negra.

Fornet Betancourt, Raúl. 2011. "Filosofía de la Interculturalidad." In *El Pensamiento filosófico latinoamericano, del Caribe y "latino" (1300–2000): Historia, corrientes, temas y filósofos*, edited by Enrique Dussel et al. México, DF: Siglo XXI.

———. 2012. "Filosofía de la Interculturalidad." In *Manual de Inteculturalidad*. Santo Domingo: Centro Bonó.

Francis, Donette. 1999. "Unsilencing the Past: Edwidge Danticat's *The Farming of Bones*." *Small Axe* 5 (March): 168–75.

———. 2010. *Fictions of Feminine Citizenship: Sexuality and the Nation in Contemporary Caribbean Literature*. New York: Palgrave Macmillan.

Franco, Jean. 1994. *An Introduction to Spanish American Literature*. 3rd ed. Cambridge, UK: Cambridge University Press.

Franco Pichardo, Franklin J. 1977. *Los negros, los mulatos y la nación dominicana*. 5th ed. Santo Domingo: Nacional.

Freeman, Carla. 2000. *High Tech and High Heels in the Global Economy: Women, Work, and Pink-Collar Identities in the Caribbean*. Durham, NC: Duke University Press.

Freites, Luis. 1995. *Mona, canal de la muerte*. San Juan: N.p.

Friedman, Thomas L. 2006. *The World Is Flat: A Brief History of the Twenty-First Century*. Updated and expanded ed. New York: Farrar, Straus and Giroux.

Fuente, Alejandro de la. 2001. *A Nation for All: Race, Inequality, and Politics in Twentieth-Century Cuba*. Chapel Hill: University of North Carolina Press.

Fujiwara, Lynn. 2008. *Mothers without Citizenship: Asian Immigrant Families and the Consequences of Welfare Reform*. Minneapolis: University of Minnesota Press.

García Cabrera, Manuel. 1992. "Laguerre y sus polos de la cultura iberoamericana." *Revista del Centro de Estudios Avanzados de Puerto Rico y el Caribe*, July–December, 50–55.

García Cuevas, E. J. 1999. *Mirada en tránsito*. San Juan: Isla Negra.

———. 2008. *Sujetos y predicados (El hijo de la mujer y diez cuentos más)*. San Juan: Editorial Isla Negra.

García Muñiz, Humberto. 2010. *Sugar and Power in the Caribbean*. Río Piedras: UPR.

García Muñiz, Humberto, and Jorge Giovanetti. 2003. "Garveyismo y racismo

en el Caribe: El caso de la población cocola en la República Dominicana."
Caribbean Studies no. 1: 139–211.

García Passalacqua, Juan Manuel. 1993. *Dignidad y jaibería: Temer y ser puertorriquño*. San Juan: Cultural.

———. 2003. Conference presentation. Caribbean Studies Association, Belize City.

García Ramis, Magali. 1995a. *Las noches del riel de oro*. San Juan: Cultural.

———. 1995b. "Retrato del dominicano que pasó por puertorriqueño y emigró a mejor vida en Nueva York." In *Las noches del riel de oro*. San Juan: Cultural.

Geggus, David P., ed. 2001. *The Impact of the Haitian Revolution in the Atlantic World*. Columbia: University of South Carolina Press.

Geggus, David P., and Norman Fiering, eds. 2009. *The World of the Haitian Revolution*. Bloomington: Indiana University Press.

Gelpí, Juan. 1993. *Literatura y paternalismo en Puerto Rico*. San Juan: Universidad de Puerto Rico.

Glave, Thomas. 2008. *Our Caribbean: A Gathering of Lesbian and Gay Writing from the Antilles*. Durham, NC: Duke University Press.

Goddard, Jacqui. 2003. "Farmers Forced Out as Global Brands Build Haiti Free-Trade Area." World History Archives. Accessed May 12, 2005. http://www.hartford-hwp.com/archives/43a/458.html.

Godreau, Isar. 2006. "Folkloric 'Others.'" In *Globalization and Race: Transformations in the Cultural Production of Blackness*, edited by Kamari Maxine Clarke and Deborah A. Thomas. Durham, NC: Duke University Press.

———. 2008. "Slippery Semantics: Race Talk and Everyday Uses of Racial Terminology in Puerto Rico." *Centro Journal* 20, no. 2: 5–33.

Godreau, Isar, Mariolga Reyes-Cruz, Mariluz Franco Ortiz, and Sherry Cuadrado. 2008. "The Lessons of Slavery: Discourses of Slavery, Mestizaje, and Blanqueamiento in an Elementary School in Puerto Rico." *American Ethnologist* 35, no. 1: 115–35.

González, Jorge. 2013. "Cada doce minutos nace haitiano en República Dominicana." *El Nacional*, February 19. Accessed February 28, 2013. http://elnacional.com.do/cada-doce-minutos-nace-haitiano-en-rd/.

González, José Luis. 1983. *El país de los cuatro pisos*. Río Piedras: Huracán.

———. 1993. *The Four-Storeyed Country*. Translated by Gerald Guinness. Princeton, NJ: Marcus Wiener.

González Echevarría, Roberto. 2004. "The Making of the Latin American Novel." In *Literary Cultures of Latin America*, vol. 2, edited by Mario J. Valdés and Djelal Kadir. Oxford: Oxford University Press.

Gónzalez-Mendoza, Juan R. 2001. "Puerto Rico's Creole Patriots and the Slave Trade after the Haitian Revolution." In *The Impact of the Haitian Revolution in the Atlantic World*, edited by David P. Geggus. Columbia: University of South Carolina Press.

González-Pérez, Aníbal. 2004. "Cultural Journalism in Spanish America." In

Literary Cultures of Latin America, vol. 2, edited by Mario J. Valdés and Djelal Kadir. Oxford: Oxford University Press.

Gónzalez Vales, Luis E. 1978. *Betances en París: Historia de una misión diplomática*. San Juan, PR: Colegio de Abogados.

Graciano, Berta. 1990. *La novela de la caña: Estética e ideología*. Santo Domingo: Alfa y Omega.

Grasmuck, Sherri, and Patricia R. Pessar. 1991. *Between Two Islands: Dominican International Migration*. Berkeley: University of California Press.

Gratacós Wys, Lizette. 1998. "Yolanda." In *Tortícolis*. San Juan: Editorial de la Universidad de Puerto Rico.

Graziano, Frank. 2013. *Undocumented Dominican Migration*. Austin: University of Texas Press.

Gregory, Steven. 2007. *The Devil behind the Mirror: Globalization and Politics in the Dominican Republic*. Berkeley: University of California Press.

Grosfoguel, Ramón. 2003. *Colonial Subjects: Puerto Ricans in a Global Perspective*. Berkeley: University of California Press.

"Grupo M y Codevi tratan planes Haití." 2011. *Listín Diario*, December 19. Accessed April 30, 2014. http://www.listindiario.com/economia-y-negocios/2011/12/18/215133/Grupo-M-y-Codevi-tratan-planes-Haiti.

Guerra, Lillian. 2003. "From Evolution to Involution in the Early Cuban Republic." In *Race and Nation in Modern Latin America*, edited by Nancy P. Appelbaum, Ann S. Macpherson, and Karen Alejandra Rosemblatt. Chapel Hill: University of North Carolina Press.

———. 2005. *The Myth of José Martí*. Chapel Hill: University of North Carolina Press.

Guridy, Frank Andre. 2010. *Forging Diaspora: Afro-Cubans and African Americans in a World of Empire and Jim Crow*. Chapel Hill: University of North Carolina Press.

Gutiérrez, Franklin. 2004. *Diccionario de la literatura dominicana*. Santo Domingo: Búho.

"Haitian Jobs Hang in the Balance in IFC-Funded Plant." 2004. Bretton Woods Project, July 26. Accessed July 26, 2004. http://www.brettonwoodsproject.org/2004/07/art-62678/.

Haiti Progrés. 2002. "Aristide Trying to Sell 1875 Km2 of Haiti." *Haiti Progrés*, July 10–16. Accessed May 12, 2005. http://www2.webster.edu/~corbetre/haiti-archive-new/msg12403.html.

Hall, Michael R. 2000. *Sugar and Power in the Dominican Republic: Eisenhower, Kennedy, and the Trujillos*. Westport, CT: Greenwood Press.

Hames-García, Michael Roy. 2011. *Identity Complex: Making the Case for Multiplicity*. Minneapolis: University of Minnesota Press.

Harvey, David. 1997. *Justice, Nature, and the Geography of Difference*. Oxford: Wiley-Blackwell.

———. 2003. *A Brief History of Neoliberalism*. New York: Palgrave Macmillan.

———. 2005. "From Globalization to the New Imperialism." In *Critical Globalization Studies*, edited by Richard P. Appelbaum and William I. Robinson. New York: Routledge.

"Hay que defender el país." 2004. *Listín Diario (Santo Domingo)*, June 11.

Hernández, Ramona. 2002. *The Mobility of Workers under Advanced Capitalism: Dominican Migration to the United States*. New York: Columbia University Press.

Hernández Cabiya, Yanira. 2005. "Cabildeo en suelo dominicano." *El Nuevo Día* (Guaynabo), August 19.

Hernández Flores, Ismael. 1983. *Luperón, héroe y alma de la restauración: Haití y la revolución restauradora*. Santo Domingo: Loteria.

Horn, Maja. 2014. *Masculinity after Trujillo*. Gainesville: University Press of Florida.

Howard, David. 2001. *Coloring the Nation: Race and Ethnicity in the Dominican Republic*. Oxford: Signal Books.

Hurbon, Laennec. 2013. "El Estado haitiano antes y después del 12 de enero de 2010: La instrumentalización del Estado débil." In *Haiti y República Dominicana. Miradas desde el siglo XXI*, edited by André Corten. Port-au-Prince: C3 Éditions.

Inoa, Orlando. 1999. *Azúcar: Árabes, cocolos y haitianos*. Santo Domingo: FLACSO.

International Organization for Migration. 2001. *La question migratoire entre la Republique Dominicaine et Haiti: Matériaux pour une proposition de politique. Document de travail pour l'Organisation Internationale pour les Migrations*. Geneva: International Organization for Migration.

"Investigan a militares por viaje de náufragos." 2004. *Hoy* (Santo Domingo), August 14.

Irizarry, Estelle. 1982. *Enrique A. Laguerre*. Boston: Twayne.

James, C. L. R. 1963. *The Black Jacobins*. New York: Vintage Books.

Jameson, Fredric. 1981. *The Political Unconscious: Narrative as Socially Symbolic Act*. Ithaca, NY: Cornell University Press.

Janer, Zilkia. 2005. *Puerto Rican Nation-Building Literature*. Gainesville: University Press of Florida.

Jarayam, Kiran. 2010. "Capital Changes: Haitian Migrants in Contemporary Dominican Republic." *Caribbean Quarterly* 55, no. 3: 31–54.

Johnson-La O, Sara E. 2001a. "The Integration of Hispaniola: A Reappraisal of Haitian-Dominican Relations in the Nineteenth and Twentieth Centuries." *Journal of Haitian Studies* 8: 4–29.

———. 2001b. "Migrant Recitals: Pan Caribbean Interchanges in the Aftermath of the Haitian Revolution 1791–1850." PhD diss., Stanford University.

———. 2005. "*Cinquillo* Consciousness: The Formation of a Pan-Caribbean Musical Aesthetic." In *Music, Writing, and Cultural Unity in the Caribbean*, edited by Timothy J. Reiss. Trenton, NJ: Africa New World Series.

———. 2012. *The Fear of French Negroes: Transcolonial Collaboration in the Revolutionary Americas*. Berkeley: University of California Press.

Karim, Lamia. 2011. *Microfinance and Its Discontents: Women in Debt in Bangladesh*. Minneapolis: University of Minnesota Press.

Kempadoo, Kamala. 1999. *Sun, Sex, and Gold: Tourism and Sex Work in the Caribbean*. Lanham, MD: Rowman & Littlefield.

———. 2004. *Sexing the Caribbean: Gender, Race, and Sexual Labor*. New York: Routledge.

King, Nicole. 2001. *C. L. R. James and Creolization: Circles of Influence*. Jackson: University Press of Mississippi.

Kinsbruner, Jay. 1996. *Not of Pure Blood: The Free People of Color and Racial Prejudice in Nineteenth-Century Puerto Rico*. Durham, NC: Duke University Press.

Knight, Franklin W. 1990. *The Caribbean: Genesis of a Fragmented Nationalism*. 2nd ed. New York: Oxford University Press.

Knight, Franklin W., and Teresita Martínez-Vergne, eds. 2005. *Contemporary Caribbean Cultures and Societies in a Global Context*. Chapel Hill: University of North Carolina Press.

Laguerre, Enrique A. 1939. *La Llamarada*. 2nd ed. San Juan: Biblioteca de Autores Puertorriqueños.

Lara, Ana-Maurine. 2006. *Erzulie's Skirt*. Washington, DC: RedBone Press.

Larrier, René. 2001. "'Girl by the Shore': Gender and Testimony in Edwidge Danticat's *The Farming of Bones*." *Journal of Haitian Studies* 7: 50–60.

Lazo, Rodrigo. 2005. *Writing to Cuba*. Chapel Hill: University of North Carolina Press.

Lee Turits, Richard. 2002. "A World Destroyed, a Nation Imposed: The 1937 Haitian Massacre in the Dominican Republic." *Hispanic American Historical Review* 82: 589–635.

Lerebours, Michel-Philippe. 1992. "The Indigenist Revolt: Haitian Art, 1927–1944." *Callaloo: A Journal of African American and African Arts and Letters*, no. 3: 711–25.

Levitt, Peggy. 2001. *The Transnational Villagers*. Berkeley: University of California Press.

Lionnet, Françoise. 2000. "Transnationalism, Postcolonialism, or Transcolonialism? Reflections on Los Angeles, Geography, and the Uses of Theory." *Emergences: Journal for the Study of Media and Composite Cultures* 10, no. 1: 25–35.

Lowenthal, Abraham. 1995. *The Dominican Intervention*. 2nd ed. Baltimore: Johns Hopkins University Press.

Lozano, Wilfredo, and Franc Báez Evertsz. 2013. "Políticas migratorias en la globalización: El caso de la inmigración haitiana a la República Dominicana." In *Haiti y República Dominicana. Miradas desde el siglo XXI*, edited by André Corten. Port-au-Prince: C3 Éditions.

Lugones, María. 2003. *Pilgrimages/Peregrinajes: Theorizing Coalition against Multiple Oppressions.* Lanham, MD: Rowman & Littlefield.

———. 2007. "Heterosexualism and the Colonial/Modern Gender System." *Hypatia,* no. 1: 186–209.

Luperón, Gregorio. 1939. *Notas Autobiográfricas y Apuntes Históricos,* vols. 1–3. 2nd ed. Santiago: El Diario.

Maingot, Anthony P., and Wilfredo Lozano. 2005. *The United States and the Caribbean: Transforming Hegemony and Sovereignty.* New York: Routledge.

Maldonado-Denis, Manuel. 1976. *Puerto Rico y Estados Unidos: Emigración y colonialismo.* México, DF: Siglo Veintiuno.

Maldonado-Torres, Nelson. 2011. "El pensamiento filósofico del 'giro descolonizador.'" In *El pensamiento filosófico latinoamericano, del Caribe y "latino" (1300-2000): Historia, corrientes, temas y filósofos,* edited by Enrique Dussel et al. México, DF: Siglo XXI.

Marrero Aristy, Ramón. 1963. *Over.* Santo Domingo: Librería Dominicana.

Martínez, Osvaldo. 2005. *Neoliberalismo, ALCA y libre comercio.* Habana: Ciencias Sociales.

Martínez, Samuel. 1995. *Peripheral Migrants: Haitians and Dominican Republic Sugar Plantations.* Knoxville: University Press of Tennessee.

Martínez Burgos, José R. 2010. "Cuidado con la invasión haitiana." *Hoy* (Santo Domingo), June 24.

Martínez-Fernández, Luis. 1994. *Torn between Empires: Economy, Society, and Patterns of Political Thought in the Hispanic Caribbean, 1840-1878.* Athens: University of Georgia Press.

Martínez Rosario, Raúl, 1993. *Puerto Rico, una ruta incierta al norte: La travesía en yola.*
Santo Domingo: Centro Editorial.

Martínez–San Miguel, Yolanda. 1998. "De ilegales e indocumentados: Representaciones culturales de la migración dominicana en Puerto Rico." *Revista de Ciencias Sociales,* n.s., 4 (January): 147–73.

———. 2001. "A Caribbean Confederation? Cultural Representations of Cuban and Dominican Migrations to Puerto Rico." *Journal of Caribbean Literatures* 3, no. 1: 93–110.

———. 2003. *Caribe Two Ways: Cultura de la migración en el Caribe insular hispánico.* San Juan: Callejón.

Martínez Vergne, Teresita. 1992. *Capitalism in Colonial Puerto Rico.* Gainesville: University Press of Florida.

———. 2005. *Nation and Citizen in the Dominican Republic, 1880-1916.* Chapel Hill: University of North Carolina Press.

Massó Vázquez, Benito, Jr. 2013. *Negro: El color que me queda bonito.* San Juan, Colombia: QuadGraphics.

Mata, Irene. 2008. "Caribbean Border Crossers: Negotiating Identity and Ideas of Home." In *African Diasporas: Ancestors, Migrations and Borders,* edited by Robert Cancel and Winifred Woodhull. Trenton, NJ: Africa World Press.

Mateo, Andrés L. 2004. *Mito y cultura en la era de Trujillo*. Santo Domingo: Manatí.

Matías, Wanda Ivette. 2004. "En buen estado los 14 cubanos en isla de Mona." *El Nuevo Día*, August 21.

Matibag, Eugenio. 2003. *Haitian-Dominican Counterpoint: Nation, State, and Race on Hispaniola*. New York: Palgrave Macmillan.

Mayes, April. 2014. *The Mulatto Republic*. Gainesville: University of Florida Press.

McClintock, Anne. 1995. *Imperial Leather: Race, Gender, and Sexuality in the Colonial Contest*. New York: Routledge.

McDonald, Janice-Marie. 1991. "A Slave by Any Other Name Is Still a Slave: The New Slavery as Depicted in the Novel *Over*." *Afro-Hispanic Review* 10: 37–41.

McGuinness, Aims. 2003. "Searching for 'Latin America': Race and Sovereignty in the Americas." In *Race and Nation in Modern Latin America*, edited by Nancy P. Appelbaum, Ann S. Macpherson, and Karen Alejandra Rosemblatt. Chapel Hill: University of North Carolina Press.

Mejía, Hipólito. 2000. "Statement by His Excellency." United Nations Millennium Summit, September 6. Accessed September 16, 2005. http://www.un.org/millenium/webcast/statements/dominican.htm.

Mella, Pablo. 2013. *Los espejos de Duarte*. Santo Domingo: Amigo del Hogar.

Méndez, Danny. 2011. "Bittersweet Affections: The Ambivalent Imaginings of Haitians in *Cañas y Bueyes* (1936)." *Confluencia*, no. 1: 113–23.

———. 2012. *Narratives of Migration and Displacement in Dominican Literature*. Hoboken, NJ: Taylor & Francis.

Mendoza, Félix Darío. 1994. *Marina de la Cruz*. Santo Domingo: Sin Sello.

Meyer, Gerald J. 2011. "Pedro Albizu Campos, Gilberto Concepción De Gracia, and Vito Marcantonio's Collaboration in the Cause of Puerto Rico's Independence." *Centro Journal*, no. 1: 87–123.

Mirabal, Nancy Raquel. 2001. "'No Country but the One We Must Fight For': The Emergence of an Antillean Nation and Community in New York City, 1860–1901." In *Mambo Montage*, edited by Agustín Lao Montes and Arlene Dávila. New York: Columbia University Press.

Morejón, Nancy. 1982. *Nación y mestizaje en Nicolás Guillén*. Habana: Unión de Escritores y Artistas de Cuba.

Moreno Fraginals, Manuel. 1985. "Plantations in the Caribbean: Cuba, Puerto Rico, and the Dominican Republic in the Late Nineteenth Century." In *Between Slavery and Free Labor*. Baltimore: John Hopkins University Press,.

Moya Pons, Frank. 1998. *The Dominican Republic: A National History*. Princeton, NJ: Markus Wiener.

Mulero, Leonor. 2001. "Rechazo boricua a su origen negro." *El Nuevo Día*, April

16. Accessed March 20, 2006. http://www.adendi.com/archivo.asp?num=44
8371&year=2001&month=4.

Negrón-Muntaner, Frances. 2007. Introduction to *None of the Above: Puerto Ricans in the Global Era*. New York: Palgrave Macmillan.

Negrón-Muntaner, Francés, and Ramón Grosfoguel. 1997. Introduction to *Puerto Rican Jam: Essays on Culture and Politics*. Minneapolis: University of Minnesota Press.

Nicholls, David. 1979. *From Dessalines to Duvalier: Race, Colour, and National Independence in Haiti*. Cambridge, UK: Cambridge University Press.

Nina-Estrella, Ruth. Forthcoming. "Ser inmigrante dominicano en Puerto Rico: Percepción de la convivencia intercultural." *Revista Estudios Sociales.*

"No son dominicanos." 2003. *Hoy* (Santo Domingo), February 2, 1–2.

"Novela explora aspectos de historia domínico-haitiana." N.d. Accessed October 28, 2003. http://www.todito.com.

Núñez, Manuel. 2001. *El ocaso de la nación dominicana*. Santo Domingo: Letras Gráficas, Fundación Soberanía.

Nuñéz Polanco, Diómedes. 1997. *Anexionismo y resistencia*. Santo Domingo: Alpha and Omega.

Ojeda Reyes, Félix. 1984. *La manigua en París*. San Juan: Centro de Estudios Avanzados de Puerto Rico y el Caribe.

———. 2000. "Ramón Emeterio Betances, patriarca de la antillanía." In *Pasión por la libertad*, edited by Félix Ojeda Reyes and Paul Estrade. San Juan: University of Puerto Rico Press.

Ojeda Reyes, Félix, and Paul Estrade, eds. 2000. *Pasión por la libertad*. San Juan: University of Puerto Rico Press.

Ornes, Germán E. 1961. "Espera decisión de Washington sea inicio de nuevo trato para exiliados dominicanos." *El Mundo*, May 4.

Ortiz Otero, Bienvenido. 1978. "Decreta libertad 5 dominicanos entraría ilegalmente a la Isla." *El Mundo*, December 10.

Ovalle, Priscilla Peña. 2011. *Dance and the Hollywood Latina: Race, Sex, and Stardom*. New Brunswick, NJ: Rutgers University Press.

Pacini-Hernández, Deborah. 2009. "Dominicans in the Mix: Reflections on Dominican Identity, Race, and Reggaetón." In *Reggaetón*, edited by Raquel Z. Rivera, Wayne Marshall, and Deborah Pacini Hernandez. Durham, NC: Duke University Press.

———. 2010. *Oye Como Va!* Philadelphia: Temple University Press.

Padilla, Mark. 2007. *Caribbean Pleasure Industry Tourism, Sexuality, and AIDS in the Dominican Republic*. Chicago: University of Chicago Press.

Padilla, Mark, et al., eds. 2007. *Love and Globalization: Transformations of Intimacy in the Contemporary World*. Nashville, TN: Vanderbilt University Press.

Paravisini-Gebert, Lizabeth. 2008. "Endangered Species: Caribbean Ecology and the Discourse of the Nation." In *Displacements and Transformations in Caribbean Cultures*.

Penson, César Nicolás. 1986. "Las Vírgenes de Galindo." In *Cosas Añejas*. Santo Domingo: Taller.

Pérez, Odalís. 2002. *La ideología rota: El derrumbe del pensamiento pseudonationalista dominicano*. Manatí, DR: Centro de Información Afroamericano.

Petras, James. 2000. *La izquierda contraataca: Conflicto de clases en América Latina en la era del neoliberalismo*. Translated by Diego Palacios Cerezales. Madrid: Westview.

Polanco, Tania. 1994. "Sacerdote amenazado." *Acontecer migratorio*, December–January 17.

Premnath, Gautam. 2003. "The Weak Sovereignty of the Postcolonial Nation-State." In *World Bank Literature*, edited by Amitava Kumar. Minneapolis: University of Minnesota Press.

Prestol Castillo, Freddy. 1943. *Paisajes y meditaciones de una frontera*. Ciudad Trujillo, DR: Cosmopolita.

Price-Mars, Jean. 1953. *La République d'Haiti et la République Dominicaine*. 2 vols. Port-au-Prince: L'Impr. Held.

———. 1958. "L'Unité politique d'Ile d'Haiti s'est-elle opérée en 1822 par la violence ou par le libre ralliement des Dominicains a la République d'Ha ti." *Société d'Histoire et de Géographie d'Haiti Revue* 9.

Puri, Shalini. 2004. *The Caribbean Postcolonial: Social Equality, Post-Nationalism, and Cultural Hybridity*. New York: Palgrave Macmillan.

Puyana, Alicia, ed. 2003. *La integración económica y la globalización*. Barcelona, FLACSO.

Quintero Herencia, Juan Carlos. 1996. "La superioridad del isleño." *Diálogo* (San Juan), September, 24.

Quiroz, Margarita. 2003. "Gagá: Una expresión de vida que une dos culturas." May 17.

Rama, Angel. 2001. Prologue to *Las Antillas para los antillanos*. 2nd ed. San Juan: ICP.

Ramos Escobar, José Luis. 1989. *Indocumentados: El otro merengue*. San Juan: Cultural.

Ramos Rosado, Marie. 1999. *La mujer negra en la literatura puertorriquea*. Río Piedras: University of Puerto Rico Press.

Ramphal, Sir Shridath. 2009. "Wither the Caribbean?" Presentation at the Roxborough Institute, Jamaica. Norman Girvan: Caribbean Political Economy. Accessed July 29, 2009. http://www.normangirvan.info/wither-the-caribbean/.

"République Dominicaine: L'encouragement au crime." 2005. *Haiti Progrés*, August 31.

"République Dominicaine: Répression policière contre une manifestation ouvrière." 2005. *Alter Presse*, September 1. Accessed September 1, 2005. http://www.alterpresse.org/article.php3?id_article=3191.

Rey-Hernández, César. 1999–2000. "Puertorriqueños y dominicanos migrantes ante el reto de la identidad nacional." *Homines* 22: 389–98.

Reyes-Santos, Irmary. 2008. "Capital neoliberal, raza, migración: Análisis comparativo de relaciones domínico-haitianas y domínico-puertorriqueñas." *Revue Européene des Migrationes Internationales* 24, no. 1: 13–34.

———. 2013a. "Afro-descendencia y pan-americanismo en el pensamiento antillanista del siglo diecinueve." *Estudios Sociales* 41, no. 154: 29–51.

———. 2013b. "On Pan-Antillean Politics: Ramón Emeterio Betances and Gregorio Luperón Speak to the Present." *Callaloo* 36, no. 1: 142–57.

Ríos, Palmira. 1995. "Gender, Industrialization, and Development in Puerto Rico." In *Women in the Latin American Development Process*, edited by Christine Bose and Edna Acosta-Belén. Philadelphia: Temple University Press.

Rivarola Puntigliano, Andrés, and José Briceño Ruiz, eds. 2013. *Resilience of Regionalism in Latin America and the Caribbean Development and Autonomy.* New York: Palgrave Macmillan.

Rivera, Miguel. 1970. "Policía sigue búsqueda de 5 dominicanos." *El Mundo*, December 8.

Rivera, Raquel Z. 2003. *New York Ricans from the Hip Hop Zone.* New York: Palgrave Macmillan.

Rivera, Raquel Z., Wayne Marshall, and Deborah Pacini Hernandez, eds. 2009. *Reggaetón.* Durham, NC: Duke University Press.

Rivera-Velázquez, Celiany. 2008. "Brincando bordes, cuestionando el poder: Cuban Las Krudas' Migration Experience and Their Rearticulation of Sacred Kinships and Hip Hop Feminism." *Letras Femeninas* 34, no. 1: 97–123.

Rivero, Yeidy M. 2005. *Tuning Out Blackness: Race and Nation in the History of Puerto Rican Television.* Durham, NC: Duke University Press.

Rodríguez, Néstor. 2003. "La isla y su envés: Representaciones de lo nacional en el ensayo dominicano contemporáneo." *Revista del Instituto de Cultura Puertorriqueña* 4: 95–109.

Rodríguez, Tony. 2002. "Define aislados casos discriminación PR." *El Nacional* (Santo Domingo), February 2.

Rodríguez Alicea, Fidel. 1986. "Indocumentados huyen de gobierno de Balaguer." *El Mundo*, May 31.

Rodríguez Beruff, Jorge. 2003. "Una pugna caribeña: Muñoz Marín y Trujillo." *Revista del Instituto de Cultura Puertorriqueña* 4: 26–39.

Rodríguez Castro, María Elena. 1993. "Foro de 1940: Las pasiones y los intereses se dan la mano." *In Del nacionalismo al populismo: Cultura y política en Puerto Rico.* Río Piedras: Universidad de Puerto Rico.

Rodríguez de León, Francisco. 2004. *Trujillo y Balaguer: Entre la espada y la palabra.* Santo Domingo: Nostrum.

Rodríguez Demorizi, Emilio. 1975. *Luperón y Hostos*. Santo Domingo: Taller.

Rodríguez-Juliá, Edgardo. 2002. *Caribeños*. San Juan: ICP.

Rodríguez Silva, Ileana. 2012. *Silencing Race: Disentangling Blackness, Colonialism, and National Identities in Puerto Rico*. New York: Palgrave Macmillan.

Roorda, Eric. 1998. *The Dictator Next Door: The Good Neighbor Policy and the Trujillo Regime in the Dominican Republic, 1930–1945*. Durham, NC: Duke University Press.

Rosa Abreu, Aida Liz de la. 2002. "La identidad cultural de la mujer dominicana de clase trabajadora en Puerto Rico: Su articulación en la comedia televisiva." Master's thesis, University of Puerto Rico.

Rosario, Ivonne Y. 2003. "Repudian expropien viviendas en Santurce." *El Vocero* (San Juan), July 23.

Rosenberg, June C. 1979. "El gagá: Religión y sociedad de un culto dominicano: un estudio comparativo." Santo Domingo: Universidad Autónoma de Santo Domingo.

Roumain, Jacques. 1944. *Gouverneurs de la rosée: Roman*. Paris: Editeurs Français Réunis.

Roy-Féquière, Magali. 2004. *Women, Creole Identity, and Intellectual Life in Early Twentieth-Century Puerto Rico*. Philadelphia: Temple University Press.

"Rubbing Shoulders: A Collective Introduction." 2014. "Ra(i)ces: Black Feminist Encounters," edited by Ana-Maurine Lara. Special issue of *Aster(ix) Journal of Art*, April. Accessed May 1, 2014. http://asterixjournal.com/issues/raices/.

Ruquoy, Pedro. 2003. "Virgen de la Altagracia une a los pobres de Haití y República Dominicana." *Ultima Hora*, January 22.

Sagás, Ernesto. 2000. *Race and Politics in the Dominican Republic*. Gainesville: University Press of Florida.

San Miguel, Pedro L. 2005. *The Imagined Island: History, Identity and Utopia in Hispaniola*. Chapel Hill: University of North Carolina Press.

Santos Febres, Mayra. 2004. *Cualquier miércoles soy tuya*. Barcelona: Mondadori.

"Santurce no se vende." N.d. Santurce no se vende campaign. Accessed March 15, 2006. http://www.santurcenosevende.org /faq.html.

Sassen, Saskia. 1998. *Globalization and Its Discontents*. New York: New Press.

———. 2005. "The Many Scales of the Global." In *Critical Globalization Studies*, edited by Richard P. Appelbaum and William I. Robinson. New York: Routledge.

Schuller, Mark. 2012. *Killing with Kindness: Haiti, International Aid, and NGOs*. New Brunswick, NJ: Rutgers University Press.

Sheller, Mimi. 2003. *Consuming the Caribbean: From Arawaks to Zombies*. London: Routledge.

———. 2012. *Citizenship from Below: Erotic Agency and Caribbean Freedom*. Durham, NC: Duke University Press.

Shemak, April. 2002. "Re-membering Hispaniola: Edwidge Danticat's *The Farming of Bones*." *Modern Fiction Studies* 48: 83–112.

Silié, Rubén. 2001. Introduction to *Seminario internacional hacia una nueva visión de las relaciones fronterizas*. Santo Domingo: Buho.

———. 2005. "Aspectos y variables de las relaciones entre República Dominicana y Haití." *Revista Futuro* 9, no. 3. http://www.revistafuturo.info.

———. 2013. "Debilidad del estado haitiano y su impacto en el manejo de la cuestión migratoria." In *Haiti y República Dominicana: Miradas desde el siglo XXI*, edited by André Corten. Port-au-Prince: C3 Éditions.

Silié, Rubén, Carlos Segura, and Carlos Dore Cabral, eds. 2002. *La nueva immigración*. Santo Domingo: Mediabyte.

Simpson, George E. 1940. "Haitian Peasant Economy." *Journal of Negro History* 25: 498–519.

Singh, Anoop. 2004. "The Caribbean Economies: Adjusting to the Global Economy." Presentation to the seminar Developmental Challenges Facing the Caribbean, Port of Spain, Trinidad and Tobago, June 11. Accessed August 2, 2008. http://www.imf.org/external/np/speeches/2004/061104a.htm.

"Solo falta que llueva." 2004. *Ahora* 1330, November 3. Online.

Sommer, Doris. 1982–83. "Populism as Rhetoric: The Case of the Dominican Republic." *Boundary 2: Engagements: Postmodernism, Marxism, Politics* 11: 253–70.

———. 1988. "La ficción fundacional de Galván y las revisiones populistas de Bosch y Marrero Aristy." *Revista Iberoamericana* 54, no. 142: 99–128.

———. 1993. *Foundational Fictions: The National Romances of Latin America*. Berkeley: University of California Press.

Soto, José Luis. 2005. "Les feux de forets, une menace l'écosysteme de la ile." *Alter Presse*, August 3. Accessed August 4, 2005. http://www.alterpresse.org/article.php3?id_article=2980#.UpYvleIljUw.

Soto, José L., and Ronals Cobert. 2005. "Produire de l'énergie alternative, une solution viable, saine et faible cout." *Alter Presse*, August 4. Accessed August 4, 2005. http://www.alterpresse.org/spip.php?article2984#.UpYwDuIljUw.

Stephens, Michelle Ann. 2005. *Black Empire*. Durham, NC: Duke University Press.

Stoler, Ann Laura. 2002. *Carnal Knowledge and Imperial Power: Race and the Intimate in Colonial Rule*. Berkeley: University of California Press.

Stoler, Ann Laura, and Karen Strassler. 2010. "Memory Work in Java." In *Carnal Knowledge and Imperial Power: Race and the Intimate in Colonial Rule*. 2nd ed. Berkeley: University of California Press.

Suárez, Ada. 1968. *El doctor Ramón Emeterio Betances y su obra*. San Juan: Ateneo Puertorriqueño.

Suárez Büdenbender, Eva-María. 2013. "'Te conozco, bacalao': Investigating the Influence of Social Stereotypes on Linguistic Attitudes." *Hispania* 96, no. 1: 110–34.

Suárez Findlay, Eileen. 1999. *Imposing Decency: The Politics of Sexuality and Race in Puerto Rico, 1870–1920*. Durham, NC: Duke University Press.

Szeman, Imre. 2003. *Zones of Instability: Literature, Postcolonialism, and the Nation.* Baltimore: Johns Hopkins University Press.

Taboada, Hernán G. H., and Sofía Reding Blase, eds. 2011. *Debates contemporáneos en torno a una ética intercultural.* México, DF: UNAM.

Távarez, A., and D. Hilario. 2004. "Rescatan a 33 yoleros tras 12 días a la deriva." *País,* August 11.

Thomas, Don. 2003. "Levi Strauss Moving to Haiti." *Edmonton Journal,* October 4. Accessed May 15, 2005. http://www.hartford-hwp.com/archives/43a/456.html.

Tinsley, Omise'eke Natasha. 2010. *Thiefing Sugar: Eroticism between Women in Caribbean Literature.* Durham, NC: Duke University Press.

Toledo, Josefina. 2000. "Ramón Emeterio Betances en la génesis de los Clubes Borinquen y Mercedes Varona." In *Pasión por la libertad: Actas, coloquio internacional el independentismo puertorriqueño, de betances a nuestros días. Paris, Septiembre de 1998,* edited by Félix Ojeda Reyes and Paul Estrade. San Juan: University of Puerto Rico Press.

———. 2002. *Lola Rodríguez de Tío: Contribución para un estudio integral.* San Juan: LEA.

Tolentino Dipp, Hugo. 1974. *Raza e Historia en Santo Domingo.* Santo Domingo: UASD.

———. 1977a. *Gregorio Luperón: biografía política.* Habana: Casa de las Américas.

———. 1977b. *Perfil Nacionalista de Gregorio Luperón.* Habana: Casa de las Americas.

Torres, Arlene. 1998. "La gran familia puertorrique a 'ej prieta de beldá.'" In *Blackness in Latin America and the Caribbean: Social Dynamics and Cultural Transformations,* edited by Norman E. Whitten and Arlene Torres. Bloomington: Indiana University Press.

Torres-Saillant, Silvio. 1997. *Caribbean Poetics.* Cambridge, UK: Cambridge University Press.

———. 2000. "The Tribulations of Blackness: Stages in Dominican Racial Identity." *Callaloo* 23: 1086–111.

Torres-Saillant (2004)

———. 2006. *An Intellectual History of the Caribbean.* New York: Palgrave Macmillan.

Torres-Saillant, Silvio, and Ramona Hernández. 1998. *The Dominican Americans.* Westport, CT: Greenwood.

Torres-Saillant, Silvio, Ramona Hernández, and Blas R. Jiménez. 2004. *Desde la orilla: Hacia una nacionalidad sin desalojos.* Santo Domingo: Manatí.

Trouillot, Michel-Rolph. 2003. *Global Transformations.* New York: Palgrave Macmillan.

Umpierre, Luz María. 1983. *Ideología y novela en Puerto Rico.* Madrid: Playor.

Urrutia, Rosario. 1993. "Detrás de la vitrina: Expectativas del Partido Popular

Democrático y política exteriod norteamericana, 1942–1954." In *Del nacionalismo al populismo: cultura y política en Puerto Rico*, edited by Silvia Alvarez-Curbelo and María Elena Rodríguez-Castro. Río Piedras: Decanato de Estudios Graduados e Investigación, Recinto de Río Piedras, Universidad de Puerto Rico.

U.S. Department of Justice. 2011. "Investigation of the Puerto Rico Police Department." http://www.justice.gov/crt/about/spl/documents/prpd_letter.pdf.

Valerio-Holguín, Fernando. 2003. "Encuentro poscolonial y diáspora caribe a." *Revista del Instituto de Cultura Puertorriqueña* 4: 87–92.

Vargas Canales, Margarita. 2011. *Del Batey al papel mojado: Campesinos cañeros y vida cotidana en Puerto Rico*. México, DF: UNAM.

Vázquez, David J. 2011. *Triangulations: Narrative Strategies for Navigating Latino Identity*. Minneapolis: University of Minnesota Press.

Vásquez, Pastor. 2004. "J. B. Aristide agradece la solidaridad de Hipólito." *Hoy* (Santo Domingo), February 1.

Vásquez Zapata, Larissa. 2003. "Una voz para todo Santurce." *El Nuevo Día* (San Juan), December 21.

Vega, Ana Lydia. 1983. *Encancaranublado y otros cuentos de naufragio*. Río Piedras: Antillana.

———. 1989. "Cloud Cover Caribbean." In *Her True-True Name*, edited by Pamela Mordecai and Betty Wilson. Translated by Mark McCaffrey. Portsmouth, NH: Heinemann.

Vega, Bernardo. 1995. *Trujillo y Haití*. Vol. 2: *1937–38*. Santo Domingo: Fundación Cultural Dominicana.

Vélez, Diana L. 1994. "We Are (Not) in This Together: The Caribbean Imaginary in 'Encancaranublado' by Ana Lydia Vega." *Callaloo* 17: 826–33.

Veloz Maggiolo, Marcio. 1977. "Tipología del tema haitiano en la literatura dominicana." In *Sobre cultura dominicana y otras culturas*. Santo Domingo: Editora Alfa y Omega.

Ventura, Miriam. 2000. "La Diáspora: Opción u obligación?" *Ultima Hora*, January 30.

Verna, Chantalle F. 2005. "Haiti's Second Independence and the Promise of Pan-American Cooperation, 1934–57." PhD diss., Michigan State University.

Viego, Antonio. 2011. "The Place of Gay Male Chicano Literature in Queer Chicana/o Cultural Work." In *Gay Latino Studies: A Critical Reader*, edited by Michael Roy Hames-Garcia and Ernesto Javier Martínez. Durham, NC: Duke University Press.

Vigoreaux, Luis Jr. 2012a. "Asientos de cuero." Part 1. *Entrando por la cocina*, circa 1995. Accessed April 15, 2014. https://www.youtube.com/watch?v=deBgTMPaWis.

———. 2012b. "Primera base." Part 1. *Entrando por la cocina*, circa 1995. Accessed April 15, 2014. https://www.youtube.com/watch?v=FPIzDbiaBGo.

———. 2012c. "El sandwich." Part 1. *Entrando por la cocina*, circa 1995. Accessed April 15, 2014. https://www.youtube.com/watch?v=eEJ3F9cwLOQ.

Wade, Peter. 1993. *Blackness and Race Mixture*. Baltimore: Johns Hopkins University Press.

———. 2009. *Race and Sex in Latin America*. London: Pluto Press.

———. 2010. *Race and Ethnicity in Latin America*. 2nd ed. London: Pluto Press.

Waller, Nicole. 2005. *Contradictory Violence: Revolution and Subversion in the Caribbean*. Heidelberg: Universitätsverlag.

Weston, Kath. 1991. *Families We Choose: Lesbians, Gays, Kinship*. New York: Columbia University Press.

Whitten, Norman E., and Arlene Torres. 1998. "General Introduction." In *Blackness in Latin America and the Caribbean: Social Dynamics and Cultural Transformations*, edited by Norman E. Whitten and Arlene Torres. Bloomington: Indiana University Press.

Williams, Erica Lorraine. 2013. *Sex Tourism in Bahia: Ambiguous Entanglements*. Urbana: University of Illinois Press.

Woodhull, Winnifred. 2003. "Postcolonial Thought and Culture in Francophone North Africa." In *Francophone Postcolonial Studies: A Critical Introduction*, edited by Charles Forsdick and David Murphy. London: Arnold.

World Bank, Caribbean Country Management Unit. 2002. "A Review of Gender Issues in the Dominican Republic, Haiti, and Jamaica." Report 21866-LAC, December 11.

Wright, Michelle. 2004. *Becoming Black: Creating Identity in the African Diaspora*. Durham, NC: Duke University Press.

Wucker, Michele. 1999. *Why the Cocks Fight: Dominicans, Haitians, and the Struggle for Hispaniola*. New York: Hill and Wang.

Wynter, Sylvia. 1970. "Jonkonnu in Jamaica." *Jamaica Journal* 4, no. 2: 34–38.

Zenón Cruz, Narciso. 1975. *Descubre su trasero: El negro en la cultura puertorriqueña*. Humacao, PR: Editorial Furidi.

INDEX

ABOUT THE AUTHOR

Alaí Reyes-Santos (also known as Irmary) is from Cidra, Puerto Rico. She finished her undergraduate studies in the Humanities Department of the University of Puerto Rico, Mayagüez, and pursued her doctoral studies in the Literature Department at the University of California, San Diego. She is an assistant professor of ethnic studies at University of Oregon, a codirector of Centro Bonó's academic journal *Estudios Sociales* in the Dominican Republic, and a member of INTEGRA (Red de Investigación Interdisciplinaria y Difusión sobre Identidades, Racismo y Xenofobia en Latinoamérica), an organization based in México City. She has published her research about literature, racial politics, migration, colonialism, and globalization in the Caribbean and Latin America in *Callaloo, Revue Européenne des Migrations Internationales*, and *Revista Estudios Sociales*.

CPSIA information can be obtained
at www.ICGtesting.com
Printed in the USA
LVOW10s1350060317
526282LV00001B/47/P